SOVEREIGNTY

HISTORY AND THEORY

SOVEREIGNTY
HISTORY AND THEORY

Raia Prokhovnik

imprint-academic.com

Published in the UK by Imprint Academic
PO Box 200, Exeter EX5 5YX, UK

Published in the USA by Imprint Academic
Philosophy Documentation Center
PO Box 7147, Charlottesville, VA 22906-7147, USA

ISBN 9 781845 401146 (paper)
ISBN 9 781845 401412 (cloth)

A CIP catalogue record for this book is available from the
British Library and US Library of Congress

CONTENTS

For Leigh

PREFACE

This book arises out of a desire to clarify in detail some of the theories taken to be canonical in the discussion of the concept of sovereignty. I wanted to do this both for conceptual clarification and because this context forms an important but under-explored part of the background and framework for the contemporary discussion of the reconceptualisation of sovereignty. As always, Quentin Skinner and Conal Condren are intellectual touchstones for my thinking.

The book also owes much to the inspiration of discussions with Rob Walker, Jef Huysmans, Neil Walker and others. I would like to thank colleagues in the Feminist Reading Group at the Open University for debates, discussions and friendships over the past seven years — Kath Woodward, Stephanie Taylor, Rachel Thomson, Jane McCarthy, Wendy Hollway, Gillian Rose, and Elizabeth Silva.

I would also like to thank Gary, Eleanor, and Conal Browning, Anna Prokhovnik, Madeline, Kaz, and Mia Cooper-Ueki, Nick Prokhovnik, Alan, Hilary, and Stuart Browning and Jen Hardwick, David Blair, Scott Pitman and Susan Danseyar, Angela Radcliffe, Lorraine Foreman-Peck, Caroline Thompson, Anne Markiewicz and Ian Patrick, and Jane Wedmore for their sustaining love and warm friendship.

Raia Prokhovnik

INTRODUCTION

Sovereignty is sometimes regarded as a concept with a fixed meaning, as something that can only be kept or lost, and which at the present time is under threat from globalisation, the erosion of the nation state, and European integration. This book develops a strong argument for sovereignty as a robust concept with many conceptualisations in the past, and capable of further fruitful reconceptualisation in the future (taken up in Prokhovnik 2007). As such it clarifies a strong new direction for contemporary debate, especially within political theory and international relations, about the meaning of sovereignty.

The subheading of the book signals one of its distinctive properties. The two elements of the subheading, *History and Theory*, point to the way in which there is both a history of the concept, reflected in a range of conceptions and a canon, and a discourse on sovereignty as a political concept within political theory. The method followed in this book takes as crucial the nuanced way in which, in the study of the history of political thought, the historical examination of the concept and the conceptual analysis of sovereignty are interdependent. Here the canonical status of the different theories is not at issue. The subheading also registers how, in a second sense, history and theory are both crucially involved in each of the constructions of sovereignty dealt with in the book, in terms of present concerns and questions. Here the canonical status of the different conceptions is part of what is under investigation. The argument, in full, is built upon the understanding that each conception of sovereignty not only has a history and is contextually-grounded, but can also be recognised as a theory contributing to Europe's intellectual history and potentially having a direct (though not causal) effect upon the structures of practice in organising the political community and relations with other polities in the contemporary world. The debate about the construction of the meaning of sovereignty in the European Union is a prime example.

The book begins by setting out the scope of the project. This Introduction examines in general terms some of the problems and opportunities of integrating historical and conceptual work, combining the methods of the history of political thought with political theory. It goes on to explore the sense in which it is helpful to refer to general features of sovereignty, and then utilises the concept/conception distinction to elucidate the diversity of conceptions of sovereignty found in the modern period. The chapter also addresses the question of the range of theorists studied here and outlines the contents of the different chapters.

Integrating historical and conceptual work

The idea that the meaning of sovereignty is fixed can be very effectively challenged by demonstrating the historical malleability of the concept over time. The dominant notion of the meaning of sovereignty as fixed can be unpicked into a set of propositions about sovereignty, of which four are briefly considered here. The first proposition is that sovereignty means *absolute* power and/or authority and relatedly that sovereignty is indivisible. However, the history of the concept of sovereignty gives us several different meanings of the 'absolute' quality of sovereignty and so the import of this proposition depends crucially upon whether it is, for instance, Bodin's, Hobbes's or Kant's meaning of 'absolute' which is being used. The supposedly indivisible quality of sovereignty is disputed very effectively by both Spinoza and Kant. The second proposition is that sovereignty is the location of *final and supreme* authority. However, we can see for instance in the case of Locke's theory, that final authority is not an active category in the way it is in other conceptions. There is not a final authority in a positive sense in Locke.

The third proposition is that the distinction between legal and political sovereignty (legal supremacy and law-making power on the one hand and legitimate power to rule on the other) sets up the primary framework for discussing sovereignty. However, I argue elsewhere that the salience of this distinction depends in particular on examining sovereignty in the modern liberal tradition, with its distrust of government, disaggregation of the source of (popular) sovereignty in 'the people' from government power to make law, its public/private distinction, and its depoliticised understanding which reduces politics to matters of government. The liberal tradition in important ways redefines political sovereignty in terms of legal sovereignty, reduces politics to the implementation of law, and so works with a depleted notion of might be called ruler sovereignty. There is scope for a reinvigorated notion of political sovereignty which fully recognises the political functions that we ask the concept of sovereignty to perform for us (Prokhovnik 2007). The fourth proposition is that sovereignty necessarily has two mutually-exclusive dimensions, internal and external sovereignty, from which the monopoly of internal legitimate force within a specified territory, and of external war- and peace-making derive.

Elsewhere (Prokhovnik 2007) I build on Rob Walker's highly-influential critique of this dichotomy, demonstrating its indebtedness to the specifically modern state conception of sovereignty and so releasing the reconceptualisation of sovereignty from its grip.

The theories outlined in Chapters 1–5, then, demonstrate how dynamic and mutable the meanings of propositions such as these are. Moreover, we can see from studying the history of the concept of sovereignty that it is a history of reconceptualisation rather than a history of progressive refinement towards a final and fixed meaning. Indeed the historicity of sovereignty leads to the recognition of the necessary multiplicity of its conceptions. There will always be a place in the political vocabulary of a polity for something like the concept of sovereignty, among other things to define the scope of politics (whatever content is given to it), distribute political powers (whatever source of legitimacy is invoked), and set the limits of the political (however those boundaries are envisaged), and to perform these functions slightly differently with respect to the domestic and international realms, however defined and whatever the perceived relationship between them. Prokhovnik (2007) goes on to argue that the fixed view of sovereignty (both its features and its problems) can be identified with a modern Western state-centric, realist IR, liberal model. When unpicked, we are free to recognise the richness of the tradition of thinking on sovereignty and reconceptualise it in a way that fits contemporary ideas and political practices such as in the EU.

The historical and intellectual contexts sketched in each of the following chapters are not seen as determining how we can understand what each thinker says, or predetermining what the writer thought about their political context, but are a way of setting the scene for readers at such a historical distance from first publication. They are a starting point for trying to set out the theory of sovereignty of each of these thinkers in its own right, highlighting the distinctiveness of each conception and so avoiding reducing them to a standard pattern. Part of this approach is to indicate if only briefly how their conceptions of sovereignty arose out of the questions they posed in the context of their historical and intellectual backgrounds. This means that the different conceptions are not seen as developmental, not leading to a greater refinement and clarity. It also means that there is an important element of contingency involved. The response each thinker gives to his own question, formulated in terms of his own understanding of his specific intellectual and political context, is not seen as the only one which could have been or was generated within that context.

Another part of recognising the distinctiveness of each conception of sovereignty is to accent how the treatment of the theorists is organised around the different clusters of key terms which each of the writers brings to bear on their conception of sovereignty, shaping the meaning of sovereignty in that political theory, and identifying how those key terms hang together to form a logic of reasoning for that author. For instance, one of the keys to sovereignty for Bodin was the idea of absolute dominion, while sovereignty for Hobbes had to include the notion of supreme power. Central to Rousseau's conception of sovereignty are the key terms of sovereignty itself, the act of association, government, the general and particular wills, general and particular laws, and the lawgiver. The important concepts in Kant's theory of sovereignty are right, international relations, publicity, law, and representation. The key concepts in Hegel's notion of sovereignty are the state, the constitution, the Crown, sovereignty at home, sovereignty in relation to foreign states, and war. Foucault's theory of sovereignty seeks to bring into the light of intellectual analysis what has previously been excluded and some of his key terms are the contrast between the covert and overt operations of power, the ways in which subjects are constructed, sovereignty as descending compared with disciplinary power as ascending, and the operation of sovereignty through concrete acts contrasted with the operation of disciplinary power through surveillance, normalising sanctions and the panopticon.

This approach is also committed to the view that the theory of each thinker is characterised by a cluster of conceptual connections (logical relations whereby one concept implies another), a particular vocabulary, the use and development of a specific line of argument, and is distinctive and unique. These are different, even if related, historical conceptions of sovereignty. They involve distinct political dilemmas and predicaments or problematics, but these are expressed in different ways in the theories and are not deterministic. The different theories involve distinct uses of language to discuss sovereignty, and this is emphasised by highlighting their different key terms and eliciting the meaning of sovereignty within distinct ways of doing politics and particular political mentalities. In this way we will see that each theory identifies a different and specific location for sovereignty, and confirms different features of political life as central to the meaning of sovereignty. In these chapters the overall political theory of each of these thinkers is refracted through their conception of sovereignty. The chapters do not attempt to do justice to the political theories of these writers as a whole, and so none of the chapters provides an exhaustive analysis of the thinker or their texts. The overall aim in making explicit these sets of key terms is to demonstrate the diversity of conceptions of sovereignty, and to indicate how differently these thinkers thought about sovereignty and the wide variation in the role sovereignty played in their theories.

The purposes of the book are to review the diversity of the major conceptions of sovereignty established in European intellectual history up to the present; to provide persuasive reinterpretations of some of those conceptions; to establish that the concept of sovereignty has a dynamic and fertile history of reconceptualisation; and to provide a resource, a broad vocabulary of ideas to help illuminate and enrich the contemporary discussions and debates about the term, and so draw out the different ways of making a relationship between sovereignty and politics. The argument seeks to make a scholarly contribution to the history of political thought in its own right. It also establishes a broad framework for a critical perspective on current discussion in political theory and international relations theory, a task undertaken in *Sovereignties: Contemporary Theory and Practice* (Prokhovnik 2007). This approach is designed to deliver a stronger and more flexible understanding of the present debate on reconceptualisation, preferable to an approach which sought to systematically 'apply' the meanings of sovereignty derived from a set of historical chapters.

The chapters endeavour to identify the role of sovereignty in the political theory of each writer, and to show that in each case his purpose in using his theory of sovereignty to answer certain questions raised in political debate, is different. Ball draws out this crucial historicity of the uses and meanings of political concepts when he notes that the 'history of *political* concepts (or more precisely, concepts used in political discourse) cannot … be narrated apart from the political conflicts in which they figure'. Graphically, Ball makes the case that '[p]olitical concepts are weapons of war, tools of persuasion and legitimation, badges of identity and solidarity' (Ball 1997, 41). Underlying Ball's purpose is the important point that the study of a political concept which seeks to encompass the specificity of the concept necessarily involves a study of the history of that political concept. As Ball puts it, histories of political concepts are 'histories of political arguments, and of the conceptual contests and disputes on which they turned and to which they gave rise' (Ball 1997, 42).

The central question in the following chapters is, what role does sovereignty play for each of these thinkers? What work does sovereignty do in the theory of each of them? What other political concepts is sovereignty clustered with, and how, in each thinker? What are the conditions of its use? For Schmitt as for Hobbes sovereignty is a solution to a problem. A strong sovereign identified with the state is the remedy to social instability that threatens the polity. For Foucault sovereignty is part of the problem, of unacknowledged power relations of domination in the social realm. For Locke, sovereignty is a dangerous concept, grudgingly recognised in the formal supremacy of the people and in their pre-political rights, and a thing to be denied to the state/government. We can also recognise that some of the theories of sovereignty studied here have operated as a regulative ideal while others have been developed in order to critique sovereignty. As a regulative ideal sovereignty becomes an 'unquestioned form of reflection'. In this way, as a regulative ideal for Rousseau and Kant, sovereignty allows for a specific kind of flourishing for the individual. In this sense as well, the presupposition of the importance of the state for Hobbes, Hegel and Schmitt has been taken as a regulative ideal. For Spinoza, sovereignty as a regulative ideal highlights a polycentric conception and the lack of importance of an over-arching and centralised state. As the object of critique, as seen in Schmitt and Foucault, sovereignty is something to dismiss, ignore, discount, or is counterposed to another concept.

These chapters are also deeply political in several respects. The conceptions of sovereignty are studied with two distinguishable focuses of attention, and the book thus has two objectives. The first objective is to interpret (and analyse, explore, and seek to do justice to the writers involved) and to the second is go beyond the history of political thought to evaluate in terms of their usefulness to contemporary reconceptualisation. In this way the argument in all the chapters has normative, analytical and descriptive dimensions. This distinction between the interpretive and evaluative objectives also relates closely to the difference identified by Skinner between 'the question of what we may be doing *in* saying something' and 'what we may happen to bring about *by* saying something', in establishing the meaning of the use of words (Skinner 2002, 104). The interpretive objective involves examining the conception of sovereignty developed by each of the thinkers against the background of the questions posed by that thinker in the light of their intellectual and political framework and the discourse of their time. The selection and portrayal of the cluster of key terms found in each of the conceptions of sovereignty is political in the sense that such acts of selection and portrayal are never simply neutral, though not in the sense of acting against the integrity of the material, since criteria of adequate reasoning, persuasiveness and judgment come into play.

The question posed by the evaluative objective is, on what basis can we assess the different arguments being made for the different conceptions of sovereignty? The perspective employed is unavoidably contemporary, shaped by the concerns, interests, dilemmas and problematics set out in current debates about sovereignty and related concepts. The evaluative objective is to contribute to contemporary debates. This is done in part by identifying the general features of sovereignty that each thinker employs, and by making a case for what we can identify as the crucial strengths and weaknesses of each conception. It is also done by teasing out what sort of realm for *politics* is established in each case, with due acknowledgment that our notion of politics is a modern and culturally-specific one. In the following chapters the question is addressed as to what kind of politics each conception allows for, and whether there is room for contestation to take place. This method aims to raise questions and open up the contemporary debate about sovereignty, as well as to lay out some of the resources for the discussion of sovereignty. The basis of the evaluation is complex. In part it concerns how the different theories, in their own terms, according to their own logics, are effective, though not necessarily in order to make judgments about the one that is most coherent and internally consistent. The evaluation also includes awareness of which theory has been ideologically the most successful (therefore it is Locke's).

The interpretations developed of these historical thinkers show that sovereignty is political in a further sense as well. The thinkers have played different roles in canon. Hobbes, or a version of his theory, has been taken as paradigmatic. Others have been marginal or recessive. Kant's theory has come to be regarded as important in recent international relations literature – constructing or making a bid to supplement the canon. Foucault and Schmitt enter a largely 'liberal' canon. Our fixation with a modern, Western and narrow dominant meaning of sovereignty taken as unchanging prevents us from immediately recognising the scope and richness of meanings of non-dominant theories of sovereignty. It also masks how sovereignty works or the reasons why it doesn't work in polities with very different traditions in the modern de-colonialised or post-colonial world. Sometimes, in both theory and practice, a version of state sovereignty has been foisted onto decolonised states replacing and erasing the value and meaning of indigenous traditional governing and ruling vocabularies and practices of inter-polity relationships.

The following chapters highlight a political issue in a final further respect. Instead of reaffirming a canon of political thought that has the effect of affirming 'the appearance of rationality or necessity' (Connolly 1993, 231), the aim is to identify some of the multiple and varied ways in which sovereignty has been conceptualised. By demonstrating the conceptual and historical distinctiveness of each of the conceptions of sovereignty highlighted in the canon, we can see that none of them aligns completely with the modern state realist liberal model of sovereignty with its exclusionary internal/external logic. This consequence brings the historical specificity of the modern conception of sovereignty into view, at the same time as reaffirming some of the rich texture of the historical resources available for the reconceptualisation of sovereignty.

General features

Coming now to the general features of sovereignty, we can evaluate with hindsight that each theory of sovereignty not only revolves around a distinctive cluster of key terms but also focuses upon a different collection of general features, attributes, marks, properties, and conditions to define and indicate the location and meaning of sovereignty, and no theory includes them all. From this vantage point it is clear that the identity of sovereignty varies distinctively across the different conceptions of it that have been developed. For Hobbes sovereignty is a hypothetical single, meaningful, performance. For Locke it is a technical requirement, and for Rousseau it is an on-going activity rather than a 'thing'. For Schmitt

sovereignty is again a performance, invoked in the decision to acknowledge an exception, while for Foucault it is a dead letter and a false alibi.

The general features of sovereignty cover a range of subjects within and
related to politics, including government, law, state theory, international
relations, ethics, diplomacy, defence, security studies and policing. The
sub-disciplinary discourses emphasise different collections of general features but these also overlap. Some of the general features highlighted in
the mainstream political theory discourse include the authority relationship between rulers and ruled; sovereignty as a recognition concept, relying upon the recognition of others in order to be established; sovereignty
as a regulative ideal establishing political order and stability; sovereignty
as a way of designating the 'whole' realm of a political unit; sovereignty
as functional rather than territorial; and modern sovereignty establishing
a modern constitutional state but also possibly overridden by the
constitution.

The legal and constitutional discourse focuses upon features such as the
idea of sovereignty as self-government; the capacity to make law but take
commands from none; as specifying the highest legal authority and establishing the rule of law; the idea of jurisdiction; the competence to initiate
constitutional change; unequalled power; sovereignty's perpetual character over time across different office-holders; independent power; self-
management; full authority; strong leadership; independence; supreme
rule; self-reliance; autonomy; and control over one's own affairs.

In the international relations discourse sovereignty is used to designate
the idea of a fixed and bounded territory; territory as marking the border
between internal and external sovereignty; security for and the boundaries of property and wealth; a monopoly on the use of violence within
that territory and in the name of the state in external intervention; the
power to declare war and make peace; to posit formal juridicial equality
between states; state infrastructure (in particular for state theorists); the
spectre and sanctioning of dominance (for state and critical IR theorists);
and relations between states as setting the framework for the ideas of —
variously — international relations, global politics, international politics,
world politics, relations between state and non-state actors, foreign policy,
international power relations, 'international society' (defined by Keal
(2003, 30) as 'a community of mutual recognition' of each others' legitimate right to sovereign independence), and international community.

We can see that when the meaning of sovereignty in the different disciplinary modes is unpacked, a wide range of features, clustered into different if overlapping vocabularies, can be discerned. The contemporary
reconceptualisation of sovereignty can draw on all the rich vocabularies of
these disciplinary traditions.

In addition, a cluster of Latin terms has been used to define and discuss
sovereignty (Bartelson 1995, Coleman 2005, Armitage 1998). Concepts

such as *imperium* (command), *jurisdictio* (administration of justice), *dominion* (rule), *potestas* (power), and *officium* (office-holding), with all the resonances these terms hold in the Western tradition since Ancient Rome, can also all shed light on the meaning of sovereignty. Franklin (1992), for instance, renders sovereignty as *maiestas* or majesty, and other authors select different combinations of these terms and give them varying weights. Skinner, in the index of *The Foundations of Modern Political Thought. Volume Two* (1978), lists sovereignty under the category of *imperium*. The significance of the use of these Latin terms is evidenced in the discussions over the meaning of sovereignty in Chapter 1.

Having set out a range of general features of sovereignty, one can ask how these features are related. Each of the thinkers studied in this book has different answers to questions such as, Do such features mutually reinforce each other? Are they interdependent, or intersect, or interlinked? Do they together form an edifice? Does one or more feature underpin the others? Is there a core to sovereignty, given that no one general feature is a requirement for all conceptions? How are the features related conceptually, and politically (for example, there is a strong connection between the rule of law and the monopoly of violence by the state)? Or are these features disjunctive, features that simply arose historically without fitting logically together but with particular histories and meanings in different places, with no universal logical theory? Moreover, what would answers to these questions mean for how the relation between the features can be reconceived? The book seeks to provide a clearer picture of some of these questions, and in this way again break down the idea of there being a single fixed meaning of sovereignty.

The diversity of conceptions of sovereignty

Studying sovereignty as a history of conceptualisations, integrating history and theory in this sense, allows for the highlighting of the diversity of the conceptions of sovereignty, because the method is an example of enabling difference to be seen, of thinking against the closure of thought.

The following chapters seek to analyse a set of distinctive and contextually-grounded conceptions that inform and enrich idea of sovereignty. These chapters also aim to identify some of the major paradigms in the (constructed) tradition of thinking about sovereignty. In both these ways the approach emphasises what is notable, characteristic and historically-grounded about these separate and contingent moments, as a sound alternative to an approach whose purpose is to form a story of linear and cumulative progress towards a final and fixed meaning.

The twin ideas of the concept/conception distinction and the essential contestability of concepts, developed by Gallie, Connolly and others, demonstrate clearly the value of recognising how our political concepts are always articulated in and contingently situated in particular languages, cultures and sets of contemporaneous questions, and can only be known through those specific conceptions. There are conceptual and historical aspects to this. On the conceptual side, Connolly notes that understanding a concept 'involves the elaboration of the broader conceptual system within which it is implicated' (Connolly 1993, 14). On the historical side, Connolly again argues convincingly for the 'constructed, contestable, contingent, and relational character of established identities' (Connolly 1993, xi), and Frazer confirms that '[m]eaning is indeterminate [because it is conventional and changes over time] and interpretation is unavoidable' (Frazer 1997, 224). It follows that even a self-conscious tradition of conceptualisation, whereby for instance Hegel is in a sense in conversation with some of those in the canon who have theorised sovereignty before him, is a history of reconceptualisations filled with dispute and re-interpretation as well as with re-imagining in the light of different political circumstances, rather than a teleological development of progressive rational improvement towards a final and fixed meaning. In this way the concept/conception distinction acknowledges the crucial historicity as well as the instability and constructedness of our political concepts.

The concept/conception distinction is also a way of gathering individual cases under universal terms without resulting in the loss that comes from eschewing the rush to identity and sameness. Identity thinking tends to make unlike things alike and to obliterate difference, whereas the concept/conception approach allows for the recognition of tension rather than attempting to resolve differences away. Another way of describing this point is to argue that the pairs of theories analysed in this book can be recognised as related in kind rather than in essence or nature, and indeed the broader cluster of conceptions of sovereignty can be identified as sharing membership of a kind rather than an essence.

The approach taken in the following chapters illustrates a number of points about the relation between concepts, politics, and history articulated by Ball, Farr and Hanson, taking their cue from the ground-breaking methodological work of Skinner and others. They emphasise that 'the concepts constitutive of political beliefs and behaviour have historically mutable meanings' and that 'conceptual histories reveal the mutations of meaning that attend all our political concepts', as well as making the case that 'the political dimension of conceptual change and the conceptual dimension of political innovation' go hand in hand. In this way this book takes the view that the writers discussed here wrote in part in response to doubts, challenges and dilemmas of their time and gave their own particular answers to them, and in so doing helped construct the shifting meaning of sovereignty. Ball, Farr and Hanson's argument is also based on the acknowledgment that 'speaking a language involves taking on a world, and altering the concepts constitutive of that language involves nothing less than remaking the world' (Ball, Farr and Hanson 1989, ix) or, as Skinner puts it, the need to focus on the role of words in 'upholding complete social philosophies' (Skinner 1989, 13). Skinner also makes the valuable point that concepts are political in the sense that we need to attend to the role of 'our evaluative language in helping to legitimate social action', in that 'our social practices help to bestow meaning on our social vocabulary', but equally 'our social vocabulary helps to constitute the character of those practices' (Skinner 1989, 22). The identification of the general features of sovereignty in three of the major discourses on it (political theory, legal theory, and international relations) provides an example of these points.

The chapters

The following chapters explore a non-exhaustive range of conceptualisations of sovereignty in the modern period, demonstrating their constructedness and their logics of reasoning within their particular intellectual and political contexts and so highlighting the distinctiveness of each conception and the diversity of the range of conceptions studied. A close reading of each writer as a theorist of sovereignty in their own terms and their own conceptual vocabulary, and an analysis of the scholarship on each thinker's conception of sovereignty, is the basis for a scholarly interpretation. Fidelity to the text governs the integration of what the text can best be interpreted as meaning and 'what its author may have meant' (Skinner 2002, 113). The examination of each theorist will then lead to a case being made in our terms for the strengths and weaknesses of each theory, indicate the general features of sovereignty accented in each conception, as well as consider the scope for politics envisaged in each theory.

After setting Bodin's conception in the context of earlier understandings of sovereignty, detailed paired accounts are provided of the theories of sovereignty in Hobbes and Spinoza, Locke and Rousseau, Kant and Hegel, and Foucault and Schmitt. Bodin's absolutist account of sovereignty is comprehensively taken as the major exposition inaugurating the modern intellectual interest in the concept. Hobbes' notion of state sovereignty is compared with Spinoza and sovereignty without a unified state. Locke and the absence of a positive theory of sovereignty is compared with Rousseau and the sovereignty of the people. Kant's equivocally cosmopolitan view is compared with Hegel and the political sovereignty of the state. Schmitt and political exceptionalism in the light of the limits of liberal constitutionalism is compared with Foucault and sovereignty's coercive face. Schmitt and Foucault offer important critiques of the mainstream tradition of thinking about sovereignty, and because there is no teleological process involved the approach taken here would argue that we cannot predict where the next critique might come from. These chapters will engage with the interpretive literature on these theorists through the debates opened up by highlighting the differences and commonalities between the pairs of theorists. In some cases the interpretations offered of the theorists go against the grain of or take issue with conventional views.

It is worth making explicit the value of comparison in the treatment of the paired thinkers. The aim of demonstrating the diversity of conceptions of sovereignty across the history of the term is mirrored on a smaller scale in the different chapters, through the comparison between bracketed sets of theorists. The method of comparison allows for the similarities and differences between thinkers to be highlighted, for resemblances and analogies to be apprehended without sameness being invoked, for the distinctiveness of their conceptual vocabularies and approaches to be accented, for equivalence between the theories as conceptions of sovereignty to be indicated without an identity between them (or hierarchy in them) being drawn, and for the lack of identity between theories to be examined positively rather than mourned. The chapters develop patterns of resemblances and shared vocabulary, and the criteria for selecting resemblances arise out of the material itself. The resemblances and distinctivenesses in the writers' logics of reasoning which are picked out are meant to be pictured as operating within a wider and open-ended field of interpretation. The explicitness of the process of selecting similarities and differences is designed to de-naturalise the criteria of classification.

Who is included in the book and why? The composition has been influenced by the (especially) political theory canon on sovereignty, but is also contingent. There is a politics of the tradition of thinking about sovereignty going on in the canon, in that what we choose to remember of that tradition is a useful cultural indicator. To a certain extent these chapters are about the politics of the tradition as well as about the recovery of ideas. Strong claims could also be made for including Grotius and Pufendorf, Marx, G D H Cole's radically pluralistic theory of sovereignty within associative politics, and Agamben. Machiavelli's concern with relations between city states, and foreign policy and relations, are grounds for his inclusion. In addition, just as the book could not deal with these extra writers with a claim for inclusion, it is clear that the orientation of the whole book privileges the tradition of Western experience. Hopefully further work could usefully explore and compare notions of sovereignty from other cultures and traditions of thinking.

The conclusion will round off the book by reinforcing the diversity of ideas found in these thinkers, and demonstrating how history and theory are integrated in the examination of their conceptions of sovereignty. In particular the conclusion analyses what this set of examples tells us about the scope and meaning of politics, and about the relationship between the concepts of politics and sovereignty.

Chapter One

BODIN AND BEFORE

The first theorist of sovereignty to be considered is Jean Bodin, and the aim will be to unpack the meaning of Bodin's association with absolute sovereignty and his reputation for setting out a model of state sovereignty. But before discussing Bodin, we need to consider what sovereignty meant before Bodin. In particular, we need to assess the view that maintains that there is a break between ancient and modern theorising that effectively derives the idea of sovereignty from its early-modern conceptualisation identified in circular fashion with the modern state. This view is evaluated against the one which posits a suitably qualified continuity in the meaning of the term 'sovereignty' across the ancient and modern worlds.

BEFORE BODIN

The received story of the Western political tradition runs roughly from ancient Greece and Rome through the European Dark Ages and the medieval period to the Renaissance, the modern period and the Enlightenment, and the rise of the modern state. The issue to be addressed in the first half of this chapter is whether 'sovereignty' is properly identified only with its 'modern' theorisation or whether it is helpful to think of there being different conceptions before Bodin, thus repealing the artificial and dismissive ancient/modern divide. In order to keep the focus clearly on the issue of the ancient/modern divide, the argument will work with the mainstream distinction between notions of political and legal sovereignty.

One factor to contend with, in coming to an assessment about whether or not the concept of 'sovereignty' accurately portrays a general and distinctive feature of polities, is that there is a shifting political vocabulary over this whole period. For instance, 'empire' does not now mean what it meant to the Romans, 'state' develops a particular meaning in the modern period, as does the meaning of 'politics' as we know it, and the dependency of legal and political terms on a religious context in the medieval period was transformed by the secularisation of the modern period. Also, the meaning of political terms resonates very strongly with the specific contexts in which they were used. The term 'sovereignty' was sometimes used before Bodin but not with all the key elements of its modern meaning. The argument that follows takes the view that typically a key political term contains an open-ended cluster of components, and its elasticity and malleability of meaning may be traced over time as components of the cluster are downgraded or invested with new meaning. Not only is it unfaithful to the modern history of conceptions of sovereignty to expect the delivery of a single, fixed, meaning, but also it is unrealistic to expect to discover and identify a single, fixed meaning prior to Bodin.

One of the components in the cluster that gives sovereignty meaning is 'constitution'. The issue of whether the meaning of sovereignty aligns only with modern state sovereignty is complicated by the historical absences and presences of a relationship of sovereignty with constitutionalism. The constitution, like sovereignty, is a part of the architecture of the polity as a whole, and the relationship between sovereignty and constitutionalism is not a given. Like sovereignty, constitutionalism has multiple meanings, and it comes in different forms. Bellamy and Castiglione (1997, 602) find it useful to distinguish the 'ancient conception of a constitution as describing the characteristics and form of the body politic, as opposed to the more modern view of constitutions as embodying a pre-political higher law'. However, if one's purpose was to examine the historical record in more detail, or to emphasise the multiplicity of forms of constitutionalism, then this broad brushstroke dichotomy would be helpful at best only as a starting point. Useful paradigms tend to dissolve into more complex stories.

With the threat of anachronism on the one hand and awareness of the continuities and transformations in political meanings on the other, it is not possible to resolve the question of whether 'sovereignty' meaningfully pre-dates Bodin simply by reference to the language, by taking the use of the term as definitional proof. Instead, the first half of the chapter will examine four lines of reasoning through the arguments of a set of mostly modern scholars and commentators. This set of writers is not meant to be comprehensive or exhaustive, nor to express 'classic' statements on the matter. The purpose of this approach is to demonstrate the strength of the fourth case, the view that there were in a significant sense conceptions of 'sovereignty' before the modern period. 'Sovereignty' did not arrive *de novo* with Bodin and, while with hindsight we can see that we have identified with Bodin a threshold to the recognisably modern meaning in terms of its cluster of components, the diversity in 'sovereignties' characterises the period before as well as after Bodin. The idea that different conceptions of sovereignty help us to understand different polities over time and space, and the idea that political sovereignty is a feature of all polities (see Prokhovnik 2007, Chapter 4), does not undermine the importance of the emergence of the modern conception of sovereignty, when as Preuss et al (2003 4) put it, 'all public authority resided in and was derived from the state'.

The question that underpins the debate is whether sovereignty is a necessary feature of politics and political community. There is an ambiguous legacy here, with at least four competing lines of argument that we have inherited. One argument identifies sovereignty with the modern period and with state sovereignty. It posits either a sharp break, maintaining that in the ancient and medieval worlds of the West other political concepts were significant but sovereignty was not, or sees uses of the term sovereignty before the modern period as precursors. The general argument held by this view is that different forms of political rule are characterised by different forms of symbolic authority, and sovereignty is the name given to the specific kind of symbolic authority in the (modern) state form. Another argument sees sovereignty as specifically associated with modernity and secular reason, and with the pattern of enlightenment dichotomies such as objective/subjective, mind/body, science/opinion, external/internal, reason/emotion, and culture/nature. A third argument maintains that there is a long and continuous tradition of sovereignty. Bodin himself makes a claim for sovereignty's pedigree and it is an important feature of his argumentative strategy. According to this view sovereignty has always meant roughly the same thing, namely ultimate authority, legal supremacy, law-making power, and the power to attempt to subdue enemies, even if distributed between different persons, bodies and institutions. Bruno Simma takes this view when he asserts that 'all states in the world possess *suprema potestas* and are thus not placed in any kind of hierarchy' (quoted in Simpson 2004, xii). Here sovereignty is equivalent to the very idea of symbolic authority, of rule by authority rather than through mere force. While all these three lines of argument contain important insights, they all have in mind (albeit different) fixed concepts of sovereignty.

The fourth argument differs in holding that sovereignty features in ancient and medieval as well as modern political forms, but that there have been many and various conceptions of sovereignty. The value of the fourth line of argument over the others lies in its recognition of change and movement over time, of contextual variety and difference, and this is expressed in the distinction between concept and conception. It emphasises, against the first view in particular, that the state and state sovereignty, and so sovereignty at all according to this fixed conception, is not universal, transhistorical in applicability, or transcendent in character. In a sense the question of whether sovereignty existed prior to the modern state can only be decided by definitional fiat, since if you hold that all the central components of sovereignty all belong to the state form, then no other conception of sovereignty is possible. However, if you hold that only some features are inherent in the modern state conception, then conceptions of sovereignty both pre- and post- the modern state are possible. This matter cannot be decisively resolved by appeals to historical material since all historical evidence is radically subject to selection and interpretation. The value of the fourth line of argument is that it takes the debate forward rather than being stuck in the discourse dominated by state sovereignty.

Attention in the first half of this chapter is focused on the first and fourth of these lines of argument. The first argument is especially significant because it contains the dominant narrative, about the emergence of the modern state and modern state sovereignty. For the purposes of this book this focus is also important because it is within this dominant story that the idea of multiple conceptions of sovereignty is lost sight of with the hegemony of the state form, and other conceptions of sovereignty are rendered invisible as the state form became a 'given' of political life and of the political vocabulary. It is also important to examine this narrative, and so to recognise that the meaning of sovereignty is more complex than portrayed there, in order to identify the ideological investment at stake in the first line of argument. By accounting for the modern state in this way we can begin to see again how sovereignty has a rich set of meanings broader than the association with the state form, and lay the ground for showing the value of the fourth line of argument.

One

The argument for the equation of sovereignty with modern state sovereignty picks up on several aspects of the meanings of 'modern', 'state', and 'sovereignty'. It also makes a strong claim about a breach and severance between the notions of 'ancient' and 'modern' sovereignty, often based on a presumption of the conceptual superiority of the modern form. We will examine a range of lines of argument put forward by a number of scholars. Loughlin argues that the key transition from the medieval period involved the assertion of royal supreme power and the sweeping away of the system of medieval city states. Habermas also subscribes to the notion of a decisive 'break' between medieval and modern modes of political organisation. Schmitt uses Hobbes to posit a 'break'. Keal gives weight to a sharp change in sixteenth century claims to sovereignty over foreign territory and indigenous groups, based now on the conquered peoples rather than on the right of the conquerors. Brod distinguishes modern polities from their predecessors in terms of the exercise of some form of popular sovereignty. Skinner's portrayal of the gradual process of emergence of the modern state is a welcome counterbalance to narratives of a 'break', but it necessarily suppresses a narrative about the metamorphosis of sovereignty.

Heiman regards the development of 'constitutional and legally ordered interaction' as the key feature of modern sovereignty. Bottici highlights the idea of the state as a *persona ficta*, and in similar vein Gough regards as crucial a shift from the personalised sovereignty of the monarch to the 'technical' modern notion of a legal sovereign. Harrison locates the suppression of church authority as the key factor. Jackson's confident assertion of sovereignty as the distinguishing mark of modern politics represents well the ideological claim of the realist tradition of international relations. Spruyt presents a more nuanced account of the Jackson argument. Franceschet draws out the ideological dimension of this story. A version of this first argument is also put forward by Brown *et al*, who contrast the emergence of sovereignty with the way political communities were envisaged in the ancient world. Keal's work complicates the received story when it identifies how the modern state definition of sovereignty was crucially constructed against a backdrop of a continuity of imperial power.

Loughlin makes a case that the concept of sovereignty is necessarily associated with the modern state, and looks to evidence from medieval history to support his claim. He argues that while the 'terminology of sovereignty was in use during the medieval period, the concept in a true sense did not then exist'. He quotes Jouvenel that although people in the Middle Ages had 'a very strong sense of that concrete thing, hierarchy; they lacked the idea of that abstract thing, sovereignty'. Loughlin contends that sovereignty was used in the medieval period to signify superiority but that even the Holy Roman Emperor could only assert 'command over those who were best placed to disobey', and he invokes the fact that 'central authority possessed only a limited hold over the governed' (Loughlin 2003, 57). Loughlin sees the major stages on the way to modern sovereignty as monarchs 'breaking the political power of the feudal magnates', and challenging the authority of the Pope and the Holy Roman Emperor, with the outcome that sovereignty gives to the modern state its internal coherence, external independence, and supremacy of the law. The first was achieved by the 'destruction of all authorities that sought to challenge the power of the royal will', and so the achievement of *plenitude potestas*, supreme power, and the second resulted in the 'assertion of royal authority and the subversion of the medieval order' (Loughlin 2003, 58–9). Habermas also takes the view that the modern sovereign state marked an important break when he refers to 'its predecessor, the dynastic absolutist state' (Habermas 1997, 120).

However, as Spinoza's conception of sovereignty will demonstrate in Chapter 2, lack of strong central authority does not on its own invalidate the use of the notion of sovereignty. More generally, in order to make his point Loughlin describes a conception of sovereignty that is very narrowly conceived. There is a strong case for recognising a wider scope for the meaning of sovereignty.

Schmitt highlights Hobbes's innovation over the medieval form. He says, '[f]or Hobbes it was relevant for the state to overcome the anarchy of the feudal estates' and the church's right of resistance as well as the incessant outbreak of civil war arising from those struggles'. The Hobbesian state did so by 'confronting medieval pluralism, that is, power claimed by the churches and other "indirect" authorities', but also through its sense of 'the rational unity of an unequivocal, effective authority that can assure protection and a calculable, functioning legal system' (Schmitt 1996, 72).

Keal seeks to distance modern from earlier forms of sovereignty by pointing out the different bases of sovereignty. He argues that, 'Christian claims [in the sixteenth century] to sovereignty rested on the "nature of the people being conquered [ie their supposed status as barbarians], instead of in the supposed juridical rights of the conquerors"' (Keal 2003, 69–70, quoting Anthony Black).

Brod finds another way of differentiating modern sovereignty from earlier forms of rule. He argues that '[e]very modern political system must in some sense claim to express "the voice of the people" and must at least give lip service to the idea of "popular sovereignty"'. Brod contends that '[c]lassical or medieval political systems, in contrast, had no such obligation'. He substantiates this view with the argument that 'Hegel's attention is on the underlying deep level of continuity and agreement in the foundations of political discourse in the modern world'. This underlying level of continuity 'makes it possible, for example, to take competing systems like capitalism and communism and cast the arguments for each in terms acceptable to the other system, to speak of competing claims to realise political and economic democracy, and to construct a dialogue with shared basic assumptions'. These things, says Brod, 'could not have been constructed between monarchists and republicans, for example, in an earlier period' (Brod 1992, 136).

Although this first narrative poses modern state sovereignty as emerging from a decisive break with the past, the historical record indicates rather a series of stages through which the modern state notion of sovereignty became entrenched, of modifications right up into the twentieth century and beyond. State sovereignty as we understand it today did not arise simply at one time fully formed. State sovereignty, and the international system of nation states that accompanies it, have both developed over time and so changed their meaning since the seventeenth century. The relationship between state sovereignty and the international system of states (so crucial to the modern sovereignty paradigm) has also varied across time, and these redefinitions can be plotted through the history in a series of treaties and settlements. The Westphalian settlement of 1648 not only sought to provide a peace treaty between warring political societies in Europe, but also set out the basis for excluding religious differences from conflicts between polities, recognised the existence of England and France as nation states, set the basis for what became the principle of an international system of nation states whereby states had sovereignty and a right to non-intervention, acknowledged a wider international system dominated by European states with colonies and empires abroad, and inaugurated the territorialized basis of states. The Concert of Europe of 1815 was set up to enforce the decisions of the Congress of Vienna. The Versailles Treaty after the First World War redrew the borders of states and the marked the final end of the Austro-Hungarian Empire, and the League of Nations was formed. The end of the Ottoman Empire had an important impact in shaping European self-definitions. The post-Second World War settlement, the establishment of the United Nations, waves of decolonisation, the Yalta agreement instituting bipolarity and the Cold War, have all also registered new meanings to state sovereignty and its international context. The end of the Cold War, the emergence of the United States as the single world super-power, waging war in Afghanistan and Iraq in the name of liberal freedom, and the growing importance of religion in politics and political judgment, marks another patterning of international politics and a new meaning for the sovereignty of the nation state.

One far-reaching effect of the development of the idea that there is a separate legal and constitutional order, that of the state, which the ruler has a duty to maintain, is that the power of the state, not that of the ruler, came to be envisaged as the basis of government. This in turn enabled the state to be conceptualised in the distinctively modern terms of modern sovereignty — as the sole source of law and legitimate force within its own territory, and as the sole appropriate object of its citizens' allegiance. Skinner, Heiman, Bottici, and Gough all express aspects of this view.

Skinner's Conclusion to his 1978 *Foundations of Political Thought. Volume 2*, traces well the historical detail of the process by which the idea of the modern state emerged. He sets out the preconditions of the modern state by the end of the sixteenth century. This is an important story, but it is not completely coeval with that of the development of modern sovereignty and its distinction from earlier ancient and medieval conceptions. The narrative of the emergence of the modern state, from the perspective of the history of conceptions of sovereignty, has the effect of depoliticising sovereignty and suppressing the story of the transmutation, translation, and metamorphosis of the concept of sovereignty over time.

Heiman also supports this first view. He comments that, '[e]qually lacking from the medieval model was that type of sovereignty which brings about a constitutional and legally ordered interaction between the numerous elements of the whole, an arrangement which allows for diversification yet retains the aims of the whole in sight' (Heiman 1971, 127–8).

Bottici also identifies modern sovereignty with a vital feature of the modern state. She articulates the view that the notion of sovereignty arose in conjunction with the idea of state as a *persona ficta*. Bodin and Hobbes are singled out, in this story, as the theorists who exploited the metaphor of the state-person, with the state as a 'unitary actor, equipped with a single will and rational behaviour' and the focus of the 'concept of a power *superiorem non recognoscens*'. Schmitt takes a similar view, Bottici notes, arguing that the force of the metaphor was achieved through a political secularisation of theological categories, with 'God's *superiorem non recognoscens* power becoming the state's sovereign power, and the omnipotent God becoming the omnipotent lawgiver'. She also recognises that the 'idea of the personality of the state is ancient, dating back to the Justinian Roman law idea of the state as an abstract subject of rights', but regards ancient Greek thought as being governed by another metaphor, an organicist one. She argues that the 'Platonic parallel *polis-soul* and the Aristotelian organicistic metaphor point instead much more to the organic composition of society, where the whole of the society is superior to the sum of its parts, but cannot be conceived of without them'. In contrast, the state as *persona ficta* is regarded as 'somehow independent of its members' (Bottici 2003, 395–6).

Gough (1963, 127) wants to make a distinction between a medieval sense of sovereignty and a modern, 'technical' sense. In the medieval sense sovereignty coincided with the monarch, while sovereignty in the modern sense is constituted by the distinction between legal and political sovereignty, for Gough. The legal sovereign is the person or assembly that can make positive law that none other can overrule, while political sovereignty is found for instance in popular sovereignty forms. In this case sovereignty has two dimensions — it can revert to the people if the government is dissolved, and it operates where the legislative body represents the people in a popular franchise.

Harrison points out that the move towards modern state sovereignty entailed in a very real sense the suppression of the authority of the church. He takes the view that 'Bodin argued that in any regime there had to be a single sovereign. Even if this is not analytically correct, it was becoming more and more true as a matter of fact in the new regimes of Europe'. Harrison notes that in 'the Middle Ages, there were two swords, Pope and Emperor. With Henry they became one', when 'Henry abolished the Pope (as a judicial authority in his country) and hence gave himself plenary power, full sovereignty'. Harrison pinpoints Henry's action as the effective claim to 'full power, this unification of authority in a single person' (Harrison 2003, 18–19).

Jackson, working within a confidently state-centric conception of sovereignty, stipulates categorically that sovereignty is 'a distinguishing feature of modern politics'. It 'points toward the modern era and away from the medieval era and all previous era'. For Jackson it is unequivocal that '[s]overeign statehood anchors our concept of modern politics just as the notion of Christian empire anchored the concept of medieval politics' and that '[p]resumably some new or renewed concept will have to anchor post-sovereign politics' (Jackson 1999, 423).

Franceschet reminds us that what we are dealing with here is not just facts but with an ideological story too. He observes that the development of '[l]iberalism is historically bound up with the coterminous rise of the modern state and the desire by certain social classes for freedom from the constraints of feudalism'. Moreover, if 'the constraints of the feudal order were to be dismantled properly in favour of individual self-determination, then another, more rational and legitimate constraining device was to be found in the modern sovereign state' (Franceschet 2002, 69).

The history of ideas about modern (state) sovereignty begins with Bodin, and in an important sense this is a constructed and political beginning. Regardless of what Bodin said (for instance about an impersonal sovereign, secularising the question of rule and politics, and providing a legitimacy away from divine right and in 'natural' law, all of which are indeed relevant to the emergence of the concept of modern state sovereignty), it acts to give modern state sovereignty a prestigiously long pedigree, identifying state sovereignty as a concern of a sixteenth century writer.

Spruyt presents a sophisticated form of the argument represented by Jackson. He contends that it was not a foregone conclusion nor natural upshot that sovereign states, and a system of sovereign states, would supersede medieval nobilities, feudal lords, burghers, city states, city leagues, confederated city leagues, centralising monarchies, emperors, and the pope as crosscutting jurisdictions and focuses of political authority. The development of the state system cannot be ascribed to a simple Darwinian survival of the fittest in terms of military power. Neither was the history of this development even nor linear in fashion. The previous 'system' was the feudal mode, characterised by rule by personal bonds, and in the late medieval and early modern period the sovereign state had serious competitors in the city league and the city state. However, Spruyt argues, the element that proved decisive was not 'the particular level of monarchical administration or royal revenue, nor the physical size of the state', but the 'new element introduced by the late medieval state ... the notion of sovereignty', a 'critical turn in the political organisation of the Late Middle Ages'.

According to Spruyt, while 'the fundamental transformations of the late medieval period were set in motion by the dramatic changes in the

economic environment' (Spruyt 1994, 67), 'it was the concept of sovereignty that altered the structure of the international system by basing
political authority on the principle of territorial exclusivity'. He states
bluntly that the 'modern state is based on these two key elements, internal
hierarchy and external autonomy, which emerged for the first time in the
Late Middle Ages' (Spruyt 1994, 3). The sovereign state is 'an organisation
that is territorially defined. Authority is administrative control over a
fixed territorial space. It is delimited in an external sense, vis-à-vis other
actors, by its formal borders. Unlike the church or empire, it advances no
superiority over other rulers' (Spruyt 1994, 36). The sovereign state exercises secular rule. Spruyt argues that the 'sovereign, territorial logic of
organisation replaced the alternative modes of authority in Europe'
because their centralised decision-making authority was 'in a better position to overcome the feudal remnants of economic and legal
particularism'. Because 'the king's interest in rationalizing and improving
the overall economy coincided with the interests of the mercantile elements in society', kings were more efficient at 'curtailing freeriding and
defection, and hence they were better at mobilizing the resources of their
societies'. Also, given 'the existence of a final decision maker, sovereigns
could credibly speak on behalf of their constituencies' and, 'because of
their territorial character, states were compatible with one another', and
their 'borders enabled sovereigns to specify limits to their authority'
whereas city-leagues could not easily do this (Spruyt 1994, 155).

Spruyt also argues that before the system of sovereign states emerged,
the identity of the political community derived from some readily identifiable shared affinity such as 'shared kinship, similar religious belief, or
highly personalistic ties of mutual aid and submission'. Similarly, says
Spruyt, the sovereign state also needs to be 'imagined and personified
before it can exist' (Spruyt 1994, 67), or in other words this transition 'required reification and objectification of authority'. Feudal relations 're-
sembled a form of artificial kinship'. According to Spruyt, the 'emergence
of sovereign, territorial rule was, therefore, not merely a fight between the
forces favouring fragmentation versus centralization; it was a contest
about the very nature of authority and kingship', and a move from a personalised to a depersonalised form of kingship (Spruyt notes that 'when
Louis XIV supposedly equated himself with the state, he contravened the
realities of political discourse of the seventeenth century'), as well as a
'radically different way of ordering international transactions as well',
based on the 'principle of juridical equivalence' between states. Spruyt is
adamant that what is at stake here 'represent[s] a cognitive shift' and that a
'pure materialist explanation does not suffice' (Spruyt 1994, 68).

Spruyt's argument is excellent in pointing out the historical specificity
of the political 'logic of organisation' in the late medieval period and at

showing how the system of sovereign states triumphed over its competitors in a non-teleological manner. Also, while Spruyt is not on sound ground in introducing the concept of the 'logic of organisation' meta-historically, nevertheless the term is useful in conveying an important aspect of what 'sovereignty' accomplishes for a polity. However, the weakness of his analysis is that he takes on a definition of sovereignty from Benn and Hinsley as a given, has a simplistic model of sovereignty (hierarchy and autonomy), and does not seek to problematise whether the concept of sovereignty might have more richness by looking for continuities with the past or broadening the range of factors involved in its meaning.

A version of this first argument is also put forward by Brown *et al*, who contrast the emergence of sovereignty with the way political communities were envisaged in the ancient world. They highlight the role of city states as ensembles of collectivities, and argue that 'cities such as Athens and Rome were founded as associations of families, and the lineage groups of the original families, the tribes, continued to play an important role in the politics of the city throughout the classical period'. Under the Roman republic, they observe, 'the Romans always voted with the tribe as the constituency rather than any territorial sub-division of the city, and tribal identities were equally important amongst the Athenians, where the large number of resident aliens—some of second or third generation or more—testified to the near impossibility of non-descendents of the founders achieving citizenship'. They note that 'Rome had a more open policy in this respect, but under the Republic the notion of descent as the basis for citizenship was preserved by the policy of adopting naturalised citizens into a particular tribe' (Brown *et al* 2002, 7).

Brown *et al* also follow the view that, in the Middle Ages, '"[p]olitical" authority was divided amongst a number of different kinds of entities, ranging from territorial magnates and incorporated bodies such as towns or universities to universal entities such as the Holy Roman Empire or the papacy. Each of these bodies exercised some authority, none exercised sovereignty in the modern sense of the term' (Brown *et al* 2002, 5). Brown *et al* endorse a picture of medieval Europe as 'a tangle of overlapping feudal jurisdictions, plural allegiances and asymmetrical suzerainties'. They characterise it as a place where not only 'kings, lords, vassals, and church officials but also towns, parliaments, guilds, and universities exchanged diplomatic missions, settled their disputes by negotiation and arbitration, and concluded formal treaties'. They support the view that 'kings made treaties with their own vassals and with the vassals of their neighbours. They received embassies from their own subjects and from the subjects of other princes', and 'subject cities negotiated with one another without reference to their respective sovereigns'. They contrast this with the situation in modern international society, whereby 'only states are "international legal persons" capable of sending and receiving ambassadors, signing treaties, or appearing before international tribunals'. Moreover, they note, medieval treaties 'were more like private contracts' because the idea of public international contract had not yet been established, and treaties 'were made under the law common to all peoples', and partly because the distinction between office and office holder had not been established (Brown *et al* 2002, 250–1).

Brown *et al* also represent sovereignty as emerging as a way of 'solving the problem' of 'how conflicting claims to ruling authority should be reconciled' (Brown *et al* 2002, 247). But they see the idea of sovereignty as 'implicit' as far back as 'the thirteenth-century French formula, "the king is emperor in his own realm" — in other words, that the law of the king of France overrides that of any other lord, baron, or noble in France'. They argue that Bodin's work was crucial in promoting the case that 'in the face of intractable religious disagreements', the 'only plausible basis for peace was shared recognition within each state of the authority of its ruler'. The criterion for delimiting the respective claims to exercising power is sovereignty (Brown *et al* 2002, 248).

The teleological and normative interpretation often found as an element of this first view, is summed up by Brown *et al* when they state that '[a]lthough a society of states has been in the making in Europe since at least the fifteenth century, the idea of a distinct body of law springing from and regulating this society remained hazy throughout the early modern period' (Brown *et al* 2002, 311).

The conventional idea about the emergence of the sovereignty political form is made more complex by directing attention to writers like Spinoza who presented a theory of sovereignty which refutes the notion that sovereignty in the early modern period was universally characterised by a unified state form, and by pointing out the ideological quality of the modern state paradigm of sovereignty. A further argument that complicates the received story is found in Keal's work, which identifies how the modern state definition of sovereignty was crucially constructed against a backdrop of a continuity of imperial power. This first story, of the emergence of the modern sovereign state, does not sufficiently take into account several points about empire. The orthodox narrative misses out the impact of the subsequent development of empires in the modern period, and the differentiated experience of countries and peoples under empires, as well as underplaying the (spurious) theoretical arguments used to amalgamate state and empire and to justify imperial domination. To make this case, Keal usefully highlights the value of Benjamin Cohen's definition of sovereignty, which emphasises the asymmetry between dominance and dependence (Keal 2003, 38). He also usefully quotes Michael Doyle's definition of empire as 'a relationship, formal or informal, in which one state controls the effective political sovereignty of another political society'. Keal makes the point that, following Doyle's definition, the 'political society' being controlled could be a state or something less than a state (Keal 2003, 41).

Keal reminds us that empire is not only a Western political form—the Ottoman, Japanese and Chinese empires are all examples of important non-Western empires. He also observes that, 'at the very time that it became clearly discernible, international society was itself a society of empires' (Keal 2003, 42). The implications for understanding the emergence of the sovereign state as the dominant political form and of international society in this context are important, according to Keal, because 'empire involves the limitation of sovereignty'. Keal quotes Doyle's phrase for empire, 'a sovereignty that lacks a community', and argues that it was in important respects the character of empires that led to claims by groups for 'self-determination and sovereignty over their own affairs' (Keal 2003, 43).

Two

The second line of argument contends that sovereignty is defined by the modern commitment to reason, social contract and individual rights. This commitment contrasts with the legitimation of political order in the previous period by ideas inflected with Christian religious sanctionings such as the divine right of the king. According to this view sovereignty is associated with the specific context in the history of ideas of modernity and secular reason, and with the pattern of Enlightenment dichotomies such as objective/subjective, mind/body, science/opinion, external/internal, reason/emotion, and culture/nature, all of which have a distinctive form in modern thinking and social practices.

According to this view, the early-modern period saw the transition from temporal rule by personalised rulers legitimated by divine sanction, to temporal rule legitimated by an abstract, non-personalised principle of sovereign right. For this view, modern sovereignty begins with Bodin precisely because this is when the modern process of de-personalisation begins. Modern sovereignty is the answer to questions about ruling that were now being asked, where the answer of a divine sanction retreated into being considered as only part of the background of an explanation.

This second story about sovereignty also argues that the shape of modern sovereignty, and the story about its differentiation from earlier political forms, is profoundly affected not only by Enlightenment processes of secularisation and the elevation of individual reason. It is also deeply informed by the process of nation-state structuring, capitalist economic developments, and the formation of international relations or the international system, which occurred during the seventeenth and eighteenth centuries.

These two processes were closely related. The development of the modern international sphere characterised by modern autonomous states as the agents with choices, mirrors the construction of the sovereign individual. The metaphorical relationship between individual and state, taken to have powerful explanatory value, developed in consequence. The new self/other dichotomy that formed during the Enlightenment period is mirrored in the notion of international relations being modelled on the self/other dichotomy between states.

Three

The third narrative, to which Bodin subscribed, is that sovereignty is a political concept which characterises any and every political form. In capturing the notion of symbolic authority itself, sovereignty applies to all polities by virtue of their having some distinction between the arrangement of public order and other kinds of social orderings, including before and outside the modern Western formulation of the distinction between public and private. Bodin's answer to the first story, about a putative break between modern and pre-modern sovereignty, was simply to argue that in the medieval period, 'the emperor is subject to the Estates of the Empire, and does not claim sovereignty over the princes or the Estates' (Bodin 1992, 16). Cole uses the same logic when he argues that we 'have only to seek out the determinate human superior in a given society, and we shall find the Sovereign', following Austin that a sovereign has no superior to whom obedience is due and receives 'habitual obedience from the bulk of a given society' (Cole 1973, xxv).

De Tocqueville takes the view that the application of the term sovereignty is general enough that it can be made both about different time periods and, perhaps, different institutions within a society. He argues that the 'principle of sovereignty of the people ... which is always to be found, more or less, at the bottom of almost all human institutions, usually remains buried there' (quoted in Connolly 2004, 31).

This third perspective on the history of sovereignty argues that if the legitimation of rulers and the establishment of political order are seen as two of the key components in the sovereignty cluster, then we can trace a history of changes in sovereignty in the Western tradition from the legitimation of rulers in ancient Greece and Rome by law and polytheistic religion. In the medieval period the legitimation of rulers (monarchs and emperors) came from divine law, a divine source, God. This political order was supplanted by one in which legitimation of the monarchs of early-modern Europe as sovereign was supplied by a developing *Rechtstaat* idea linking law and morality. With Rousseau we have the argument for the legitimation of the ruler from the people, from popular sovereignty in the *Rechtstaat*. In contemporary practice the legitimation of rulers comes from democratic principles and procedures (rather than from the people directly) in a moral and legal *Rechstaat*.

The third narrative can also be supported by reference to important continuities with older political forms such as the Roman. A primary contribution of the Roman period to political thought, lies in the areas of legislation and the definition of governmental offices and institutions. Roman law is the basis of all European jurisprudence, not excluding the 'common law' of the Germanic peoples of Northern Europe whose 'Romanisation' was mediated by Christianity. Armitage's analysis of the term *imperium*, for example, is useful in showing the strong links and continuity between sovereignty and the early classical understanding of empire, because of the Roman origin of the term. His description of the meaning of *imperium* resonates as strongly with the concept of sovereignty as it does with the concept of empire. *Imperium* was the term for authority in Roman public law, and it had been 'invested with a spatial dimension during the late Roman republic and early principate'. The term 'originally signified the supreme authority held by a military commander', but took on the meaning of 'rule' more generally, and then came to refer to the 'territory over which such rule was exercised'. Armitage traces the way early-modern uses of 'empire' (and the later meaning which put together empire and 'imperialism') were 'distilled from these Roman precedents', such that from meaning 'supreme authority, *imperium* became used to denote any power that recognized no superior and, by extension, a political community that was self-governing and acknowledged no higher allegiance' (Armitage 1998, 103–4). Armitage's analysis is also useful from the point of view of this third narrative, in highlighting the 'wider conceptual field' of order, hierarchy, independence, and political community, within which contemporaries debated the meaning of empire and, we can add, sovereignty. Furthermore, Armitage's reminder of the persistence of Roman classics in the educational curriculum, and so the basis of intellectual life, well into the eighteenth century, demonstrates also the indebtedness of the meaning of sovereignty to those Roman sources (Armitage 1998, 104).

Vincent also takes the view of a long and continuous tradition of sovereignty but with a fixed conception of it, specifically in relation to conceptualising the power and authority of Popes in the medieval period. Vincent quotes Figgis that 'there was a belief, that true sovereignty, ie independence and unquestioned authority, had been derived from appropriation by each kingdom of rights originally confined to the Empire' in the medieval period (Vincent 1987, 66). He writes that 'Gierke and Figgis consciously identified the source of this principle of sovereignty with Roman law. The doctrines of *imperium* and *legibus solutus* were taken on board originally by Popes'. Vincent notes that the 'doctrine of the "pleni-

tude of power" (*plenitudo potestatis*) was adapted by Popes such as Innocent to justify their absolutist claims' (Vincent 1987, 199). He makes the
case that Roman law ideas certainly played a key role, from the twelfth
century onwards, in the development of the absolutist theory of the state,
of which the idea of sovereignty as absolute, perpetual, indivisible, and
inalienable was a central concept. Vincent argues that this 'is specifically
the case with doctrines such as *plenitudo potestas* and *princeps legibus solutus
est*. These doctrines tended to focus and concentrate power, authority and
law into the ruler'. Such doctrines, he claims, 'were attractive ideas to theorists looking for an alternative to the strife of civil war'. Initially, 'canon
lawyers were fascinated by the use of such doctrines to describe papal
rule. Papal monarchy was first formulated by Pope Leo I (440-6), although
later, much more vigorous, formulations of it were offered by popes Greg-
ory VII and Innocent III'. According to Vincent, religious 'discussions of
papal sovereignty and the constitutional role of the Church were gradually laicized in the sixteenth century', and the transformation was 'accomplished during the Reformation' (Vincent 1987, 48).

Hinsley's perspective straddles the third and first narratives. He argues
that the concept of (internal) sovereignty is ancient and extends back at
least to Roman times, but that sovereignty was not applied to the international domain until the end of the sixteenth century. He accounts for this
situation by holding that it was not until the end of the sixteenth century,
when another formulation of internal sovereignty was made, that the
authority relationship at the heart of the concept was applied to the international realm. Only then did 'men first grapple with the problem of
extending' the idea of sovereignty 'to the relations between states'. Moreover, Hinsley relates, and expressing the teleological perspective explicitly, 'it was not until the eighteenth century that they finally solved it'.
Hinsley maintains that while the 'idea that there is a sovereign authority
within the single community involves the corollary that this authority is
one among other authorities which are ruling other communities in the
same sovereign way', in practice 'this logical consequence was not recognized for hundreds of years'. Neither the 'Romans nor their Byzantine suc-
cessors, both of whom had developed the notion of internal sovereignty,
ever applied it in its international sense' (Hinsley 1969, 275-6).

Four

The fourth line of argument builds on the third but differs from the previous three in taking conceptual and historical change seriously. The
concept/conception distinction enables us to identify a multiplicity of
conceptions of sovereignty across ancient, medieval and modern political
forms. Attention to historical change and specificity enables us to
acknowledge contextual variety and difference. This fourth perspective

emphasises that no conception of sovereignty, including the modern state one, is universal, transcendent in character, or transhistorical in its reach. After outlining the abstract form of the argument, evidence from Coleman, Franklin, Loughlin, Teschke, Bartelson, and Reus-Smit is brought to bear to support this view.

In answer to the question of whether sovereignty is a necessary dimension of politics and political society then, this fourth line of argument says, yes in a weak sense but no in a strong sense. In the same way that all political regimes have conceptions of something like politics and law, all have an organising principle for living in political society together. But sovereignty is not necessarily allied to a capitalist economic market, an impersonal bureaucratic state system, a state with a monopoly of power and violence, and fixed territory. All polities have a role for law, though not necessarily a 'rule of law' or *Rechtstaat*. Not all polities have a secularised conception of political principles, and not all polities distinguish political theory from civil and legal theory. All polities have mechanisms for dealing with social conflict, political differences, a principle for social coherence and identity, social cooperation and methods of enforcement, but their means of legitimating and achieving these things vary widely.

Similarly, this fourth viewpoint responds to the question of whether one can talk about sovereignty independently of its subject – of the specific form of polity with which it is associated – by saying that, as with all political concepts the answer is both yes and no. Yes – in order to operate with a concept/conception distinction, there must be a thin notion of the concept which is shared by all thick conceptions but which is expressed differently in the various conceptions. The Greek polis, medieval city-states, the early-modern absolutist state, and the modern nation state, all share a thin concept of sovereignty, this fourth argument maintains. At least in the Western tradition, moreover, the category of empire with reference to ancient Greece and Rome and medieval Christendom can, with some adjustments, be discussed in terms of sovereignty. But no – they don't all share the same thick conception. In addition, when discussing non-Western forms the meaning of the term is stretched and at some point becomes anachronistic and can only be considered by analogy, and so loses some explanatory force. In these senses then, at least within a Western tradition, all polities, all political forms have a conception of sovereignty, just as they all have some form – however much unwritten or unformulated – of a constitution, an explanation of relations of order, political institutions, ideas about rights and duties, and a sense of law.

The question of what sovereignty meant in the medieval (and possibly) ancient period is complicated by the absence, as Coleman documents, in the earlier time, of the modern notion of self-ownership associated with classic liberal writers. She complains that, in reading the earlier period, 'there is still a tendency to conflate ownership with powers of self-gover-nance' (Coleman 2005, 135). Coleman's work is important in that it helps to de-naturalise the equation of sovereignty with modern liberal sover-eignty. She notes that there has been 'an easy contemporary conflation of sovereignty over oneself and ownership of that self' (Coleman 2005, 126). In the earlier period, she shows, '[s]overeign jurisdiction—the word in Latin was often *dominium* but it meant *jurisdiction*—was a duty of care of a superior over an inferior'. Another meaning of the word *dominium*, she adds, '*did* refer to private property ownership and to say that someone has a property *in* something, in some exterior material good, meant he had a material interest in it and this required that the something be alienable'. Coleman gives the example of how 'a judge could have a range of jurisdic-tional powers over, say, a criminal's body and his material possessions', but 'he could no more "own" that body than he could "own" the man's soul'. Moreover, Coleman argues, 'the individual could be said to be *dominus* or proprietor of his body but only in the sense that his directive intellect was ultimately charged with the care of his body so that one could say he had a *ius* or right, which was really a power to care for himself, from God, and so long as he did no injury to others'. To emphasise the differ-ence between medieval and modern notions, Coleman confirms that the 'kind of absolute property right in oneself that could imply that the self was alienable was not possible for medieval scholastics or indeed for Locke since it would give a licence to suicide or self-mutilation, which under natural law is forbidden' (Coleman 2005, 135).

Franklin expresses a good understanding of the nuances of historical and conceptual change, important to this fourth perspective, in his work on Bodin. He makes a useful point in the context of making a judgment that Bodin's insistence on indivisible sovereignty was wrong and that the scholars before Bodin were simply confused in classifying some regimes as instances of 'mixed sovereignty'. Franklin describes how, in the six-teenth century, 'the king was still addressed as sovereign even though he might require the consent of the Estates or other body [because of their customary legal rights and 'privileges'] for the conduct of some of his affairs' (Franklin 1992, xviii).

Loughlin underlines the way the instability and stretched meanings of political terms leads to the conclusion that no single attribution can be taken as authoritative, and that these terms are slippery and overlap. He distinguishes *dominium*, that is force and material power over another —'the power of mastery'—from political power, which is 'a product of a relationship between individuals (natural persons) that, in form at least, conceives them to be equals'. Loughlin argues soundly that this political power 'becomes public power proper only when taking some institutional form', and when it retains a sense of 'some form of partnership', and of 'formal relationship constituted by a system of rules' (Loughlin 2003, 62).

Teschke supports the case for multiple conceptions of sovereignty by arguing convincingly that the medieval, absolutist and modern conceptions of sovereignty need to be distinguished from each other. He also has insightful comments on the relationship between sovereignty and politics. While he takes the view that 'a strict historical semantic would avoid the terms sovereignty or state', nevertheless he argues that 'for comparative purposes it is acceptable to say that sovereignty was "parcellized" or "divided", in the sense that each lord was a "fragment of the state"'. However, he adds, 'since the feudal "state" was neither a corporate entity nor a "legal person", since it lacked an abstract institutional existence beyond the life-spans of individual rulers, it is more precise to define the political in terms of a concrete praxis of personalized domination'. Indeed, Teschke notes, 'since the medieval world lacked a "state", it also lacked an "economy" and a "society" as separate institutions with autonomous mechanisms of social integration and developmental logics'. Moreover, it also follows from the 'interpersonal character of medieval domination for determining the sphere of the political' that because 'domination was personal, noble families — dynasties — were perforce the "natural" transmitters of political power' (Teschke 2003, 62). Adding weight to the notion of the utility of the idea of sovereignty prior to the modern conception of it, Teschke refers to 'Roman law and the Justinian conception of undivided sovereignty flowing from one supreme source' (Teschke 2003, 179).

Teschke also works with a concept/concept distinction when he usefully classifies 'geopolitical core institutions' central to conceptions of sovereignty. The term 'geopolitics' refers here to 'relations between public carriers of political power' (Teschke 2003, 12), 'such as political authority and public power, peace and war, territoriality and border, legitimation and coercion, empire-building and geopolitical fragmentation, alliance formation and the resolution of conflicts'. Teschke identifies such connections between 'public carriers of political power' as having different meanings and references in different historical periods (Teschke 2003, 4).

The concept/conception approach is also evident in Bartelson's insightful work when he takes the view that something like sovereignty has been a generic feature of political communities. He says that 'most human societies have confronted problems of power and authority, and where they should be located' (Bartelson 1995, 3). In the context specifically of European political thought, he argues, the trend has been that the source and locus of 'authority is distributed downwards in a slow chronological series, ranging from God to king, and then from king to people' (Bartelson 1995, 4). He makes a case that a different and 'specific arrangement of sovereignty' is found in three historical periods, which he calls the

Renaissance, the Classical and the Modern, the last of which is characterised by the modern subject, the modern state and the international system
(Bartelson 1995, 7).

Within this context, Bartelson argues that among the 'conceptual ante-
cedents' to sovereignty, articulated within the 'logical conditions of possibility within theological, legal and political writings in the Middle Ages
and in the Renaissance' (Bartelson 1995, 88), there is 'an array of concepts
with overlapping and sometimes contradictory connotations, as as *potesta,*
potential, majestas, gubernaculums, regnum, imperium, dominium, status,
republicae' (Bartelson 1995, 263). He also cautions that the framework in
which to discuss sovereignty is also made more complex by the recognition that before the modern age, there was 'no object of knowledge called
the *international system'* (Bartelson 1995, 137). According to Bartelson, the
'very tem sovereignty was not present within political discourse until
Beaumanoir introduced it in the thirteenth century', and that even after
that date, there is no autonomous discourse on sovereignty, if we by
autonomous mean a discourse which has a single system for the formation
of statements'. Consequently he uses the term 'mytho-sovereignty' to refer
to 'the mimetic paradigm of rulership in the early and high Middle Ages,
when the legitimacy of the ruler is founded on his resemblance with Christ
or God', and he uses the term 'proto-sovereignty' to refer to 'the polity-
centred paradigm of rulership in the late Middle Ages, when the legitimacy
of the ruler derives from more profane sources' (Bartelson 1995, 88–9).

Bartelson makes the case that a profound shift marks the meaning of
sovereignty from the late Middle Ages and the Renaissance to what he
calls the Classical Age, the sixteenth, seventeenth and eighteenth centuries. He contrasts sovereignty in the earlier period, as 'a mark of superiority or a sign of divine origin, known and disseminated by analogy,
resemblance and *exempla'*, with the later period when 'the concept of sovereignty becomes linked with individuation, identification and order.
Sovereignty here, for Bartelson, 'has the power of individuation since [as
Bodin noted] it is "it selfe a thing indivisible"'. As a result, Bartelson maintains, 'sovereignty itself becomes "sovereign" in political discourse as
[again in Bodin's words] "the most necessarie point for the understanding
of the nature of a Commonweale"' (Bartelson 1995, 138). Sovereignty is a
principle of identification in the sense that it is no longer 'exclusively
linked to the person of the prince', but is also identified with the political
unit. Bartelson argues that in this period, sovereignty ambivalently
referred to both 'the intense divinisation and personalisation of authority
in the hands of the sovereign', and to 'an abstract notion of a naturalised
state as a symbol of depersonalised authority'. Sovereignty became in this
period also a principle of order, in the sense that 'its concept defines the

domain of objects of an autonomous discourse, a science of states' (Bartelson 1995, 139).

Reus-Smit also employs a concept/conception procedure when he argues for sovereignty as a concept with a history going back to Ancient Greece, whose meaning has been underpinned by values current in different historical situations, and so revised and recast over time. He relates that when 'sovereign states were constructed in ancient Greece, when they were championed again in Renaissance Italy, when absolutist states were carved out of the declining heteronomous order of medieval Europe, and when the age of revolutions spurned the development of modern nation-states', the 'idea of sovereignty did not emerge in a moral vacuum'. In each case, he notes, sovereignty 'had to be justified, and that justification has always taken the form of an appeal to higher-order values' or moral purposes. Such values and purposes, Reus-Smit continues, 'define the identity or *raison d'etre* of the state, whether they entail the pursuit of justice', the 'cultivation of *bios politikos*, a distinctive form of communal life', the 'achievement of civic glory', the preservation of a divinely ordained, rigidly hierarchical social order', or the advancement of individuals' rights and the celebration of the nation' (Reus-Smit 2001, 527–8).

This way of looking at sovereignty is valuable for breaking down the not very helpful ancient/modern sovereignty formula, for seeing the history of sovereignty as a history of changing conceptions tied to specific circumstances, and for showing in this way the constructedness of sovereignty. However, it is worth noting that Reus-Smit's theory is less convincing when he argues that configurations of sovereignty are always determined by revolutionary ideals of legitimate statehood and new ideas about the moral purpose of the state challenging the existing political order. In his tripartite scheme of sovereignty, ideals of moral purpose, and political order, it is possible that the other two elements could also drive change, not just the ideals of moral purpose. Reus-Smit's theory also places too much weight on moral considerations in politics, when sometimes instrumental and strategic considerations can be recognised as playing a stronger part, and sometimes all considerations are so intertwined that it would be difficult to isolate moral considerations as primary.

Reflecting back over the first and second lines of argument, we can see that they contain a dominant and triumphalist narrative about modern sovereignty that sees it emerging from the entanglement of politics with religion and dynastic monarchies in the medieval period, equates it with state sovereignty as a new secular, rational form of political organisation based on nations, and regards it as bringing about a progressively more egalitarian expression of popular sovereignty. From the perspective of the fourth line of argument it is possible to contest all these points. First, it is clear that the past is misrepresented as an irrational web of loyalties and obligations, that modern sovereignty is misrepresented as a rational and neutral system, and that both are much more diverse. Secondly, there is a strong case for the view which highlights the powerful but *mythical* status of state sovereignty and which identifies the presence of continuing diversity, for instance in that not all political communities even today are states. Thirdly, one can argue strongly against the teleological view and demonstrate the diversity of conceptions. The canon of thinking about sovereignty does not simply support the view of the emancipatory nature of modern sovereignty. One can point, for example, to the way that the only really positive conception of popular sovereignty in the mainstream canon is Rousseau's and he is considered equivocally from the liberal perspective on the grounds that too much popular sovereignty can result in totalitarianism. Moreover, Schmitt's theory is no more egalitarian than was Hobbes's.

Having made a case for the fourth argument, for the continuity of a thin concept and existence of a multiplicity of thick conceptions of sovereignty over time, we turn to Bodin.

BODIN

Jean Bodin was born in 1529 or 1530 in Angers in France and died in 1596. He made an early change of career after three or four years in a Carmelite order, and then gained an up-to-date humanist education in Paris. Franklin describes Bodin as a 'religious maverick' (1992 xii) although he continued throughout his life to observe Catholic religious practice. After studying and teaching law but not gaining a permanent appointment, Bodin became a barrister in the *Parlement*, and was given a number of administrative and political appointments under Henry III's government in France in the mid-sixteenth century. He was very proud to be elected to the assembly of the States General in 1576, but his act of trying to persuade the assembly to resist the king's taxation proposals (despite his being a public figure recognised as an enlightened royalist and his being against civil war) meant an end to further advancement in public office. His treatise on public law and policy, *Six livres de la république*, first written in French and now translated as *Six Books of the Commonwealth*, was published in 1576, during the French religious wars, to considerable acclaim.

To contextualise further, the *Six Books* was published sixty years after two crucial events had taken place. Publication occurred sixty years after Luther nailed his Ninety-Five Theses to the door of the Castle Church at Wittenberg, which initiated the Reformation, the Protestant challenge to the hegemony of the Roman Catholic Church in Europe. The appearance of the *Six Books* also happened sixty years after Machiavelli's works were written, cautioning against the inevitable corruption of political forms. Bodin's approach is more legal and philosophical than Machiavelli's, but like Machiavelli, Bodin places great significance on the idea of power in his understanding of the state. This account of Bodin's theory of sovereignty is indebted to Quentin Skinner's fine *Foundations of Modern Political Thought. Volume Two* and Julian Franklin's edition of Bodin's writings on sovereignty.

Four chapters in the first and second books of the *Six Books* deal specifically with the definition of sovereignty, the marks of sovereignty, the refutation of mixed forms of state, and with whether it is permissible to kill a tyrant. These chapters on sovereignty, while clearly central to Bodin's purpose, are part of a much broader political theory, examining the way political communities differ from the family and from patriarchal power; providing a detailed exploration of monarchy, aristocracy, and democracy; a discussion of senates, magistrates and other powers within the political community; consideration of the cyclical character of commonwealths and the role of officials and princes in them; an examination of the diversity of commonwealths and peoples, and of alliances and treaties between princes; and surveying matters such as censorship, finance and coinage; ending with a comparison demonstrating that royal monarchy is the best form of state.

Bodin's *Six Books* was shaped to a considerable extent in reaction to the intense religious and political conflict between Catholics and Huguenots which threatened the unity and survival of the French monarch. The Huguenots argued that the religious duty to resist tyrannical monarchs could be translated into the political concept of a moral right of resistance. The Puritans in the English Civil War a century later argued the same case, and Locke gives the classic liberal articulation of this political right of resistance at the end of the seventeenth century. In Bodin's earlier work, written in Latin, the *Method for the Easy Comprehension of History* of 1566, he had shared with a group of other writers a plea for toleration towards the Huguenots, and as Vincent notes, 'Bodin was a member of the *politiques*, a Catholic royalist group who advocated some toleration' (Vincent 1987, 34). Interpreters of Bodin have different views about whether the move from the *Method* to the *Six Books* represents a continuity or a sharp break. While this debate does not have a crucial bearing on the examination of Bodin's ideas here, it is important for assessments of Bodin's wider theory. Vincent characterises the positions in the debate. For Franklin the *Six Books* involved a dramatic shift from the more constitutionalist view of his earlier work. The line of argument is that in the wake of the force of the Huguenots' claim for constitutional limits on monarchical power, Bodin in the *Six Books* abandoned his earlier constitutionalist position. Vincent argues that, for Franklin, Salmon and Skinner the *Six Books* was 'a reaction to the views of Huguenot monarchomarch constitutionalism after 1572', and the work advocated more limited forms of sovereignty. On the other side of the debate, Vincent contends that Preston King however, 'maintains that the *Six Bookes* simply "argues more forcefully than the *Methodus* for unrestrained public power — not that it contains fewer arguments for greater restraint upon public power"' (Vincent 1987, 52).

Another aspect of the historical context in which Bodin asserted this conception of sovereignty is attested to by Vincent. Vincent notes that the 'independent life of many thirteenth-century Italian cities fostered the image of sovereign units independent of the prince'. He quotes A J and A W Carlyle to the effect that 'as late as the middle of the thirteenth century the civil or Roman lawyers were unanimous in holding that the *populus* was the ultimate source of all political authority, that they recognised no other source of all political authority than the will of the whole community' (Vincent 1987, 110).

The most important concepts in Bodin's political theory — examined in turn below — are the rejection of a right of resistance, the theory of sovereignty, and the idea of the state. The three concepts are closely inter-connected. What emerges crucially from this investigation is that Bodin theorised the 'state' as the locus of power rather than theorised absolute monarchy, and that while he places limitations on the power of the prince they do not mirror corresponding rights of resistance by the people, legislative representative or other officials. What is most distinctive about Bodin's theory of sovereignty is the notion of sovereignty as majesty, within the context of the office-holder theory and asymmetrical limitations just noted. The general features highlighted in Bodin's theory include sovereignty as the highest legal authority, sovereignty as absolute and indivisible, and sovereignty as a regulative ideal establishing political stability and identity.

As Skinner assesses, the *Six Books of the Commonwealth* contains several crucial lines of argument, the first of which is an uncompromising defence of the power of the French monarchy, in the form of a theory of sovereignty. Sustaining the conception of sovereignty is a compendious and wide-ranging wealth of scholarship in the *Six Books* drawn not just from French history but from the histories and legal codes of other contemporaneous European countries and ancient Rome and Greece, as well as further afield. Examples from Poland, Denmark, Persia, and Egypt are regularly used. This feature of Bodin's writing serves not just to illustrate his points but also to form an interpretation of history to support his particular conception of sovereignty. One of the primary ways in which Bodin uses his examples is as evidence for his argument that his conception of sovereignty is and always has been a necessary feature of all political communities. In illustrating his theory with this breadth of knowledge, Bodin often — significantly — uses the rhetorical strategy of finding other and earlier authors to be 'confused'. The breadth of Bodin's intellectual background is indicated by Vincent, who compares the rationalistic and utilitarian features of Hobbes's thinking and his scepticism about religion with the view that 'Bodin's ideas on politics were rooted in his interests in astrology, climatology, geography and cosmology' (Vincent 1987, 51). The *Six Books* also contains, as Skinner attests, an ideological assault on and repudiation of the Huguenots' constitutional case, and a call (that directly follows from the logic of the theory of sovereignty) for the outlawing of all theories of resistance. Bodin held that no public act of resistance against a legitimate sovereign by a subject can ever be approved or vindicated. Skinner also underlines that the *Six Books* contains a call for order, peace and political harmony to be recognised as the primary value in political life, even above liberty. In contrast with his earlier tolerationist and constitutionalist emphasis in the *Method*, it was the fragility of order and the importance of political stability that now preoccupied Bodin.

Lindahl makes an observation in support of this view, linking Bodin's theory to a deeper 'loss of order' than the religious wars on their own created. He argues that the mainstream reading 'has him devising the concept of sovereignty to hold at bay the disintegration of society in the face of bitter religious wars'. But, Lindahl notes, this interpretation does not account for why sovereignty, 'became a philosophical theme at the threshold of modernity; after all, there was no dearth of civil wars prior to Bodin's time'. He contends that the significance for Bodin of these civil wars was that they were occurring in the context of a more profound 'loss of order', the loss of a unifying framework previously supplied by the Catholic Church and the political institutions of the papacy and the Holy Roman Empire. Lindahl identifies this loss of order with the inauguration of modernity, politics in a secular framework, and political community as a unity achieved in the context of contingency (Lindahl 2003, 88).

Once the basic doctrines of no right of resistance and the primacy of order have been propounded, Bodin does introduce a qualification — if the ruler is a tyrant who has usurped power, he can be lawfully slain. This qualification is perhaps surprising, given Bodin's reputation for theorising absolutist sovereignty, but he is able to propose the qualification without compromising his theory because what he seeks to establish is absolute sovereignty through law, or legal absolute sovereignty. So, on the question of killing a tyrant he says unequivocally that 'a tyrant … may be justly killed without form or shape of trial'. Again, deliverance by a virtuous foreign prince from a sovereign tyrant who is 'cruel, oppressive, or excessively wicked' is 'glorious and becoming', in Bodin's view (Bodin 1992, 112–13). However, Bodin adds, if the tyrant 'becomes legitimate', in that 'having encroached upon sovereignty by force or fraud, he has himself elected by the Estates', then that 'solemn act of election is an authentic ratification of the tyranny', and it is not permissible to kill him (Bodin 1992, 111).

Bodin does not regard his validation of killing tyrants as in any way providing an ambiguous clause licensing widespread claims that sovereigns were tyrants and so killed. Secure in his belief in the lucidity of the close abstract relation between the concept of law as legitimate and the concept of sovereignty, Bodin evidently thinks he has made it sufficiently clear that such exceptions to absolute sovereignty do not in any way infringe the fundamental argument against a right of resistance. He asks rhetorically, 'if it is not permissible for a subject to pass judgment on his prince, or a vassal on his lord, or a servant on his master — in short, if it is not permissible to proceed against one's king by way of law — how could it be licit to do so by way of force?' (Bodin 1992, 115).

Bodin's assault on the ideas and conduct of the Huguenots is translated in the *Six Books* into a positive theory of sovereignty. The importance Bodin attaches to sovereignty is seen in his designation of it as 'the principal and most necessary point for the understanding of the nature of a commonwealth'. As Skinner argues, since the 'aim of government must be to secure order rather than liberty, any act of resistance by a subject against his ruler must be altogether outlawed' in order 'to preserve the fragile structure of the commonwealth'. In this way, Skinner notes, Bodin is 'drawn by the logic of his own ideological commitment into arguing that in any political society there must be a sovereign who is absolute' (Skinner 1978, 287).

By 'absolute' Bodin means something quite precise, the asymmetry of unaccountability to another of a sovereign who governs but is never governed. Bodin adopts the view that 'persons who are sovereign must not be subject in any way to the commands of someone else and must be able to give the law to subjects, and to suppress or repeal disadvantageous laws and replace them with others — which cannot be done by someone who is subject to the laws or to persons having power of command over him' (Bodin 1992, 11). We can see how the terms 'majesty' and 'absolute' do crucial work for Bodin in his theory of sovereignty when we observe that, in practice, this means for Bodin that 'the main point of sovereign majesty and absolute power consists of giving the law to subjects in general without their consent' (Bodin 1992, 23). It is in the nature of sovereignty, for Bodin, that a sovereign prince 'cannot tie his hands even if he wished to do so' (Bodin 1992, 13). Bodin begins Chapter 8 of Book 1 with the statement that sovereignty 'is the absolute and perpetual power of a commonwealth' (Bodin 1992, 1), and he defines sovereignty as 'the most high, absolute and perpetual power over the citizens and subjects in a commonwealth'. For Bodin, a commonwealth is 'a just government, with sovereign power' (Bodin 1992, 1). The absolute sovereignty of the sovereign protects him, by definition, from lawful and well as from unlawful resistance. In this way, the meaning of sovereignty is in part constituted by the rejection of the right of resistance.

Philpott introduces an important point when he defines absolute sovereignty as the 'scope of affairs over which a sovereign body governs within a particular territory', but poses the question as to whether that requires it to be 'supreme over all matters or merely some'. Philpott notes that initially, 'non-absoluteness might seem to contradict sovereignty's essential quality of supremacy'. After all, if 'sovereignty is supreme, how can it be anything but absolute?' Indeed, this is the line taken by James, that sovereignty 'is either present or absent, never only partially realised' (James 1986, 112). However, Philpott makes a case to 'understand absoluteness... to refer not to the quality or magnitude of sovereignty, for if sovereignty were less than supreme in any particular matter, it would not indeed be sovereignty at all'. It remains the case, though, that 'a holder of sovereignty need not be sovereign over all matters' (Philpott 1999, 571).

Bodin stringently distinguishes the perpetual possession of sovereignty from all the many ways in which there may be 'trustees and custodians of that power until such time as it pleases ... the prince to take it back, for the latter always remains in lawful possession'. The prince still remains 'lawfully possessed of power and jurisdiction, which the others exercise in the manner of a loan or grant on sufferance' (Bodin 1992, 2), or on commission. His power is undiminished, no matter how much power is delegated for how long a period of time, and is 'revocable at the good pleasure of him who granted it' (Bodin 1992, 6). Bodin is at pains to reaffirm that sovereignty 'is not limited either in power, or in function, or in length of time' (Bodin 1992, 3). And when Bodin adds that 'it makes no difference whether the officer is high or low' (Bodin 1992, 2), he is affirming that the same rule applies to magistrates, regents, deputies, lieutenants, governors, agents, guardians, and senates as to less important officials. None can have a legitimate veto over or right of appeal against the sovereign power, and all similarly exercise authority or power (even if it is 'absolute power') only on condition or proviso of the sovereign (Bodin 1992, 5). As Bodin emphasises, the 'power of commanding and judging, and the action and the force of the law, do not lie in the person of the deputy'. Sovereignty itself is only granted when a sovereign dispossesses and strips himself of power and vests it in another, transferring 'all his power, authority, prerogatives, and sovereign rights to him and placed them in him, in the same way as someone who has given up the possession of, and property in, something that belonged to him' (Bodin 1992, 7).

While Bodin often refers to the sovereign as 'prince', he also states that, strictly speaking, the status of a prince conveys that he is merely 'first in the state' (Bodin 1992, 18). Moreover, it follows from the logic of his argument that, for Bodin, 'sovereignty given to a prince subject to obligations and conditions is properly not sovereignty or absolute power' (Bodin 1992, 8). Furthermore, Franklin points out that, perhaps surprisingly, 'Bodin does not reject election as inherently incompatible with the principle of monarchy, but only the idea that the power to elect entails a power to depose' (Franklin 1992, 19). It also follows, for Bodin's conception of absolute sovereignty, that no power of any form with political import can be held by an independent agent. In consequence the sovereign can never be legitimately hindered by any of his subjects, even if his commands are not honest or just. Furthermore, as Franklin notes, the king's absolute sovereignty eclipses the right to exercise *imperium* that had been held by magistrates and public officers in more decentralised medieval practice. Now such a right belonged only to the king, and even high officers of state only acted according to a delegated authority (Franklin 1992, xiv).

Sovereignty for Bodin refers to the locus of effective power, held in a determinate location. According to Bodin, it follows from absolute sovereignty that it is indivisible. Some later theorists have taken the view that sovereignty need not be indivisible, on the grounds that it is perfectly possible to share or distribute sovereignty, for instance in the idea of the state as a federation or corporation, without sovereignty dissolving. This comparison throws into relief the radical force of Bodin's logic. Indeed, Schmitt identifies a strong parallel between the conceptions of sovereignty generated by the political crises of sixteenth-century France and inter-war Germany. He claims that, 'despair about the religious wars led the well-known originator of the modern concept of sovereignty, Jean Bodin, to become a decisionist in the sense of sovereign state power' (Schmitt 1996, 43). This quotation is also interesting in that it shows how closely Schmitt identifies the origin of modern sovereignty with his own concept of decisionism. Schmitt's appropriation of Bodin is in many ways not surprising, given the resemblances between the theories of these two lawyers steeped in jurisprudence who both conceptualised sovereignty primarily in relation to the law but as crucially overriding the law.

What Bodin added to previous discussions about these matters, as Skinner outlines so well (1978 287-9), were the idea that sovereignty is analytical, a new conception of forms of rule, and the essentially legislative quality of sovereignty. The central point of the idea that sovereignty is analytical is not just that it is an abstract concept. Moreover, the idea of sovereignty as analytical does not just contrast with the idea of sovereignty as a historical aggregation of the 'marks' or necessary prerogatives of the sovereign that in concert configured absolute sovereignty, or with the idea of sovereignty as a prudential basis for political stability. Sovereignty as analytical also means much more forcefully for Bodin that, as Skinner puts it, 'the doctrine of non-resistance' is 'an analytical implica-

tion of sovereignty', and that absolute sovereignty is 'an analytical implication of the concept of the state' (Skinner 1978, 287). What we see here is
the tight conceptual interconnection between the rejection of the right of
resistance and the meaning of sovereignty.

Coming now to the idea of the state, for Bodin the specification of sovereignty in terms of 'marks' of sovereignty is his way of registering that sovereignty is signalled in attributes that belong to the office rather than to the
person, and are exercised by the office-holder rather than shared with
subjects. Loughlin's argument that the differentiation of public power from
private power is central to the meaning of modern sovereignty is something
that is found in Bodin. Loughlin's view, that 'political power derives neither
from force nor from the power that property confers', and that it 'cannot be
possessed like property, nor applied like force' (Loughlin 2003, 61), reflects
Bodin's insistence that sovereignty lies in the monarch's office and not in his
private property or power as a private person. Bodin's insistence on the
sovereign monarch as office-holder can be seen as drawing on an older
tradition. Loughlin, for instance, notes that the concept of office, *officium*,
had previously been used to describe the power of office-holders in ecclesi-
astical institutions, and 'drew concurrently upon the dual Roman and
canonical tradition of service to the public realm and the common good'.
He also confirms that *officium* indicated a 'position of some permanence; the
position assumes the status of an institution' (Loughlin 2003, 64).

Bodin devotes a chapter (Chapter 10 of Book I) to 'the true marks of
sovereignty', and does list 'marks' of sovereignty in the conventional
manner — the power to legislate, to declare war and peace, hear final
appeals, appoint and remove higher officials, impose taxes, grant pardons
and dispensations, determine the coinage and regulate weights and measures, and receive oaths of fealty and homage (Bodin 1992, 58-9). Bodin
added extra 'marks' in the *Six Books* to those listed in the *Method*, and ele-
vated the legislative power to first place. It is critical to Bodin's argument
in the *Six Books* that the power to make and repeal laws is primary. Indeed
it follows from the logic of the argument, for Bodin, that this legislative
power 'includes all the other rights and prerogatives of sovereignty', such
that 'strictly speaking we can say that there is only this one prerogative of
sovereignty, inasmuch as all the other rights are comprehended in it'
(Bodin 1992, 58). However, the lesser significance of the 'marks' of sovereignty for Bodin is seen in that the underlying contention in the chapters
on sovereignty is that the idea of the pre-eminence of the state cannot be
fully equated with such a list of 'marks'. The concept of sovereignty
denotes for Bodin an exclusive 'high, absolute and perpetual power over
the citizens'. 'Majesty or sovereignty' is located in the state, and in the
political supremacy expressed in the sovereign person. In this way we find
in Bodin the first systematic modern use of the term 'sovereignty'.

Franklin argues that Bodin derived the 'marks' of sovereignty from 'the concept of supremacy itself', and that Bodin's line of reasoning asked 'what prerogatives a political authority must hold exclusively if it is not to acknowledge a superior or equal in its territory' (Franklin 1992, xv). Franklin's case is strengthened by Bodin's clear message in Chapter 1 of Book II, that the combined set of prerogatives of sovereignty themselves, as well as the logic of the principle of sovereignty, is indivisible, because the right to legislate assumes all the other marks, and because they cannot be considered separately since functionally they imply each other (Bodin 1992, 104). Franklin argues persuasively that Bodin's use of the term *iura* (rights or prerogatives) in his Latin edition of the *Six Books* comes closer to his meaning than does his use of the term *marques* (marks) in the original French edition. According to Franklin, the French term suggests that 'the problem was to show the ordinary subject how to discern which of the many authorities placed over him was entitled to ultimate obedience'. However, Franklin maintains, 'since the distinctive marks of a sovereign in Bodin's account are a state of juridical prerogatives (and not force or ceremonial honors *per se*), the idea perhaps is better expressed by the Latin' (Franklin 1992, 46).

Bodin defines the marks or indications of sovereignty in the following way — in order to be able to recognise a person as a sovereign, 'we have to know his attributes (*marques, nota*), which are properties not shared by subjects' (Bodin 1992, 46). The marks of sovereignty are those things that are 'proper to all sovereign princes to the exclusion of all other lords having administration of justice, magistrates, and subjects'. These, he says, are 'by their very nature ... untransferable, inalienable, and imprescriptible' (Bodin 1992, 87). Bodin thus distinguishes sovereign rights from the more minor regalian rights that can apply to 'dukes, counts, barons, bishops, officers, and other subjects of sovereign princes' (Bodin 1992, 48), and concludes that 'the prerogatives of sovereignty have to be of such a sort that they apply only to a sovereign prince' (Bodin 1992, 49). Thus pronouncing justice, appointing and removing officers, and taking counsel on affairs of state, are not marks of sovereignty (as Aristotle had contended), according to Bodin, because these are all things that can be shared with subjects or officers (Bodin 1992, 50). The same applies to the laws of a magistrate, which bind only those under his jurisdiction. In contrast, 'the power of the law lies in him who has the sovereignty and who gives force to the law' (Bodin 1992, 55). This is the primary prerogative of the sovereign, and is distinguished from the less important edicts of magistrates and decrees of a Senate. In addition, the power to order the death penalty is a punishment attached only to the laws of a sovereign and not to the orders of lesser agents (Bodin 1992, 56).

In his earlier works Bodin made two significant changes to current humanist legal scholarship at the time that was dissatisfied with the legacy of Roman law at their disposal. Bodin sought to derive the principles of law not from the defective and culturally-specific Roman source but from a systematic inquiry into (and perhaps reinterpretation of, to give historical validity to his specification of sovereign power) the legal codes of a variety of countries, and he developed a notion of the locus of sovereignty adequate for public law summed up in five essential rights. Franklin highlights Bodin's radical innovation here in relying neither on the Roman code that had been primarily concerned with private law, nor on 'the lists of regalian powers taken from feudal law [that] were mere catalogues of particular privileges' (Franklin 1992, xvi).

Skinner highlights the second change when he identifies Bodin as having significantly added to previous discussions of forms of rule. For Bodin a vital distinction needs to be made between the system of sovereign rule, found in the state, and the various forms of organised political community over which the sovereign rules. Previous categorisations of forms of rule by political theorists had tended to identify three approved ones (monarchy, aristocracy and democracy), three corresponding defective ones (tyrannies by one, by several, and by all), and the mixed state, which was often regarded as the most stable form of rule. In contrast with this commonly-held categorisation, Bodin argued that only monarchy, aristocracy and democracy are valid forms of rule because only in these forms is the sovereignty relationship exercised correctly. The defective forms of rule are thereby disqualified, and crucially there can be no valid mixed state, according to Bodin, since by definition sovereignty must be held by some identifiable person and persons within the commonwealth. Franklin underlines that Bodin's antipathy to the mixed state is not 'merely prudential or political', since for Bodin the 'unity of a legal system seemed logically to require the unification of power in a single ruler or single ruling group' (Franklin 1992, xvii).

Another innovation and radical change from past practice identified by Skinner follows from Bodin's idea that sovereignty has an inherently legislative quality. Franklin also indicates how Bodin's elevation of lawmaking to the supreme prerogative of a sovereign represents a fundamental shift. He notes that throughout Bodin's discussion of the mark of sovereignty concerning appeals, 'the term "sovereignty" is linked to the term "appeal" almost as a synonym, as though echoing an older usage in which the primary meaning of sovereignty was the right to hear appeals in last instance' (Franklin 1992, 134). Bodin stresses the importance of being able to make law in the constitution of the meaning of sovereignty when he argues 'for a sovereign prince to have power over the laws in order to govern well' (Bodin 1992, 24). Franklin emphasises that for Bodin this legislative power includes constitutional change (Franklin 1992, xvi). The highest, and in a sense single, 'mark' of sovereignty is now conceived as that of making laws for subjects without their consent, in contrast with the previous tradition of thinking in which the sovereign's capacity to judge was primary and the key 'mark' of sovereignty was the appointment of magistrates.

It follows from Bodin's line of argument that the sovereign is not subject to his own laws nor those of his predecessors, and that the sovereign's role is no longer understood in terms of the normative commitment to, as Skinner notes of the earlier period, 'upholding the sense of justice already embodied in the laws and customs of the commonwealth' (Skinner 1978, 289). Bodin's sense of the sovereign standing above the legal order, of all legal codes as grounded in culturally-specific norms requiring elucidation, and the impossibility of an abstract universal science of jurisprudence trumping the edicts of the sovereign prince, would also appeal strongly to Schmitt. At the same time, however, Bodin sought to provide in the *Six Books* an historically and sociologically-informed account of the laws common to all successful commonwealths (Skinner 1978, 292–3).

However, again perhaps surprisingly in the light of his modern reputation as the annihilator of constitutionalism, for Bodin sovereignty is not unlimited. For while Bodin defined sovereignty as absolute, this did not imply for him that sovereignty is without limits. There are three important limitations on the sovereign's sovereignty. These limitations are things whose authority is in some sense prior to the authority of the sovereign, namely the male royal line, the distinction between office and individual office-holder, and the role of natural law. Bodin accepted the condition on sovereignty set by the customary Salic law, the law that guaranteed the succession of the male line to the throne, ensuring that France had only kings and not queens. The next limitation was the idea that the ruler has a 'use only' rather than full possession of lands, attached to the role and position of sovereign. The palaces and estates of the king belonged to the office of monarch, not to the monarch as a private man. For Bodin, the sovereign and the commonwealth are not identical, and the private 'patrimony of the prince' must be distinguished clearly from 'the public treasure' (Bodin 1992, 42). As Skinner aptly puts it, 'the domain is annexed to the sovereignty rather than the sovereign' (Skinner 1978, 294). Franklin identifies the specific nature of these limitations when he notes that both the rule prescribing the succession to the throne and the rule 'forbidding alienation of the royal domain without consent', were 'designed to keep the state intact, rather than to limit the royal right of governance' (Franklin 1992, xxv).

The final limitation was that while the form of positive law was made by the sovereign alone, its contents must accord with natural and divine law. Bodin argues that 'if we say that to have absolute power is not to be subject to any law at all, no prince of this world will be sovereign, since every earthly prince is subject to the laws of God and of nature and to various human laws that are common to all peoples' (Bodin 1992, 20). He is at pains to stress the gravity of the law of God and of nature, to which the sovereign 'is more strictly bound than any of his subjects, from which he cannot be dispensed either by the Senate or the people, and for which he is always answerable to the judgement of God, whose inquiry ... is very rigorous' (Bodin 11992, 31). This is affirmed by Bodin in a hierarchical argument about ascending legal instruments — whereby he argues that 'just as the contracts and testaments of private persons cannot detract from the ordinances of magistrates, nor the edicts of magistrates from custom, nor customs from the general laws of a sovereign prince, so the laws of sovereign princes cannot alter or change the laws of God and of nature' (Bodin 1992, 32). He emphasises that sovereignty is 'the power of overriding ordinary law', but not 'the laws of God and of nature' (Bodin 1992, 13). It is also worth noting, as Philpott rightly observes, that while natural law was understood at this time as a universal standard of morality, it 'did not prescribe offices or powers in the way that the United States Constitution, for instance, does' (Philpott 1999, 579).

It might be considered that this point, by reinforcing the prior duty of the sovereign to natural law, kept open qualifications to a monarch's absolute sovereignty — such as that subjects have a duty to disobey if the sovereign's orders run counter to natural and divine law; that the ruler must honour contracts, including those with subjects, since they involve a promise and reciprocity that derive from natural law; that on the same grounds subjects must be allowed to own private property that cannot be touched by the ruler; and that, as a consequence, the taxation of subjects requires their consent. Bodin does indeed hold that it 'is not that the prince is bound by his own or his predecessors' laws, but rather by the just contracts and promises that he has made, whether with or without an oath, as is any private individual', and stresses the difference between laws and contracts (Bodin 1992, 13–14). Skinner makes a strong case that the emphasis Bodin places on the importance of natural law overcomes any inconsistency between his pointed defence of subjects' right to be taxed only with their express consent and his definition of sovereignty as a power of 'giving laws to the subjects in general without their consent' (Skinner 1978, 297).

However, as Franklin stresses, such qualifications do not in practice inhibit the sovereign prince. The restrictions that Bodin placed upon the king, for instance regarding taxation of subjects' property, crucially 'could never be a ground for legitimate resistance, since for violations of the law of nature the king was answerable to God alone' (Franklin 1992, xxiv). In addition Bodin argues that while a king cannot *justly* set aside a promise made to subjects, nevertheless he can do so without his subjects having any right of appeal (Bodin 1992, 14). As a result, for Bodin, 'neither the law of nature nor the fundamental law could justify a challenge to absolute authority, or resistance to a sitting king'. In sum, Franklin argues, these limitations on the sovereign's power, rather than specifying possible sources of popular sovereignty and resistance, actually represent the 'systematic elimination of binding institutional restraints' that were a tightening up of previous constitutional practice (Franklin 1992, xxv). While they represent limitations on sovereign power, these limitations are no longer anchored in the stronger basis of binding customary law. In this way, as Franklin sums up, 'Bodin had thereby undermined the legal force of checks upon the king' (Franklin 1992, xxvi). Bodin's stipulation that 'he is absolutely sovereign who recognises nothing, after God, that is greater than himself', and the blunt statement that 'a sovereign prince ... is answerable only to God' (Bodin 1992, 4), are meant by him to be taken in a strong sense that disbars redress by subjects.

In making the argument so forcefully that sovereigns solely make positive law but are not bound by it, and are subject only to natural and divine law but can override it with impunity from the people, Bodin in effect contends that for the purposes of temporal life there is a strict divide between civil and divine law. His conception of sovereignty is very much a secular one, and natural and divine law and oaths owed to God by the sovereign can effectively be broken by the sovereign, insofar as they are in relation to his subjects, at his discretion. While natural and divine law is said by Bodin to be binding on the sovereign, the people do not have any right to ensure his obedience to it. Rhetorically, the great stress laid by Bodin on the solemnity of the sovereign's obligation to natural and divine law has the contrary primary effect of reinforcing the powerlessness of his subjects in curbing the prince. Bodin's statement, 'it is the law of God and of nature that we must obey the edicts and ordinances of him to whom God has given power over us, unless his edicts are directly contrary to the law of God, who is above all princes' (Bodin 1992, 34), might seem to suggest a right against the sovereign prince. However, Bodin argument that a sovereign's infringements of natural or divine law are not subject to redress by the people precludes this possibility. Likewise, when Bodin states that 'a prince who has contracted with his subjects is bound by his promise should ... be beyond all doubt' (Bodin 1992, 36), his meaning is, as Franklin notes, 'not that the prince is bound by civil law, but rather that having made a contract in accordance with civil law, he is bound by the law of nature to keep it strictly' (Franklin 1992, 36). In other words, the other party to the contract has no civil remedy on a sovereign's breach of the contract.

The people have no basis for a claim against a sovereign's violation of either natural equity or his good faith. Bodin's argument that even the pope or the emperor cannot simply act without licence, and the statement that it 'is a kind of legal absurdity to say that it is in the power of the prince to act dishonestly', for 'absolute power extends only to setting civil law aside ... and that it cannot do violence to the law of God' (Bodin 1992, 39), operate on the same basis. Bodin's argument here is further augmented by his explicit rejection of an independent role for reason. He makes the argument that many authors 'mistakenly say that a sovereign prince cannot ordain anything against the law of God unless it seems well founded upon reason'. Bodin ripostes, 'what reason can there be to contravene the law of God' (Bodin 1992, 32). At the same time, Bodin seeks to give some weight, but not to the extent of a right of resistance, to the prudential idea that 'it is seemly for a sovereign prince to keep his own law, for there is nothing that makes him more feared and revered by his subjects, whereas, on the contrary, there is nothing that more abases the authority of his law than his own contempt for it' (Bodin 1992, 31).

Thus, the net effect is that the third limitation on absolute sovereignty is no limitation at all. In addition Bodin withdrew constitutional safeguards for subjects that he had included in the *Method*. These checks were part of what was called '*la police*', '*la religion*' and '*la justice*', and under which the limitations on absolute sovereignty had been specified. So while introducing conditions on sovereign power, Bodin specifically removed a range of traditional constitutional rights and checks of subjects, which previous practice had acknowledged, and which he himself had allowed in his previous work. The check of '*la police*', whereby the king was limited by customary law, was revoked. Specific restraints on the ruler, derived from '*la religion*' and '*la justice*', were abolished. For instance, the powers of the Estates General apart from that of withholding consent to taxation were curtailed, and the coronation oath was no longer seen as qualifying the king's powers. The ambiguous power of the French *Parlement* was curbed, according to Bodin's theory, and he explicitly rejects the view of earlier authors who upheld the power of the Estates over the prince. Previously, as Franklin puts it, the 'Parlements did not assert a veto on royal legislation, so much as a right of continued remonstrance until such time as their complaints were heeded' (Franklin 1992, xxv). Bodin affirms a particular interpretation of the role of the *Parlement* when he insists that 'the grandeur and majesty of a truly sovereign prince is manifested' when 'the Estates of all the people are assembled and present requests and supplications to their prince in all humility, without having any power to command or decree, or even a right to deliberate', and 'whatever the king pleases by way of consent or dissent, command or prohibition, is taken for law, for edict, or for ordinance' (Bodin 1992, 18–19). A similar ambiguity concerning the independence of judges was likewise tightened up in favour of the sovereign, in Bodin's account of sovereignty.

The effect of retracting these checks was to dramatically increase the scope of the power of government over the individual, defining — in a negative way — what subjects can and cannot do. The king's explicit powers and discretionary powers were increased, and the idea that delegated powers could be reclaimed at will was clarified. Correspondingly, the authority of customary law and habitual practice was demoted, and the active role of natural and divine law minimised. Thus the limitations on the sovereign's powers were severely diminished by the withdrawal of these constitutional safeguards protecting the subjects. However Bodin, probably sincerely, held that his conceptualisation of sovereignty was 'compatible with civilised and law-abiding government'. As Franklin puts it, Bodin 'confidently believed that the complaints and administrative pressures of the magistrates would restrain impulsive rulers, and he optimistically expected that the political value of the Estates was sufficient to assure their consultation' (Franklin 1992, xxvi).

Having examined Bodin's theory we can come to an assessment. In one sense Bodin's significance lies in his attempt to explain the political associations of the emerging modern state in completely autonomous terms, and in morally neutral terms. The idea of the state political form was only developing in the middle of the sixteenth century. It is no accident that Bodin's theory was developed in France, the first place to develop a centralised 'state' in this sense. This idea of the commonwealth as a 'state', charged with the maintenance of order, rather than with the promotion of goodness, was used by Bodin to great effect. Sovereignty, or the power to make and enforce laws, belongs he says to the state by definition. In the absence of this power it would quite simply cease to be what it is. Supreme authority and power constitute the essence of the state.

In the previous medieval period in Europe, a complex relationship was understood to exist between an individual and several different kinds of power and authority, deriving from local squires, feudal lords, town charters, work guilds, the prince, the king, the emperor, and the pope. These relationships, and their modes of expression, were differently organised in different places. The emperor was usually a very distant power, probably with no visible effect on ordinary people's lives, except in times of war in the case of conscription to fight in an emperor's wars. With his theorisation of sovereignty Bodin cut through these complex layers of power and authority over the lives of subjects. He defines a single, unitary and primary line of power and authority between the subject and the absolute sovereign. Sovereignty must be located in a determinate place and cannot be shared between different layers, he insists. Magistrates and ministers of the crown exercise powers delegated by the king, not in their own right.

But it is important to emphasise that at the heart of Bodin's theory is the analytical distinction between the office of the king, the sovereign, and the personal rule of particular kings. He is defining the 'state' as a locus of power, rather than simply justifying the power of absolutist monarchs, and this is the greatest restriction on the power of an individual ruler. Furthermore, for Bodin, sovereignty means the absolute and perpetual legislative power, a notion influenced by Roman law. According to this definition, the laws of nature and of God, and customary laws of the land represent limitations, if only theoretical provisos, on the sovereign.

Franklin argues that Bodin's account of sovereignty left an important legacy in two crucial respects. Firstly, Bodin's theory did not itself fully enunciate but prepared the ground for the notion of royal absolutism. Indeed, when Bodin says that '[c]ontempt for one's sovereign prince is contempt toward God, of whom he is the earthly image' (Bodin 1992, 46), he takes steps toward (though does not reach) that point. The attention he gives to aristocracy and democracy as valid forms of sovereignty also belies that conclusion in full. He also clearly spells out in Chapter 5 of Book II that a sovereign is not only associated with divine right but can come about by several means — by 'election, or right of succession, or lot, or a just war, or a special calling from God' (Bodin 1992, 220). Bodin's description was controversial, since it did not accord with current practice in relatively centralised states like France and England let alone in more medieval European forms.

Franklin's assessment is that Bodin's aim was not to promote the idea of royal absolutism as such but to give due weight to the complex forces at play and so to 'reconcile the new idea of royal dominance with the French juridical tradition of which he was a great admirer and connoisseur' (Franklin 1992, xiv). With his legal training and strong belief in the importance of law, Bodin drew a sharp distinction between the absolute sovereignty of the holder of the kingly office, and a personalised despotic kingship unmediated by office or law where the relationship between king and subjects is reduced to that between master and slaves. In addition, Bodin asserts an intimate link between the meanings of law and sovereignty. He asserts that 'law is nothing but the command of a sovereign making use of his power' (Bodin 1992, 38). Bodin also argues that 'the prince is not subject to the law; and in fact the very word "law" in Latin implies the command of him who has the sovereignty' (Bodin 1992, 11), and Franklin notes the derivation of the Latin word for law from the verb 'to bind' (Franklin 1992, 129 n23). Reinforcing this point, Bodin ends the key Chapter 8, 'On Sovereignty' in Book 1, on the note that 'if justice is the end of law, law the work of the prince, and the prince the image of God; then by this reasoning, the law of the prince must be modelled on the law of God' (Bodin 1992, 45).

Secondly, Franklin argues that Bodin introduced the erroneous but 'seductive notion that sovereignty is indivisible'. Franklin defines indivisibility here with reference to Bodin's theory of 'ruler sovereignty', as distinct from the idea that 'every legal system, by its very definition' is 'an authoritative method of resolving conflicts' that 'must rest upon some ultimate legal norm or rule of recognition which is the guarantee of coherence'. Indivisible sovereignty for Bodin, says Franklin, referred not to the power of 'the constituent authority of the general community' (as in popular sovereignty), and not to 'the ultimate coordinating rule that the community had come to recognise' (as in a constitution), but to the power of 'the ordinary agencies of government'. Franklin argues that Bodin 'lacks a concept of constituent power and cannot imagine any power remaining in the people authoritatively to take cognizance of a violation of the law of nature'. For according to Bodin, 'that act of cognizance would imply retention of ordinary governmental power, which, *ex hypothesi*, has been entirely vested in the prince' (Franklin 1992, 129 n17). Whereas Skinner emphasised legislative capacity and analytical logic as the key innovations in Bodin's theory, Franklin highlights Bodin's definition of the indivisibility of sovereignty. For Bodin, according to Franklin, the unity of sovereignty lay in the idea that 'the high powers of government could not be shared by separate agents or distributed among them', but must rather be centralised 'in a single individual or group' (Franklin 1992, xiii). The authority to exercise powers could be delegated by a king but could not be held by right by anyone or in any public office other than that of sovereign. Franklin concludes that 'Bodin would have done better ... to have defined the ruler's sovereignty as absolute (except with respect to the law of nature and fundamental [constitutional] law more narrowly defined)', and to have 'conceded that its functions were divided among the king, the Parlements, and the Estates' (Franklin 1992, xxii).

Brown *et al* make the same point as Franklin. They argue that Bodin 'concludes, erroneously, that the sovereign authority in a state cannot be divided'. They say that it 'is true that in any single legal system there must ultimately be one and only one way of settling legal disputes', that there 'must be a single ultimate criterion by which the question "what is the law?" is decided'. But, they contend, Bodin is confused, because 'it does not follow that the authority to enact and apply laws cannot be shared among different branches of government' (Brown *et al* 2002, 249).

However, while Bodin clearly regarded monarchy as the most appropriate and clearest form of sovereign government, he does acknowledge in many places (for instance 1992, 24) that sovereign power can be vested in an aristocracy and a democracy as well as in a monarchy. Thus, indivisibility refers in Bodin very specifically to the lack of a framework for sovereign power, provided in an ultimate but largely dormant power vested either in the people or in a constitution, rather than to the rejection of forms of sovereignty held by an assembly or other collective body, wherein 'the person who presides has no power and has to obey the orders of the governing body' (Bodin 1992, 19).

The value of Bodin's theory of sovereignty lies in its articulation of the asymmetrical character of absolute sovereignty, meaning that the sovereign commands but cannot be commanded, its analytical approach to sovereignty, its legislative form, its pinpointing of sovereignty as perpetual power and its insistence that, at the same time, sovereignty is not unlimited. The way in which Bodin combines absolute, perpetual and limited dimensions of sovereignty, opens up the conceptualisation of sovereignty beyond its seemingly binding association with early-modern absolute monarchy. This point is very important is supporting the contention of this book that attention to conceptual change and historical specificity render with clarity the particularity of the multiple conceptions of sovereignty that have been formulated.

Bodin does not seek with his theory of absolute sovereignty to eliminate or foreclose political debate, and in this sense his theory is more open than Hobbes's to a space for politics. The *Parlement*, the Estates, and magistrates may all engage in real debate. However, their role in political life is circumscribed by only being able to advise and counsel the sovereign, and by holding only delegated authority. For Bodin, so long as the line of authority and its one-way, non-reciprocal nature is well comprehended, then political life can flourish and the sovereign can exercise power, most importantly to legislate, in an effective fashion.

Bodin's place in the canon as the inaugurator of the modern theory of sovereignty rests upon his conception of absolute sovereignty (or sometimes a misrepresentation of it) and upon his theorising of sovereignty in the context of an impersonal state, whereby the distinction between the person holding the office and the office itself is a crucial element of the theory. But more importantly, and underpinning these aspects of Bodin's work is his formidable legalism—found in the importance he accords to law within a political community; his understanding of sovereignty as primarily a legal concept; the way his thinking is rooted in a jurisprudence discourse; the pre-eminence he gives to legislating as the key function of the sovereign and in the definition of sovereignty; in his preoccupation with legal distinctions; the political significance he invests in legal technicalities; and the centrality of the legal relationship between subject and sovereign. Whether by accident or design, Bodin's role in the canon as initiating the modern conception of sovereignty imports a strong legal flavour to the concept.

Bodin's legalism is of course closely linked to the absolute sovereignty and state sovereignty for which he is famous. It is precisely as a consequence of the legal character of sovereignty for Bodin that there exists that asymmetrical relationship whereby the sovereign prince alone can make law for his subjects, and whereby any infringements that his positive law might have against natural and divine law are not answerable to the people. This absolutism then denies the possibility of a right of resistance. Likewise it is as a direct implication of the status of the sovereign prince as lawmaker within the political community rather than as personal ruler that the necessary framework in which the sovereign operates is a modern state as we understand it. The other interesting dimension of Bodin's conception that this chapter has noted is that sovereignty, according to Bodin, and notwithstanding his (even if mistaken) emphasis on its indivisibility and his own preference for monarchy, can perfectly legitimately be expressed in democratic and aristocratic as well as monarchical forms of commonwealth.

To conclude the evaluation of Bodin's theory, we can register the disjunction noted by Teschke and Vincent between Bodin's proposals and on-going practices 'on the ground'. Bodin's conception of sovereignty remains enormously important for its analytical interest and its significance for later writers, but the persistence of older patterns in political life in France distort and make more complex the impact of the theory. Teschke gives two examples to support his case for the disjunction between Bodin's theory and French political practice. He argues persuasively that, however much Bodin may have analytically distinguished the sovereignty of the state from the personal powers of the monarch, in practice the 'non-separation of public authority and private property' that characterised European feudalism 'persisted in most European states well into the eighteenth and nineteenth centuries'. France is the model for this pattern of 'dynasticism and proprietary kingship' (Teschke 2003, 171), and England is the anomaly. Teschke gives weight to the history of political patterns in France, and criticises Spruyt for conflating the experiences of early modern France and England 'under one type of successful territorial state'. He makes a strong case for recognising the significance of the contrast between the way 'seventeenth-century England turned into a parliamentary-constitutional state based on an expanding capitalist economy in which sovereignty came to lie with Parliament', while 'France started to perfect its patrimonial-dynastic absolutist state form based on a non-capitalist agrarian economy while sovereignty came to be personalized by the king' (Teschke 2003, 38).

Using historical detail to great effect, Teschke is also cautious of accepting legislative sovereignty — the 'conventional benchmark of absolutism' associated with Bodin — as critical to continental and especially French practice in the early-modern period. He argues that although 'real steps towards "legislative sovereignty" through the expansion and refinement of royal law' did take place in this period, the 'alleged transition of the king from personal dispenser of justice, based on feudo-theological conceptions of divine kingship, to sovereign lawmaker was arrested by strong countervailing forces', in the form of 'widespread venal officialdom and regionally autonomous political institutions' (Teschke 2003, 179). For example, 'autonomous seigneurial courts' persisted, 'even though they tended to become integrated into an appellate system'. Even more tellingly, 'the higher courts did not draw their legitimacy from royal delegation but from a real devolution of authority'. Teschke argues convincingly that '[h]igher magistrates had authority not by virtue of their function, but by virtue of their status'. Furthermore, he notes that the 'patrimonial character of legal office — proprietary, hereditary, and irrevocable — turned the legal system into an incongruous network of patronage'. Not only did clientalism run 'beyond royal control, developing its own self-reproductive logic', but also the 'idea that legal uniformity imposed by the king implied the formal equality of "equal citizens before the law" ran time and again into traditional social hierarchy, based on the possession of land, title, and privilege' (Teschke 2003, 179–80).

Evidence from Vincent provides another example to support this case. He observes that although 'Bodin himself was not a proponent of divine right, his notion of sovereignty was quickly adorned with the robes of divinity by later thinkers' (Vincent 1987, 67). Vincent notes that from 'Henry IV's reign (1589–1610) up to Louis XIV's (1643–1715), legislative absolute sovereignty gradually mutated into divine right. The king was regarded increasingly as a mortal god'. He argues that 'divine right theory reinforced the idea of property in the realm and legislative sovereignty and also gave an added credence and lustre to the idea that the monarch *was* the State'. Vincent observes that 'it is not often realized that divine right is a modern doctrine, a bridging point between the medieval and modern conceptions of politics', for 'Papal and imperial authority had come to rest finally in the person of the king' (Vincent 1987, 68).

Chapter Two

HOBBES AND SPINOZA

During the sixteenth and seventeenth centuries in early modern Europe, two contrary ideologies of sovereignty were under construction — the ideology of absolutist sovereignty and the 'divine right of kings' to which the monarchs of France and England subscribed, and the theory of popular sovereignty, the view that all political authority inheres in the body of the people. Bodin and Filmer were taken as contributing in different ways to the absolutist ideology, while the tradition of theories of popular sovereignty develops with Locke and later with Rousseau. Hobbes has been taken as contributing to both ideologies.

Hobbes's theory of sovereignty also has a crucial place in the discourse through having been taken as providing the paradigmatic definition of sovereignty not just for the modern state but also (and inter-relatedly) for the modern international system. For both mainstream political theory and across the study of international relations Hobbes is variously acclaimed or condemned for the influential paradigm we have taken from him. This chapter seeks to present a more rounded and contextualised and also more open view of Hobbes. Since the main lines of Hobbes's theory of sovereignty are so familiar the emphasis here is on drawing out some less well known aspects of his theory which render the iconic version more ambiguous, more interesting, and also as fitting squarely into the view that there are a diversity and plurality of conceptions of sovereignty.

The argument of the chapter is centrally concerned to critically compare Hobbes's and Spinoza's theories of sovereignty as a means of illuminating both theories in ways not normally brought to light. It is also concerned to show that Spinoza is not the simple follower of Hobbes's political theory he is often taken to be, and to identify Spinoza's tactical uses of the theory of sovereignty to intervene in the political debates of his day. The misguidedness of the dominant interpretation of Hobbes's conception of sovereignty, and the relevance of Spinoza's conception, are addressed in the final chapter of Prokhovnik (2007), on the retheorisation of sovereignty in contemporary Europe.

The key elements of sovereignty for Hobbes are that the relation between rulers and ruled is one of authority (necessarily having a popular basis) rather than brute power, that the sovereign holds the highest authority to make law and that this establishes the rule of law, the monopoly on the use of force, and the power to declare war and peace. Spinoza did not subscribe to a modern division between internal and external sovereignty but in his own terms he distinguished between two areas of attention. The key elements of the external face of sovereignty for Spinoza are self-government, self-management, independence, self-reliance, having control over one's affairs, not subject to external interference, and understood in terms of government by aristocracy. In its internal face, important elements are that sovereignty governs the relation between the provinces, establishing political stability through dynamic tension, that sovereignty is a recognition concept, depending on mutual recognition among the provinces, and the perpetual character of sovereignty over time and with different office-holders. The relationship between the external and internal faces of sovereignty for Spinoza is complex because of the loose confederal character of the United Provinces and the independence of the separate provinces.

Ultimately the strength of Hobbes's theory as a robust conception of sovereignty is the appeal of its prescription and claim to be universal, indivisible and unconditional, while its weakness is the other side of the same coin, its inability to acknowledge cultural and other forms of specificity. Spinoza's theory demonstrates the opposite strengths and weaknesses, in that it is open to the value of customary practice and difference within the polity while being unable to fully generalise its propositions. In the subsequent chapters space is devoted separately to each of the pair of thinkers. In this chapter the argument is more intertwined and the two theorists are considered together.

The idea of sovereignty is the lynchpin in Hobbes's political theory and it has multiple significance and multiple sources of legitimacy. In its most highly developed form in *Leviathan* it emerges as the highpoint of a train of logical reasoning in Chapter 16 about actors who authorise agents to act on their behalf. In the more important of the two forms of sovereignty discussed by Hobbes (Hobbes 1946, 113), the sovereign office is filled not by an active agent imposing their will (acquisition) but by a mechanism in which the sovereign agent plays no role but is *instituted* as sovereign as a result of reciprocal agreements between the group of relevant persons. In this sense (similar to Franklin's notion of 'constituent power'), and it is a sense that Hobbes wishes to emphasise, sovereignty crucially has a popular basis. Hobbes is neither a populist nor a democrat but perceives that the strongest bond of obligation—in this case by ordinary people—is one taken on oneself.

Sovereignty is also, for Hobbes, the conclusion of a line of analysis about the conditions of a hypothetical social contract as a means of escaping a hypothetical state of nature as a state of war, and is also the solution to the predicament of a radically egalitarian or levelling, but untenable, form of individual freedom, in the sense of being unhindered by others in the pursuit of one's ends, in conditions of civil unrest and fear, in Chapter 13. It is also, more prosaically, a theory about the emergence of a political leader who cannot be resisted (the popular basis of the institution of the sovereign being non-reversible) because the process of 'authorising' was accompanied by an obligation which could not be withdrawn. Hobbes's theory of sovereignty is also about the abolition of politics — the unlawfulness of public dissent from and contestation of the sovereign's promulgations (Chapters 29 and 30). Moreover it is a theory about the primacy of law, of the urgency to follow the natural law imperative to seek peace, and of individuals' obligation to obey the positive law enunciated by the sovereign (Chapter 26). While Hobbes is often portrayed as primarily highlighting the force of instrumental motives and reasons his theory is more complex and also has significant elements of both moral and prudential reasoning.

There are several claims that can and have been made about the derivation and originary status of Hobbes's notion of sovereignty. While for the most part this has led to entrenched defences of contradictory positions it can also be seen as indicating the richness of Hobbes's theory as a source of debate amongst interpreters of Hobbes. One claim is that Hobbes is a traditionalist, providing a secular version of the older medieval idea of the sovereign as the highest authority in the temporal world, directly in the tradition of King James who told Parliament in 1610 that 'the state of monarchy is the supremest thing upon earth' (quoted in Harrison 2003, 2). The importance of natural laws for Hobbes, if taken seriously, supports this view. The importance of natural law is also used to see Hobbes's theory as fundamentally religious and theological in motivation. Another claim is made about the primary role of reason in Hobbes's theory, triggering the idea of sovereignty as governed by reason and the view of Hobbes as a proto-Enlightenment figure. Both modern popular sovereignty and modern state sovereignty can be and have been derived from Hobbes's theory of representation and authorization. There are widespread claims for Hobbes's conception as the origin of the theory of state sovereignty, and here Hobbes's text is open to interpretations in turn that he advocated a benign, authoritarian, or totalitarian dictator. He can also be taken to be espousing a theory of monarchy, or in contrast a theory of leadership by a person or assembly without dynastic or hereditary warrant. He has been painted as both a deeply conservative and as a radical egalitarian thinker.

Perhaps most significantly, aspects of Hobbes's theory have been appropriated in later liberal and realist perspectives. Hobbes's descriptions of a universalised and abstract individualism and of an unregulated negative freedom in a secular context are vital planks of liberal ideology, while the vision he presents of the hypothetical state of nature has been taken over by realist international relations as a viable 'real' description of the default position of states in the international realm. Hobbes's view of sovereignty has been taken as fundamental to both the internal and external self-definition of the state in modern Western political thought. Both of these sources of appropriation have entailed a severe distortion and limited reading of Hobbes's complex theory. Elsewhere I have made the case for taking more seriously those elements in Hobbes's theory such as the role of artifice, which contribute to a social constructionist reading of his work (Prokhovnik 2005) and mitigate the dominant picture of him as having a wholly abstract and analytical viewpoint.

Hobbes does not say much about international relations (it did not exist with our meaning at the time) or the relations between states but he does explicitly enjoin political communities to listen to the imperatives of the laws of nature in their dealings with each other. He does not licence the raw play of power politics and does not unambiguously sanction instrumental over moral reasons for action. He is therefore much more than a theorist of state power in international anarchy. Hobbes gives a greater role to natural law than the dominant interpretation allows. He makes it plain at the end of Chapter 30 of *Leviathan* that commonwealths are related to each other through the same laws of nature that apply within commonwealths when he says, '[c]oncerning the offices of one sovereign to another, which are comprehended in that law, which is commonly called the *law of nations*, I need not say anything in this place; because the law of nations, and the law of nature, is the same thing' (Hobbes 1946, 231–2). Whereas Hobbes has been taken to be sanctioning the right of states to pursue self-interest in international anarchy, he in fact goes on explicitly to recommend states to seek a condition of reciprocal peace when he says, 'the same law, that dictateth to men that have no civil government, what they ought to do … dictateth the same to commonwealths, that is, to the consciences of sovereign princes and sovereign assemblies' (Hobbes 1946, 232). While it is a commonplace within the sub-discipline of international relations to regard Hobbes as sanctioning the idea that the relation between actors on the world stage is of states in a *state* of nature, this view is achieved through a failure to recognise that Hobbes's description of the state of nature only represents the logical prelude to his introduction of the *laws* of nature, all of which follow from the first law of nature, to seek peace. The state of nature is not meant by Hobbes to be a historical reality nor to have any other ontological status, but rather to be a logical point in the development of the resolutive-compositive method of argument.

Hobbes's theory of sovereignty occupies a central position in his political thought. It is epitomised by the figure of the Leviathan, the commonwealth, a whole, a unity, composed solely of the individuals without whom it could not exist. On the importance of the figure of Leviathan and on metaphor more widely for understanding Hobbes's philosophy, see Skinner (1996), Schmitt (1996), and Prokhovnik (1991). For Hobbes, sovereignty is not the automatic or teleological product of a universal natural law, though that law plays a part in guiding individuals. The transformation from multitude to unified whole is mediated by the work of human artifice, as Hobbes makes clear in the opening lines of the Introduction. There are no preconditions, in the form of customary arrangements, religious or political institutions, or a social hierarchy, to the setting up of the commonwealth by radically equal individuals. Hobbes's theory of sovereignty is the theoretical high point of the argument of the first two parts, the secular parts of *Leviathan*, and is the construction which dominates the discussion of the role of religion in the political commonwealth, in the third and fourth Parts. It is the image which Hobbes brandishes, with which he can lead into that discussion. It is plausible to regard the topics discussed by Hobbes in the second Part of *Leviathan*, after the generation and definition of sovereignty at the beginning of that second Part, as amounting to an extended elucidation of the implications and consequences of the concept of sovereignty. In this light the topics covered in the second Part do not substantively advance the theoretical nexus, which lies in the interconnection of authority, authorisation, representation, sovereignty and law outlined in Chapters 14–17. Martinich's religious reading of Hobbes, that in a strong sense 'sovereign-making covenants rest upon the power of God' (Martinich 1992, 161), seems unconvincingly to undermine all the theoretical work Hobbes does to establish a viable conception of sovereignty on the basis of human authorisation.

Hobbes's theory of sovereignty is characteristically analytical, composed of, revolving around and hinging upon the relationship between a set of interconnected definitions about authority or authorisation, obligation and law, which then define legitimacy, power, obedience, justice, peace, the autonomy that is available to the state and to the individual, and individual rights and liberty (Forsyth 1981, Kaplan 1993, Skinner 1993, Goldsmith 1993, Okin 1993, Kraynak 1993, Malcolm 1991b, 542). Hobbes's primary theoretical and preferred form is sovereignty by institution. By sovereignty by acquisition, Hobbes accounts for the less conceptually interesting historical existence of settled government and rulers. Sovereignty, for Hobbes, arises from the multitude of separate individuals promising to give up the absoluteness of their rights to all things, and thereby volunteering to be the authors of the acts of one person or assembly, to act in their name, or represent them. It is often overlooked that Hobbes prescribes only the renunciation of a 'right to *all* things', not the transfer of '*all* rights to things'. The laws of nature are specified immediately after the definition of the unlimited right of nature. While the right of nature gives 'every man [a] right to every thing', the second law of nature advises that we 'lay down this right to all things' (Hobbes 1946, 85). The reading which stipulates a complete transfer of rights and utter submission is in context unconvincing, whereas the reading which affirms a crucial qualification to the wholesale transfer of rights by individuals is supported by Hobbes's further statement concerning the scope of the liberty which remains to the individual. This latter reading postulates individuals giving up only the unreasonable fantasy of entirely untrammelled freedom and accepting the constraints that necessarily accompany living together in a political community. The bargain that individuals make in Hobbes's theory of sovereignty then looks considerably less draconian.

In making this process of authorisation, freely giving authority to act and to use coercive power, each individual legitimises the sovereign, and in so doing voluntarily takes upon themselves a political obligation, which is a promise to obey and submit to the laws of the sovereign in perpetuity. Thus each individual irrevocably gives authority and takes on the obligation with respect to law. But here Hobbes enters another qualification for the obligation is not to any law however formed by whatever whim of the sovereign, but to publicly-known and easily intelligible positive laws (Hobbes 1946, 176, 178). Such laws in turn constitute justice in more or less circular fashion for Hobbes, for whatever laws the sovereign produces are thereby by definition just. Nevertheless, Hobbes again qualifies the authoritarian tendency suggested by this circular argument by insisting that such laws must be based on natural law (Hobbes 1946, 174), which enjoins all persons to seek peace, keep their promises and in sum do unto others as they would be done to. Given the important role of natural law in Hobbes's system, especially in the logical move from the hypothetical state of nature to civil society, his injunction regarding the underpinning of positive by natural law can be taken to be more than lip service.

Hobbes's theory has been criticised for setting out the authorisation process as logically prior to the operation of sovereignty. In practice, giving authority and taking on an obligation always take place in the context of an understood set of practices and norms about how politics is done in a particular polity. Even though the focus of Hobbes's attention here is only on the logical mechanisms involved, and so there is a sense in which he should not be criticised for failing to take account of cultural specificities and values, there are strong grounds for arguing that the net effect of Hobbes's argument is to suggest that contextual factors are very much secondary. King (1974) challenges effectively the universal claim of Hobbes's theory of sovereignty in this respect. Authorising and obligation are never pre-political or un-political and are substantively affected by the broad cultural framework in which they occur. Even the logical mechanisms are not neutral and context-free. However, a strong case can be made (Prokhovnik 2005) for Hobbes's awareness of elements which we might see as part of a constructed and embedded sense of both authorisation and sovereignty, including Hobbes's recognition that all law is subject to interpretation (Hobbes 1946, 180).

A crucial and complex concept in Hobbes's theory is the notion that sovereignty is 'absolute', and he means by this something distinctively different, though not unrelated, from what Bodin meant. According to Hobbes sovereignty, the defining attribute of a ruler, comes not from the positive actions of the sovereign but from the active and deliberate deeds of the people in relation to each other (Hobbes 1946, 112). Sovereignty for Hobbes could not be sustained unless the analytical interconnection between authority, obligation and law were absolute. Sovereignty must be absolute because the authority given and the obligation taken on by subjects are unconditional, within the limits established in law and by the presence of law. One of the most important features of Hobbes's conception of sovereignty is his articulation of the idea of sovereignty as a regulative ideal. Part of what this means lies in Hobbes's insistence that sovereignty is absolute. The non-reversible institution of the sovereign through the processes of covenanting and authorising, and the way an obligation cannot be withdrawn are at the heart of the meaning of this term, for him. As Hampsher-Monk puts it, given his abstract conception of sovereignty Hobbes insists that this mechanism is true of all forms of government. His argument about absolutism is an argument about the nature of sovereignty itself, and not an argument in favour of locating sovereignty in any particular form of government. In the context of sovereignty as defined by a specific set of conceptual relations, absolutism was 'the unique exercise of unbounded authority' (Hampsher-Monk 1992, 47–8) that characterised sovereignty, not the person or persons in whom it was located.

Hobbes was not advocating simple 'royal absolutism' and the modern negative connotations of absolutism are placed in context by Baumgold's evidence (1988, 60) that absolutism only took on a pejorative meaning of arbitrary government, outside the law, after 1640. Sommerville (1991, 356) notes similar evidence from the 1620s. Hobbes's theory of sovereignty marks a crucial shift in the meaning of 'absolute' sovereignty, from the absolutism of monarchs who regard their power and superiority in entirely personalised, non-negotiable and non-accountable terms, to a logical sense that the concept of sovereignty must have an absolute, all-encompassing scope in defining the relationship between rulers and ruled. In this second sense, in practice the sovereign need not behave like an 'absolute ruler' or dictator at all, and indeed forms of popular sovereignty can also be regarded as absolute as we shall see with Rousseau and others later on. However, in Hobbes this shift remains ambiguous because, while Hobbes's argument is concerned to specify the logical requirements of sovereignty as a concept, his prescription can also be taken to sanction an 'absolute ruler'. Loughlin defines a part of this absolute character of sovereignty when he notes that sovereignty is 'absolute from the perspective of its own particular way of conceptualising the world' (Loughlin 2003, 79). This is an important factor in Hobbes's meaning — not absolute as a licence to act on whim, or unconstrained by any rules or institutions, or a personal power exercised by an individual simply in their own interests. Rather sovereignty is exercised as a public office-holder, and through institutional processes.

Because sovereignty is absolute, it follows for Hobbes that it cannot be shared or divided between the sovereign and anyone else. Sovereignty must be unitary and independent. There are several practical consequences in Hobbes's theory of this analytical argument. It legitimises the centralised control of executive, legislative and judicial state powers in the hands of the sovereign (Baumgold 1988, 66). Moreover, sovereignty is unitary and independent because any division or limitation would encourage private or differing judgment (Lloyd 1992, 64). Sovereignty involves subjects 'accepting direction by a single judgment' (Lloyd 1992, 66). Thus sovereignty is designed by Hobbes both to prevent political and doctrinal disagreement, and to preclude accountability. In addition, as Tuck notes, the 'power of Hobbes's sovereign was … above all an *epistemic* power, to determine the meanings of words in the public language' (Tuck 1991, xvii, Prokhovnik 1991, ch. 4).

Goldsmith (1993 773) provides a useful exploration of Hobbes's absolutism, pinpointing that the crux of sovereignty for Hobbes is the notion of ultimate superior authority (Goldsmith 1993, 771). But Goldsmith also convincingly argues that Hobbes's view, 'that there must be a sovereign, not just sovereignty', is a fallacy. In other words Hobbes is criticised for drawing particular practical effects from the logic of the concept of sovereignty. Goldsmith's evaluation, as we shall see, also sharpens the comparison with Spinoza's notion of sovereignty in terms of balanced authority.

In contrast to the situation in which the individual subject finds themselves, the sovereign does not operate under rules except the law of nature (Hobbes 1946, 173–4). While the law of nature is in practice ineffective where no security prevails, it becomes effective in the stable commonwealth and so, according to Hobbes's argument, could and should inform the sovereign's actions, at least with respect to his subjects. Nevertheless the sovereign has no contractual obligations at all and makes no promises to other individuals. His powers are informally qualified or limited by stipulations about the public character of positive law, but because positive law is identified with the commands of the sovereign there is (necessarily) written into Hobbes's system no formal protection against the sovereign's civil law being no more than the caprice a ruler, and so there is no sufficient safeguard against despotic government. In practice, though, the sovereign's viability in Hobbes's theory, rests ultimately upon his ability to protect, not the individual's life, as this may justly be taken by the sovereign (Hobbes 1946, 139), and may be expended in war up to the point at which 'the forces of the enemies get a final victory' (Hobbes 1946, 218), but upon his ability to protect the commonwealth from dissolution.

According to Hobbes's view the sovereign is a person or assembly (acting as one person), solely entitled by authority (and in sole possession of authority through 'representation') to exercise legal and coercive decision-making power (thereby eliminating collective political activity through dispute, conflict, negotiation, bargaining, factions, alliances, parties, or requests for consultation), not subject to the legal control of another will, free from redress from civil law, located at the apex of a hierarchical structure of governmental powers. Sovereignty is for Hobbes in a very important sense the expression of the unity of the state formed by the authorisation of each individual subject (Hobbes 1946, 107). This conception of the sovereign and of sovereignty is still recognisable in the dominant notion that universal, absolute, but also in the West liberal and neutral, state sovereignty, defines what sovereignty means. In looking at another plausible seventeenth century conception, the universal claims of the theory which has been derived from Hobbes can be challenged.

The dominance of the conception derived from Hobbes overshadows the value of another seventeenth-century view, that of Spinoza. In taking seriously another perspective on sovereignty, with an alternative conceptual basis, this chapter argues that a theory of sovereignty can be detached from the necessity of regarding it as indivisible in Hobbes's sense.

Harrison expresses the view of some commentators, that 'Hobbes, as I see him, is a normative thinker (as opposed, for example, to Spinoza who, similar as he is in many ways, nevertheless seems to me to be merely descriptive in intention all the way down' (Harrison 2003, 252). To read Spinoza this way is to form an evaluation by overlooking the importance of the political, theoretical and religious contexts in the United Provinces in which he was writing, in which his work represented answers to particular problems. Harrison's assessment of Spinoza also neglects the effect on his theory of the Dutch mentality (Prokhovnik 2004) within which Spinoza was writing and which he was in some respects transgressing. To regard Spinoza as a merely descriptive version of Hobbes is to impose a meaning of sovereignty in a context where it does not fit. It involves ignoring that in the Dutch case in which Spinoza was heavily involved, either there wasn't a supreme instrument of government that sovereignty established, because sovereignty in the Dutch case is shared, or there was a supreme instrument of government (the Spanish king earlier on and the Estates General of the United Provinces later on) but it did not hold decisive supreme power. On the ladder of hierarchical powers the Spanish king and later the Estates General rested at the apex, but nevertheless effective power rested with the separate provinces or States or even with town councils within the provinces. However, the argument will show that absence of state-centrality can work for sovereignty too.

Spinoza wrote two political treatises, the *Tractatus Theologico-Politicus* (TTP) published in 1670, less than twenty years after *Leviathan*, and the unfinished *Tractatus Politicus* (TP), which was published posthumously in 1677. It is known that Spinoza read Hobbes, including *Leviathan*, though this was probably only after the Dutch translation of *Leviathan* became available in 1667, or after Hobbes's new Latin version was published in 1668. Spinoza is reported to have had *De Cive* in his library (Hampshire 1951, 179), and is reputed to have read *De Cive* and possibly *Leviathan* during the construction of his two political treatises. There are two direct references in print by Spinoza to Hobbes. In one of his letters (Spinoza 1955, 369), Spinoza distinguishes his conception of natural right from that of Hobbes. And in a note to Chapter XVI of the *Tractatus Theologico-Politicus* (Spinoza 1951, 276 n. 27), Spinoza differentiates between his own and Hobbes's notions of reason. In turn, Hobbes is known to have read Spinoza, and is reported by Aubrey as describing his as a brave man.

While there are clear indications of the awareness by the two writers of each other's works, the nature of a connection between them remains a complex and open question. Two features of Spinoza's theory of sovereignty immediately strike the reader. First the discussion of the authority of the sovereign and the obedience of subjects (which seems to draw heavily on Hobbes) is supplemented by a strong sense of the significance of customary practice, traditional legal privileges, and history. It is clear that Spinoza's aim in writing about politics was to defend the notion of the strengthening of existing practice and institutions of a community, and not to present a blank-slate, purely rational conceptual correctness. The crucial importance of practice in Spinoza's political theory deserves to be much more fully explored. The second feature, which follows from the first, is that Spinoza, in contrast with Hobbes, does not outline a conception of sovereignty expressing the *unity* of the community.

Spinoza's view of sovereignty seems, at first, rather surprising. Known to philosophers through the *Ethics* for his contribution to the development of Rationalist metaphysics, and having in mind the widespread presumption amongst commentators that his political theory, for the most part follows that of Hobbes (Allison 1987, 177; Curley 1988, x; Delahunty 1985, 226; Hampshire 1951,180-81; Harris 1992, 101; Harris 1995,104; Scruton 1986, 27; Strauss 1952, 184; Wolfson 1934, 245; Yovel 1989, 196), we are not led to expect the very important dimension of Spinoza's conception of governing which emphasises the value of social practice, expressed both in his theoretical approach and in his repeated and profound concern with the specific polity of the United Provinces. Moreover recent work on the *Ethics* by Lloyd (1994, 1996), Gatens (1996) and Lloyd and Gatens (1999) suggests important continuities with the political works through, amongst others concepts, the notion of liberty.

Five aspects of Spinoza's conception of sovereignty are discussed here — the irrelevance to him of the state form, shared sovereignty, the importance of reason and liberty, the communitarian character of the theory, and the significance of local conflicts. Spinoza is not discussing sovereignty with reference to the emergent nation state. He is not dealing with a determinate territory with permanently specified borders, a precise measure of population, or with a centralised form of government. Moreover, for Spinoza sovereignty is not about the power to make new law or with identifying the supreme legal authority but about holding in balance the sovereign parts of the United Provinces (TP 322, 330, 336, 340). His many allusions to Holland and the United Provinces make it clear that he is considering sovereignty within the context of city-states loosely giving allegiance to provinces, within a republic which was reluctant to acknowledge itself as a state. Rather than, as in Hobbes, the state being an active self, an agent, figured as a man, represented in the sovereign and achieved by rational artifice, for Spinoza the polity is an unfixed group of independent provinces which themselves contain proudly independent cities.

Neither is Spinoza concerned with a centralised location of ultimate power and authority. Crucially, political decisions are subject to negotiation in his theory (TP 376). This means that politics is a vital and valued activity in a dynamic and active sense of sovereignty. Instead of a designated individual or assembly entitled to make sovereign decisions, a group of assemblies bargain to reach consensus over each important decision. The group of provinces is entitled to make decisions together in Estates General (TP 372), but there is no single dominant power relationship that determines in advance which participants will carry decisive weight in the proceedings.

It follows that at the level of the republic, some elements of sovereignty are shared among a strictly limited number of institutions, and that the principles of constructive tension, balance and proportion guide their conduct. The overall emphasis is on the authority of the separate (aristocratic) assemblies which represent the provinces and *their* freedom from legal control by another will, rather than on the group as a whole. Spinoza notes with regard to his favoured aristocratic form of government in the *Tractatus Politicus*, that cities must be able to 'remain, as far as possible, independent' (TP 371). Spinoza's concern in the *Tractatus Politicus* is not with identifying a central location of sovereignty, but with confirming that cities and provinces should be able to safeguard their independence, by holding on to considerable powers.

The group of provinces which loosely formed the United Provinces did not, and were not interested in a strong sense in acting as one. This is demonstrated by their reluctance to accept invitations from other states to recognise them as a unified Republic. In Spinoza's case sovereignty is not located at the apex of a hierarchical structure of governance powers, and does not express the unity of the polity. The primary allegiance and obligation of each individual is to a province or even to a town. Towns and provinces thus act as two separate levels mediating and providing a buffer between citizens of aristocratic regimes and the weak confederal structure. The suppression of central power, already noted in Spinoza's claim that the only 'bonds' fastening the dominion together are in the senate and court of justice, is reinforced by him in the limits he ascribes to the powers of those bodies. For instance a federal law could not be repealed without a majority of the cities agreeing to it (TP 372).

Spinoza's endorsement of Dutch practice on sovereignty finds theoretical support in Krasner's analytical classification that disaggregates elements of sovereignty. Krasner (2001) argues that domestic sovereignty in the sense of public authority and effective polity control represents the oldest but only one of four usages of the term 'sovereignty', the others being interdependence sovereignty (control over transborder flows), international legal sovereignty (mutual recognition) and Westphalian sovereignty (no higher authority). Krasner's categorisation is useful not just in plausibly parcelling out the different functions of sovereignty but also in providing a convincing alternative to the tendency to prioritise a legalistic and depoliticised conception, especially in its Austinian form, in the modern tradition of thinking about sovereignty. Krasner makes the case that, 'Bodin and Hobbes wanted to establish the legitimacy of some one single source of authority within the polity', but that '[l]ater liberal theorists recognized that there need not be one single fount of legitimacy'. Krasner draws on the evidence that 'indeed, the Founding Fathers in the United States wanted to divide authority among the different branches of the federal government and between the federal government and the states'. Krasner's recognition of the difference between concept and conception and that sovereignty can legitimately be shared indicates that the Spinoza conception is not simply an anomaly to be dismissed. Krasner takes his argument for disaggregating the functions of sovereignty further when he contends that the 'organization of domestic authority within the polity is irrelevant for international legal or Westphalian sovereignty', except in the case of confederal structures such as Switzerland, where the component entities as well as the central government have authority to negotiate with other states (Krasner 2001, 7).

Spinoza's notion of sovereignty is also anchored in conceptions of liberty and reason which dictate what is for him the proper relationship between rulers (whether in a monarchy, aristocracy or democracy) and ruled. A key meaning of liberty in Spinoza is that the liberty of individual towns, held in the form of their non-negotiable legal 'privileges' from higher forms of political power such as an emperor or even monarch, is a concrete thing. Spinoza sees the notion of sovereignty not as an abstract principle to be safeguarded, but in practical terms of the distribution of powers and duties (TTP 10). Indeed in this passage Spinoza speaks of the 'powers of rulers' rather than the more theoretical term sovereignty, and he generally speaks of 'sovereign power' rather than sovereignty, indicating a predilection for discussing political theory in concrete terms. The radical difference in approach between Hobbes and Spinoza on this point is demonstrated in relation to the idea of law. Whereas Hobbes makes a conceptual link between positive law and the pronouncements of the sovereign, Spinoza's emphasis is not on positive (rationalistic) civil law but on the value of tradition, in customary privileges (TTP 242, TP 336).

The idea of traditional privileges which protect the people from the encroachment of monarchical or imperial power, expressing the civil and political rights of citizens under the law, is one of three distinct meanings of liberty for Spinoza in the political works. It is closely connected with both of the other meanings, the liberty of the individual and the liberty of the commonwealth. Individual liberty for Spinoza means the personal freedom to pursue the love of God — which requires religious liberty and toleration on the part of the civil government (TP 299). The liberty of the commonwealth means two things. It requires independence and self-government (TTP 258–63), and a 'free state' is one which is not governed by fear or superstition. The different meanings of liberty are also, additionally, interconnected, since for Spinoza both men and commonwealths are most free when in tune with necessity (TP 295, see also Thayer 1993). Individuals are most free when in tune with the necessity of reason, and both citizens and states are most free when in tune with the necessity of custom and tradition. In his chapter on natural right in the TP, Spinoza outlines a relationship between necessitated nature, freedom and reason, which defines man's natural rights (TP 96–7).

For Hobbes reason is a procedural capacity expressed in a process of reasoning that is useful to make sense of the passions. The passions, for Hobbes, are what drives us, and the role of reasoning is to show the way to achieve a moral end. For Spinoza reason is a goal and exemplifies the combination of freedom and necessity. For Spinoza individual reason is not overridden by the claims of sovereignty as in Hobbes's theory. In the best and most natural form of government in principle, which in the TTP Spinoza equates with democracy, 'everyone submits to the control of authority over his actions, but not over his judgment and reason' (TTP 263). In addition, for Spinoza there is a strong link between reason and history. He stresses the moral function of the polity's institutions in maintaining the protection of privileges, rather than attending to the formal aspects of the state such as a precise location of sovereignty.

This notion of sovereignty and the role of reason in it are distinctively communitarian in spirit, highlighting community, history, and practice. Sovereignty is enacted through the participation of citizens; there is no redress beyond the community nor conceptual apparatus beyond it to appeal to; and the relevance of history to political debate is explicit. For example, Spinoza condemns attempts by the Count of Orange to wrest sovereign power away from the provinces, arguing that sovereign power has 'always' been with the States (TTP 244). In other words, for Spinoza the invocation of historical time in the notion of 'always' is sufficient to establish the legitimacy of the provinces' claim. Another example of the importance of history and cultural specificity for Spinoza's reasoning is his argument that the 'form of the dominion ought to be kept one and the same' (TP 376) on the grounds that 'a multitude that has grown used to another form of dominion will not be able without great danger of overthrow to pluck up the accepted foundations of the whole dominion, and change its entire fabric' (TP 339–40). While Hobbes wants the constitutional arrangements of his civil society to be conceptually watertight, Spinoza appeals to a kind of pragmatic natural justice in law, under the banner of liberty and tolerance, as superior to mere abstract argument as in Hobbes (TTP 10). For Spinoza, the value of tradition means that abstract 'novelties' are both repugnant and suspect (TTP 189). According to Spinoza, every government has a burden of responsibility to maintain continuity with the pre-existing customary network of rights and freedoms established in law (TTP 242).

The role of practice also accounts for the ambiguity whereby Spinoza subscribes to Hobbes's argument that sovereignty entails that there can be no source of authority beyond or as well as the sovereign, but also grants to 'reason' the role of independent arbiter of a sovereign's actions, as we saw earlier. This is a point which Hobbes would never have conceded. A final example concerns Spinoza's acceptance that, even if theory prescribed otherwise, in practice the sovereign's power and the citizen's giving up of rights is never as universal as the ideal account of the formation of the state suggests. His willingness to accept the pragmatic dictates of practice against the ideal is very striking and characteristic. Hobbes would never have accepted this; what he lays down as an ideal is what matters to him.

This conception of sovereignty, based on social practice, is used by Spinoza to address local conflicts from a republican position (TTP ch. XVI). For instance, Spinoza has a vested interest in arguing that the contract by which the commonwealth is formed may be is explicit or tacit, that the ruler does not take over all the citizens' rights, that citizens may resist if the ruler does not act in their interests (TTP 10), and there is no sense of the tight bind between authority and obligation which is found in Hobbes. Again, without an account that recognises the role of local social practice Spinoza's ambiguous treatment of democracy in the earlier treatise is inexplicable, given some of his Hobbesian strictures about undivided sovereignty which he then turns on their head. Another example is found in the ambiguity in Spinoza's use of the term 'dominion', which could equally well refer to the physical tract of land over which a ruler governs, saying nothing about the character of his rule, or it could refer to the sovereignty held by the ruler in relation to his subjects. The problem is compounded by Spinoza's habit of talking about 'dominion', 'authority' and 'power' without properly distinguishing between them. The ambiguity is increased in the Latin original, where the terms, *potestas* and *imperium* are involved in dominion, power and authority, and *dominatio* is translated as both dominion and absolute power. The linguistic slippage in Spinoza's account of sovereignty provides his theory with the flexibility to position him clearly in the republican camp.

While Spinoza in many ways restates Hobbes's conceptual argument only to allow it to be trumped by the greater claims of an argument from practice, there are two specific thrusts of Spinoza's political argument which draw upon principles of Hobbes's theory of sovereignty to great effect. In being able to argue very strongly that states must be either democracies, aristocracies or monarchies, but not a mixture of all three, and that the sovereign must hold civil *and* religious authority, Spinoza is able to use Hobbes's theory of undivided sovereignty to contribute forcefully to two very local political debates. Spinoza allied himself politically with the Dutch republicans, and these two arguments were extremely valuable in opposing, on the one hand the political challenge posed by the House of Orange, and on the other the claim of the Calvinists to authority beyond the civil law.

Looking briefly at each of these arguments in turn, supporters of the House of Orange's political aspirations drew upon the Aristotelian notion of mixed government which dominated academic political theory in the United Provinces, readily accepting the Count of Orange as the monarchical element in this formula. The House of Orange's aspirations also drew for support upon an ambiguous historical precedent. Traditionally during the late medieval period, when the Netherlands were part of the Habsburg Empire, the Counts of Orange had occupied the official post of Stadholder, representing the distant imperial authority, particularly in foreign, diplomatic and defence matters. In practice this had not generally interfered with the internal self-government of the different provinces. But, by the middle of the seventeenth century, after the end of the Revolt against the Spanish and when the obligation to the empire had receded, the House of Orange's ambition to establish itself as the royal house of the United Provinces was in conflict with the desire of the provinces to maintain their independence, not only from any form of monarchical or centralised authority, but also from each other. The persistence into the seventeenth century (and beyond) in the Netherlands, of medieval legal structures and patterns, remained the basis for defining legal liberties, specific and local ancient privileges and the rights of the individual in society. The persistence of these medieval patterns is reflected also in the continuity of expectation and assumption of feudal notions of rulership and sovereignty. Without a feudal monarch or emperor, sovereignty had come, almost by default, to be seen to reside in the separate provinces, who continued to send mandated delegates to the assembly called the Estates General.

Spinoza and the republicans asserted the principles of provincial autonomy, commercial and colonial aggression, combined with isolationism in Europe, all within a Holland-centric perspective legitimised by a tradition-centred idiom of political language based on ancient privileges and liberties, validated by law. Despite being, at the time, the most important European power after France, the United Provinces pursued a policy of isolationism in Europe, acted several times as mediator in disputes between rival neighbours, and was shy of recognising sister Republics. Holland led and was the most prosperous province in the union but did not simply dominate it.

In this political climate no theoretical or constitutional innovation was possible, except when framed as endorsing the continuity of tradition. This definition of a republic held no place for an active monarchical element and Spinoza sought, by using Hobbes's conception of sovereignty, to reinvigorate the communitarian basis of the republican conception of sovereignty and to secure the exclusion of the House of Orange from any monarchical role. In consequence, Spinoza's notion of sovereignty is designed as an instrument to defend the constitutional tradition which the republicans had forged but presented as customary, and not as an instrument to unify and strengthen the state. Its purpose was to check the development of centralised government, not to promote it. Sovereignty is not territorial for Spinoza and the republicans because they are not promoting a territorially-defined entity with fixed borders but a flexible union of independent parts. Spinoza inherited and enthusiastically defended reliance upon a collection of feudal political patterns and medieval legal arrangements.

In the 1640s and 1650s Hobbes was one of many who saw the breakdown of royal authority in England and the seizure of power by Parliament and the Army as a terrible rupture in the desirable and traditional continuity of sovereign power, tangibly located in centralised and unified fashion in the monarch. Continuity in the highest power to exercise rule was seen by him as being crucial to the wellbeing of civil society. Hobbes wrote in 1640 that power and rights were inseparably annexed to the sovereignty (Dick 1946, 310; Hobbes 1984, 414; also quoted in Malcolm 1991b, 530). He held that as Parliament did not dispute that sovereignty lay with Charles I, they should not maintain any rights or power against the king. Spinoza, incidentally, sees the English Civil War as dreadful proof of what happens when a people try to change the nature of the government to which they are best suited, in this case monarchy (TTP 243).

In the United Provinces however, the issue of the continuity of sovereign power had not been so crucial to the perceived wellbeing of civil society. Netherlanders were accustomed to seeing the issue of sovereignty as quite separate from that of the power to rule, and indeed saw the two things as necessarily separate. The United Provinces in the seventeenth century was not a modern European nation state and did not become one until the nineteenth century. These different backgrounds, then, help to account for the very different understandings Hobbes and Spinoza have of the relationship between public and private, state and society, and the role of sovereignty in sanctioning these relationships. In Spinoza's theory the whole is not as important as the separate parts; there is no nation state because there is no whole. Thus when Spinoza used Hobbes's notion of sovereignty, it was not in order to cojoin sovereignty with rights and power as such, in the sense Hobbes meant. The Revolt had been won by the United Provinces in order to reaffirm this separation, and even long after the end of the Revolt the two principles were not fully merged.

Spinoza's argument against the Calvinists follows from the thesis developed early in the first political treatise, that the reason used in philosophy and the faith on which scripture depends, are separate and distinct expressions of truth. It follows, for Spinoza, that the state which allows man to pursue a life devoted to the love of God, which is after all man's highest goal, says Spinoza, is a state which has a sophisticated understanding of the need for religious toleration, and so necessarily holds sovereign power and authority in both civil and religious affairs. The sovereign's laws in both areas must override any other law, and so dictate the terms of civil religious pluralism, though not, of course, of faith. Spinoza sought to promote a form of toleration and a real religious alternative to the dogmatic view that the Calvinists in the United Provinces and the Puritans in England both held, that scripture provides all the answers and reason none. The force of Spinoza's use of Hobbes's theory of sovereignty at this point is to support his argument that sovereignty should be indivisible in the sense that civil sovereign power in matters secular should not be divided from civil sovereign power in matters spiritual. Spinoza's purpose in using Hobbes here is fulfilled when he can argue that freedom to worship God as the individual's conscience dictates, within the dominion where the sovereign has power to make civil law over both secular and religious matters, can 'be granted without prejudice to the public peace, but also, that without such freedom, piety cannot flourish nor the public peace be secure' (TTP 10, 6). It is worth emphasising that this championing of toleration, conscience and individual judgment is a very different outcome, from the same premise of absolute sovereignty, from Hobbes's advocacy of a compulsory state church.

Spinoza's successful use of Hobbes's argument in these two areas is not followed up by an analysis of sovereignty as a concept, similar to that of Hobbes. For Hobbes, sovereignty provides several crucial political functions. It identifies the locus of political authority, and the corresponding political obligation of citizens, and it involves the sovereign's right and power to make and implement law. But, perhaps most importantly, sovereignty expresses for Hobbes the political identity and unity of a commonwealth. For Spinoza, however, such an enterprise – the analysis of sovereignty as a concept, is not required. Instead of talking in terms of a sovereign, Spinoza refers loosely and interchangeably to 'the authorities' (TTP 260), 'the holders of sovereign power'(TTP 10), 'the rights of rulers'(TTP 265), 'the civil authority'(TTP 6), 'legitimate rulers'(TTP 6), 'him...who holds supreme dominion'(TP 309), and the 'supreme authorities'(TTP 301-310). And in his chapter entitled 'The Best State of a Dominion', in the second political treatise, Spinoza notes that it should be independent, free and peaceful (TP 313–15), but he does not discuss sovereignty as a criterion. Spinoza's theory exhibits strongly the Dutch mentality in its preference for expressing matters in concrete form, in its veneration of practice, and in its linguistic shifts. This predisposition accounts for Spinoza's repeated assurances at the beginning of the second political treatise that he would only entertain those arguments that are 'consistent with experience or practice', and advocate only those proposals which 'agree best with practice' (TP 288).

While for Hobbes sovereignty crucially expresses the political identity and unity of the commonwealth, such that the abstract concept could be, in theory, cashed out into a number of different forms of government, in which the sovereign is either a natural person or an artificial person, Spinoza's political thought is developed, particularly in the second political treatise, through an analysis of the three types of civil government, in a sequence of chapters on monarchy, aristocracy and democracy. It is instructive, from the point of view of sovereignty, to look at what Spinoza does regard as the best state of a dominion. For having used Hobbes to argue that the sovereign powers are indivisible and must not be shared, in the sense either of the mixed government formula or between separate civil and religious authorities, Spinoza then advocates two things, one theoretical and one practical.

At the theoretical level Spinoza holds the view that the fundamental basis of the authority and legitimacy of all governments, and the sovereignty of all dominions, rests upon their conformity with the spirit of traditional practice, a notion crucially entwined with that of liberty. Thus one could say that Spinoza's conception of sovereignty is based upon a non-transcendent, but historically-embedded, natural law of custom and tradition, in direct contrast to Hobbes's notion of sovereignty as brought about by rational artifice. Spinoza's own political works demonstrate that he is not proposing an unreflective conservatism here. His statements that for instance, 'every dominion should retain its original form' (TTP 244), that 'I am fully persuaded that experience has revealed all conceivable sorts of commonwealth, which are consistent with men's living in unity' (TP 288), and that political arrangements 'may be devised in every dominion agreeable to the nature of the situation and the national genius' (TP 382), must be read in the light of his commitment to liberty, summed up in his phrase that 'it is exceedingly difficult to revoke liberties once granted' (TTP 74). However, in the first of these quotations Spinoza does not address the problem of the conceptual weakness, and lack of clear historical definition, in the term 'original'. In the third quotation Spinoza need not be seen as advocating ethnic nationalism, given his own Marrano Jewish background, his belief in toleration, and the United Provinces' political climate which did not pursue nationalist policies.

At the practical level Spinoza advocates in the *Tractatus Politicus*, in what is his most consistent position, that his preferred form of government is an aristocratic dominion where sovereignty would be shared between a number of provinces and between cities within each provinces (TP 348, 370, 384). For Spinoza, this practical preference is not in contradiction with his argument that, in principle, democracy best fits with man's nature because in it everyone submits control over their actions to government (TTP 263). Spinoza argues for this preference for aristocracy expressed in multiple centres on several grounds, one of which is that power resting in more than one place results in a better balance being achieved, and is therefore better able to defend liberty from tyranny, either from within or without. The Dutch notion of shared sovereignty and the role in it of Dutch practice, to which Spinoza is indebted, is examined well by Van Gelderen (1993, xxix).

This perspective corresponds closely to the political values of the United Provinces in the 1660s, where sovereignty was seen to reside in numbers of self-governing cities ruled by aristocratic elites, in autonomous and independent provinces, held in constructive tension or balance in a formal but scarcely-acknowledged union. The United Provinces did not have a federal or confederal constitution in the modern sense, but rather a constitution in an older sense which focussed on separate provinces and towns. Again the outcome arrived at by Hobbes, from the idea of indivisible sovereignty, was very different, Hobbes's logical preference being for a monarchy, since one person could most easily reflect the unity of an indivisible and absolute sovereignty. Spinoza however, argues, again in terms which make sense in the light of traditional practice in the United Provinces, but not in terms of a theoretical analysis based on Hobbes's theory, that the liberty of the commonwealth is protected from the corrupting effect of power on particular men, more adequately by a 'sufficiently large council' than by one man (TP 346). A dominion with a constitution that recognises a balance of central and decentralised powers will be independent (in particular of the multitude) to rule, and establish a balance which is both dynamic and everlasting. A balanced institution, composed of the correct proportion of councillors to multitude, best represents its constituency, Spinoza contends; not electorally, since he is not advocating elections, but in the dynamic tension established between valid and competing interests. But it should be quickly added that Spinoza is not thereby endorsing the idea of pluralism in the form of political parties or factions. Both of these he condemns, on the grounds that they dissolve the council's ability to act as one. Neither does Spinoza advocate limited government in the manner of Locke. He upholds the practice of strong government by the towns and provinces, and severely restricted federal institutions to keep the others in balance.

It has been worth tracing the close connection between Spinoza and the political practice of the United Provinces in the second half of the seventeenth century, in order to demonstrate the point that although Spinoza's perspective on sovereignty may look theoretically untenable to us, used as we are to the requirement that sovereignty must be absolute in Hobbes's sense, it reflected a practice which was extremely successful, which worked in its own terms. Spinoza's estimation of the worth of the political practice of the United Provinces, above the value of the cogency of Hobbes's strictures that the primary reason for the weakness of a commonwealth is want of absolute power (Hobbes 1946, 210), and that 'powers divided mutually destroy each other' (Hobbes 1946, 213), is not to be dismissed. Spinoza's conception is the theoretical vindication of the flourishing political system and of the understanding of sovereignty obtaining in Holland and the United Provinces at the time. Contrary to Hobbes's argument that supreme power must be located somewhere definite in every state, the United Provinces thrived and prospered on the basis of its practice of polycentric sovereignty.

The way in which Spinoza nowhere argues directly for a republic, nor for republican government as such, while at the same time being concerned to outline the basis on which De Witt's republican government could be both justified and reformed, is a prime example of this approach to politics, and indicates Spinoza's considerable skill in responding the Dutch mentality with his theoretical expertise. Spinoza recognised the need for reform. His view is not simply bound by tradition (see for instance, TTP 189). For him, as for all Netherlanders, government is warranted by its maintenance of the traditional balance. But Spinoza's contribution is also exceptional in attempting a theoretical vindication of practice at all. The general lack of attention paid to reforming actual legal and formal constitutional arrangements and the shunning of theoretical discussions of sovereignty, meant that these issues were and could only be dealt with through involvement in political debate and practice.

In sum, what Spinoza advocates is, in Hobbes's terms, neither absolutism or state sovereignty on the one hand, nor popular sovereignty on the other; but a shared sovereignty which reaffirms the separateness of the parts and holds them in dynamic tension. Shared sovereignty is of course one of Hobbes's primary examples of things that tend to the dissolution of commonwealths, for if it is shared it is necessarily divided. Hobbes does, incidentally, refer directly in *Leviathan* to the United Provinces and roundly condemns their victory in the Revolt against the Spanish (Hobbes 1946, 213). Sovereignty is not the most crucial political concept for Spinoza. He does not operate with a modern distinction between state and society, and he defends an implied constitutionalism, dependent on law, rather than a modern notion of sovereignty. In doing so he expresses the values of Dutch practice. This implicit constitutionalism, as opposed to a modern rationalist written constitution, draws upon customary notions of its institutional 'foundations' (which are static) and law, and on the values of 'proportion' and balance. The constitutionalism provides the key to the accurate expression of the relationship between right and power at three levels, namely between the ruling council and the multitude, and between cities, and between provinces. Underpinned by his notions of national genius and liberty, for Spinoza it is the defence of traditional practice, as embodied in the legal and administrative arrangements of the constitution, that is vital. He lays great emphasis on the practical arrangements which will 'see that the constitution of the whole dominion is preserved unbroken' (TP 374), and later argues that 'if any dominion can be everlast-

ing, that will necessarily be so, whose constitution being once rightly instituted remains unbroken'. According to Spinoza, 'the constitution is the soul
of a dominion. Therefore, if it is preserved, so is the dominion' (TP 383).

In conclusion, for Hobbes, sovereignty is absolute in several senses, the
most important of which in this comparison with Spinoza, is that Hobbes
regarded sovereignty as analytically absolute. Furthermore, Hobbes saw
himself as disclosing the inherently universal and transcendental character of sovereignty (Kraynak 1990, 168–9). In addition, for Hobbes sovereignty is associated with centralised political control and power, a natural
territorial boundary, and is unchallengeable by supremacy claims by rival
powers (Kraynak 1990, 170). For Spinoza however, it is perfectly possible
for sovereignty to be mediated through other institutions and loyalties.
This reflects the persistence of the medieval mentality of the United
Provinces, which persevered in the seventeenth century despite the
United Provinces being highly aware of the development of modern states
in England and France. Furthermore, in a radical difference with Hobbes's
analytical absolutism, Spinoza stipulates in his second political treatise
that no-one can be considered as holding a position above the law in any of
the three forms of dominion. The king in a monarchy, and patricians,
syndics and senators in aristocracies, are all bound by the law (TP 364).
Spinoza is also explicit about the accountability of judges and senators (TP
360, 366). For Hobbes, in comparison, it is a defining attribute of sovereignty that a sovereign is not only the maker of positive law but is also
above that law.

Hobbes's and Spinoza's theories of sovereignty also result in very different conceptions of politics and political activity. Spinoza has a positive
view of political practice as a matter of negotiating disputes and differences toward consensual outcomes within the framework of the constitutional tradition embodying customary practice and conventional usage.
For Hobbes, however, as Kraynak puts it, the 'power that sets the limits
must itself be the supreme power and hence must be sovereign' (Kraynak
1990, 167). Politics is abolished by Hobbes.

This chapter has been in part concerned to demonstrate that Spinoza's
theory of sovereignty does not simply follow that of Hobbes. It has also
sought to disclose something of the importance of the Dutch context for
understanding Spinoza's political views. It is clear that Hobbes's text can
also be better understood in the light of the relevant political and intellectual contexts. Aspects of context important to understanding the absolutism of Hobbes's theory of sovereignty include the huge political upheaval
of the Civil War, the increasing centralisation of the English state, the religious disputes involving the state church and Puritans, Presbyterians and
Catholics, the growing absolutism of Stuart kings, shifting European
alliances and the development of the British Empire, as well as the

significance attaching to the natural territorial boundaries in Great Britain. These and other contexts are admirably reconstructed by Tuck (1989), Malcolm (1991b), Sommerville (1992), Skinner (1978, 1994, 1996), Goldsmith (1980), Condren (1994), and Burgess (1991, 1992). However, in the case of Hobbes, the direct connection between text and context is interestingly masked by the analytical and abstract character of *Leviathan*, which leads some readers to discount their value in understanding his theory.

This chapter has also been intent upon identifying a strong interpretation of Spinoza as a republican thinker to rectify the picture of his adoption simply into a liberal democratic tradition, and upon laying some of the groundwork for identifying the role of Hobbes's theory of sovereignty in the subsequent influential myth of state sovereignty. In articulating another view of sovereignty, the polycentric one of Spinoza, with an alternative and plausible basis, it has been shown that Hobbes's theory, whatever its universal claims, is itself historically-embedded and culturally-specific, and that therefore conceptions of sovereignty can be detached from the necessity of regarding them as indivisible in Hobbes's abstract sense.

LOCKE AND ROUSSEAU

LOCKE

This chapter compares the conceptions of sovereignty developed by Locke in the *Second Treatise* of 1689 and by Rousseau in the *Social Contract* of 1762. What are being compared are two versions of popular sovereignty — one account in which the term sovereignty itself is barely mentioned, and the other in which the term is very prominent. Locke's and Rousseau's meanings of popular sovereignty are diametrically opposed. Sovereignty does a lot of work in Rousseau's political theory. Locke is much more cautious and indeed negative about the notion, but the idea of sovereignty is nevertheless also very important to the construction of his theory. It needs to be borne in mind that the sovereignty of the people, for Locke, is provisional, conditional, qualified, disaggregated, and limited.

However, Locke's and Rousseau's theories are also signally similar in that in both sovereignty is notably performative rather than juridical. Both writers trace a strong link between the voluntary act of making a social contract and sovereignty on the one hand, and the later enacting of sovereignty (in a weak sense for Locke in 'revolution' and in a robust repeated sense for Rousseau) on the other. Both take the idea of a social contract seriously, and it is a substantive element of each theory, whereas for Hobbes and Spinoza the social contract functions primarily only as a formal and abstract mechanism in a line of reasoning. Locke appeals to an 'original compact' while Rousseau refers to the 'social pact' or 'social contract'. It is through the notions of a social contract and either rare 'revolution' or regular performance that both Locke and Rousseau have cogent, though very different, theories of popular sovereignty. For Locke the social contract helps to protect what would later be called liberal rights, while the social contact in Rousseau is a part of a republican vision. It also needs to be borne in mind that the features of Locke's position (individualism, pre-political rights, suspicion of government etc) are strongly associated with what became known as the liberal view, while his position is not that of what became held by liberal democrats. It was not until the much later development of liberal democracy that the notion of popular sovereignty was given institutional expression. What is most distinctive about Locke's theory of sovereignty is its ingenious logic, popular and yet not popular, and the deliberate absence of the term 'sovereignty' as a political concept.

The *Second Treatise* was published in 1689, the year after the Revolution of 1688 and the inauguration of the constitutional monarchy of William and Mary. Laslett's case, that the *Second Treatise* was not written to justify the Revolution as previously thought (Laslett 1965, 78), still carries considerable weight. Laslett argues that the *Second Treatise* was instead drafted between 1679 and 1683 as a call for revolution at the time of the Exclusion Crisis amid fears of a Catholic monarch, when Charles II was being entreated to disbar his Catholic brother James from the succession. Locke was instrumental at this time in articulating the political position of his powerful friend and political ally, the earl of Shaftesbury, a leading Whig politician. Certainly, Locke's antipathy to 'absolutism' and so to subscription to the 'absolute' sovereignty theorised by Hobbes, can be seen as mixed up with his fear of the threat of 'royal absolutism' associated with the reign of James II, the idea that a Catholic monarch would overturn the rule of law, jettison parliament, govern by standing army and persecute Protestants. More recently Wootton and others have contested Laslett's dating of the writing of the *Second Treatise*. Wotton argues that 'it is almost impossible to make sense of the *Second Treatise* as a work written in 1679–80'. He contends that the '*Second Treatise* is obviously a work written in defence of revolution, and yet supporters of Shaftesbury in 1679-80 were not thinking in terms of revolution: their concern was to demonstrate the urgent need for Exclusion, and the legal right of King-in-Parliament to determine the succession' (Wootten 1993, 50). What is meant by 'revolution' here needs to be carefully identified. Ball elucidates that the idea of revolution meant something quite different for Locke and his contemporaries from its meaning for us. They 'understood a revolution to be a coming full circle, a restoration of some earlier uncorrupted condition; we understand it to be the collective overthrow of an old regime and the creation of an entirely new one' (Ball 1997, 41). Whether Laslett or Wootten is correct about the date the *Second Treatise* was written, it remains the case as Dunn bluntly states, that 'the *Two Treatises* is a work principally designed to assert a right of resistance to unjust authority, a right, in the last resort, of revolution'. It was a work that 'attacked the pretension of absolute monarchy and ... drew firm conclusions from this attack about the constitutional limits on the prerogative powers of the King of England' (Dunn 1984, 28).

The first question to address here concerns whether one can attribute a conception of sovereignty to Locke at all, given that he did not use the term as a political concept at all in the *Second Treatise*. Gough takes the view that Locke deliberately 'avoided the term "sovereignty"' (Gough 1963, 127). Locke does refer to 'Sovereign' and 'Sovereignty' in relation to the individual that is born free and rational (II section 61). He uses the term 'absolute power', which is sometimes regarded as a synonym for sovereignty, for instance to argue that absolute power is utterly inconsistent with the notion of the free and rational individual who holds pre-political rights derived from natural law (II sections 17, 23, also 4, 108, 115). Absolute power is identified by Locke with absolute monarchy, and by 'absolute' he means the much simpler 'arbitrary government' than the philosophical points about sovereignty made by Bodin and Hobbes. Locke is an interesting figure in this intellectual tradition because, while on the face of it 'sovereignty' is not one of his key terms, his work is very important in the history of the concept.

Locke does use the term sovereignty in several places in the *First Treatise*. The sophisticated awareness of the meaning of the term that he demonstrates in these examples, reinforces the view that the general absence of the term in the *Second Treatise* is intentional. For instance in section 64 of the *First Treatise* Locke claims that the injunction, 'Honour thy father and mother, cannot mean an absolute subjection to a sovereign power'. It derives, he says, from 'an eternal law' only about parents and children, and so cannot be an analogy with political power. In section 68 Locke discusses the way in which 'the unlimited and undivided sovereignty of Adam's fatherhood' refers to a natural paternal power only. In section 75 he maintains that 'fatherhood and property [are] distinct titles to sovereignty'.

Some Locke scholars would attribute the absence of the term sovereignty in his *Second Treatise* not to deliberate avoidance but to the essentially pragmatic and political character of his work, arguing that he was not attempting political philosophy but was doing a kind of political theory which is much less abstract. A case can be made for thinking that this is not the only reason. Again, some historians of political thought would take the view that we cannot, without anachronism, discuss Locke's theory of sovereignty if he did not use the term. We create inaccuracies and misunderstandings about writers' work, and impose views they did not hold, if we use terms to discuss and evaluate their work that they did not employ themselves. For example Karl Popper famously accused Plato of developing a totalitarian theory, a term only invented in the Cold War in the mid-twentieth century. Popper has famously been berated for doing so. However, there are strong grounds for considering that Locke has a conception of sovereignty, so long as we are careful in clarifying what we mean by saying that. A case will be made here that crucial to Locke's the-ory is a fully intentional conception of sovereignty that is formal, power-ful, and ingenious in the following way. Locke can be understood as splitting the 'supreme power' between a constituent meaning (that resides but is normally dormant in the people) and an ordinary meaning (located in the legislative branch of government under normal conditions). This crucial distinction, together with his fundamental commitment to the pri-ority of pre-political individual rights, means that there can be no mean-ingful collective rights in Locke's schema. He is thereby able to put forward a form of popular sovereignty that successfully, at the same time, establishes narrow constraints on and for government, allows for a right of resistance, prevents the emergence of a populist common good, and is a defence against absolute monarchy.

The case for regarding Locke as having a conception of sovereignty, even if only covertly, is strengthened by evidence discussed by Ivison, locating Locke's theory in the context of the implications of the Westphalia treaties and the key debate in early modern political theory about empire. Ivison notes that 'Locke was writing in the immediate aftermath of the treaties of Westphalia. These treaties were intended to tie the various European states into a system of reciprocally guaranteed security by mini-mising the grounds for interferences in each other's affairs, in essence, by guaranteeing their territorial sovereignty, but it could at least be regulated by a principle of non-interference'. In contrast, outside Europe, 'in areas where no sovereign states (or civil societies) existed … states could pursue their extra-territorial expansionist ambitions without necessarily upset-ting the balance of powers within Europe'. (Ivison 2003, 96). Westphalia established a settled agreement at the same time as empires were develop-ing and the potentiality of accruing European wealth from foreign parts was beginning to be systematically realised. It is no accident that the two things were happening at the same time. As Ivison puts it, '[i]n short, Westphalia helped constitute not only the international *system* of states, but also the sovereignty of the states themselves; that is, their exclusive and pre-eminent right to govern their territories and the populations therein' (Ivison 2003, 96).

Taking this argument a step further and comparing Hobbes and Locke, Keal highlights the difference in the role played by natural right in their theories of sovereignty. He says, 'Hobbes's concern over natural rights was, in part, with the obstacles they posed for transferring the rights of European peoples to a sovereign'. However, for 'Locke it was a matter of whether whatever natural rights inhered in the state of nature were an impediment to dispossessing Amerindians of their land'. The net result was the same for indigenous peoples, though, for in both cases, the effect 'amounted to a loss of rights for non-Europeans; the absence of civil society justified both the assertion of sovereignty, albeit without their consent, over non-Europeans and the dispossession of their lands' (Keal 2003, 80).

As well as there being a strong case for arguing that Locke has a conception of sovereignty as regards political society, his theory also sets out the paradigm of liberal individual sovereignty in terms of the autonomy, freedom and power of the individual. Moreover, Ivison again locates this development in early modern debates about empire. He registers that 'the connection between liberalism and imperialism is not merely chronological but metaphysical'. He argues that 'the analogy between the sovereign state and the sovereign [autonomous, rights-bearing] individual acting on the basis of their natural rights, constrained by the recognition of the basic rights of others (but not much more than that), represents an influential vision of liberal freedom'. He also shows that another aspect of 'the deep connections between liberalism and colonialism trades on the apparent paradox of liberal universalism', namely, 'how universalistic premises applied to politics', for instance, 'that every man is naturally free and possesses "natural political virtue" ... can result in particularistic and exclusionary practices and institutions' in colonial practice (Ivison 2003, 98).

It is worth exploring this issue a little further, since conceptualising colonial expansion was of importance to Locke and can be seen as one of the contexts in which he developed his theory of sovereignty. Ivison outlines three lines of argument that were used to justify colonisation in the sixteenth and seventeenth centuries. The argument from conquest 'tied the extension of sovereignty to the propagation of the Christian faith, and hence the legitimacy of waging war against those who were perceived to reject Christianity and thus the foundation of natural law' (Ivison 2003, 88). The argument from grace was that the justification of empire 'rested on the dispensation of a higher authority'. As Ivison puts it, the 'authority of the prince depended not on God's laws but upon his grace, and thus if one fell from grace then he might be legitimately deposed by his subjects and replaced with a more godly prince'. This was a Lutheran-inspired argument that contended that 'no non-Christian ... could hold legitimate *dominium* of his [own] lands' (Ivison 2003, 89). Thirdly, the argument from *res nullius*, which had its roots in Roman law, claimed that 'all "empty things", including unoccupied lands (*terra nullius*)' remained 'the common property of mankind until put to proper use' (Ivison 2003, 89). It is well known that Locke contributed to this debate as well as being involved in colonial expansion in America, and this side of his thinking and activities demonstrate a close familiarity with contemporary discussions on sovereignty in relation to both the individual and the polity.

Having addressed the question of whether Locke had a theory of sovereignty at all and made a case for a powerful if covert role for sovereignty in his theory, and sketched the context of arguments about European and extra-European sovereignty, we come to the central terms involved in Locke's conception of sovereignty. These are 'trust', 'revolution' or 'dissolution of government' and the right of resistance, and the separation of powers, but in order to understand their meaning for Locke it is important to identify a couple of the background points of the more general theory. The crucial categories of Locke's theory as a whole are 'individual rights under natural law', and the two-stage process from the state of nature to government. Individual rights to 'life, liberty and estate', as Locke conceives them, are pre-political and trump any claim upon the individual by the state. As Lowe describes, Locke 'sees the restraints on governmental authority as arising out of the very nature and purpose of the original "compact"'. Lowe continues that Locke's 'reasoning extends, in particular, to individual *property* rights — which is why he maintains, contrary to Hobbes, that the government is never entitled to appropriate an individual's private goods, land or money without his consent' (Lowe 2005, 189). The transition from the state of nature to government is achieved through the intermediate mode of civil society. The first stage of the process, from the state of nature to civil society is arrived at through the consent of each person. In the second stage, from civil society to society under government, the choice of government is accomplished through majority decision. 'Political society' is arrived at when any number of men in the state of nature voluntarily enter into society to make one people, one body politic under one supreme government, and authorises the legislative to make laws for it.

Because of the manner in which it is created, Locke is able to claim that this government is entrusted with four and only four specific functions. It is charged with making laws, with punishing an injury done to any of the members of civil society, with exercising the power of war and peace with other communities, and in some ways most importantly with ensuring the preservation of the property of the members of civil society. In Hobbes's theory individuals are propelled into authorising the sovereign partly through the logic of the 'ferocious misery' (Cole 1973, xv) of extreme fear of war and death (and they see a way forward through their reasoning and the laws of nature). For Locke, in contrast, in general terms, civil society and government are entered into through the consent of individuals, with composure, merely to remedy the 'inconveniences' of the state of nature, and so civil government is intentionally designed as the opposite of absolute monarchy. For Locke, absolute monarchy is totally inconsistent with civil society, and limited and conditional government is the only form compatible with 'individual rights under natural law'.

Coming now to the features of sovereignty in the *Second Treatise*, Locke's conception of popular sovereignty is guaranteed and safeguarded by the notion of trust, a specific right of resistance linked to 'revolution' and the 'dissolution of government', and the separation of powers. Trust is the primary condition that must be satisfied for legitimate government to occur, according to Locke. Government is conditional on trust. Locke is very clear that government in a civil society can only operate on a trust basis. It follows that the only powers the government has are 'fiduciary' powers, a legal term given political significance which implies that powers are given according to a contract, and on the basis of trust. In consequence Locke's argument is that the powers of government are revoked if the trust is broken. The reason Locke specifies this fiduciary character of government power is to ensure a restraining logic on the state. The state can develop no overall object or purpose or aim or moral value of its own, separate from the individual people who make up the body politic in civil society. It follows from this that Locke places, as Ashcraft (1994 228) puts it, a 'structural constraint' on the exercise of self-interest, which is allowed free reign between individuals operating in a market society and owning private property, but which is forbidden in the realm of government.

It is in the light of this distinction that we can understand Locke to be employing the term 'common good' only in a very weak sense. Locke is intent upon prohibiting a ruler who imposes their own interest over that of the individuals with their pre-political rights. Ashcraft makes the point that 'with respect to the exercise of political power, not only will the common good always take precedence over self-interest but, also, government will have to be constituted in such a manner as to rule out a Hobbesian sovereign or a divinely instituted monarch who retains an interest which is distinct and separate from that of his subjects' (Ashcraft 1994, 228). The aim of the term 'common good' is not to specify a substantive good but only to disbar the imposition of self-interest by a ruler. The force of Locke's emphasis on trust, as a key conception in his theory and underpinning this negative sense of 'common good', is that it provides for him the only acceptable means by which individuals, with their pre-political rights, can accede to being governed and can protect those rights.

The effect of Locke's conception of government on trust is to secure the sovereignty of the people, which is the perpetual residual power of the people to change the personnel of government and reshape the type of government. Although Locke's theory appears to be ambiguous in referring to both the people and the legislative power as holding 'supreme power', the difference is actually quite clear in this context. Locke argues that the supreme power of the legislative is only conditional, dependent on observing is fiduciary nature. Otherwise 'supreme power' reverts to the people, in civil society.

Locke does not make it clear whether the trust relationship between people and government is part of the original compact, or a continuing understanding between governed and governors. Locke suggests, rather than demonstrates, that it is both. The trust relationship is referred to as originating in the compact of society, giving the governed an identity. But it is also continuously maintained, because the governed go on existing and go on entrusting. 'Trust' is not a thing given once and for all: it is by its nature an on-going process.

Having outlined Locke's theory of trust, we turn to his understanding of the right to resistance and the dissolution of government or revolution. Wootten highlights the radical character of Locke's theory here when he notes that Locke's 'conservatism was deeply subversive' (Wootten 1993, 48). Government is conditional on trust. It is also limited by the specific right to resistance, which all individuals retain when they enter into the relationship with government. The government—and Locke means by 'government' all the branches of it taken together—can be dissolved when it acts contrary to the trust placed in it. For if government is not preserving and protecting the people, their liberties and property, then it is going against what it was set up to do. Power then reverts to the people, who can then empower a new legislative and executive. This process can occur, according to Locke's two-stage process, without reversion to the state of nature.

Crucially, it is the people (the public, the community) who decide when a breach of trust has occurred and how the dissolution is to take place. This is the flip side, according to Locke's theory, of the way in which it is the people who granted power and entrusted government. In resisting and dissolving government, the people trigger the performance of their sovereignty, their residual supreme power to recognise the actions of a government *as* a breach of trust. The act of abolishing a government and establishing another, is the same as the people using their ultimate right to resist and to revolt. The same action means these two things. However, Locke drew back from the most radical interpretation of this resistance theory. For although his individualistic theory comes close to justifying anarchy—the idea that no government has the right to infringe individual liberties and rights—Locke does regard government, if properly arranged and qualified by the trust condition, as beneficial. He judges that there are advantages to be gained from government, if properly constituted, in terms of creating a settled order for the expression of individual rights. In cases of dispute, the final appeal is to God, Locke states. In using this construction Locke can be taken as giving a coded message understood at the time as representing a call for revolution.

Locke's theory leaves a series of questions unanswered. For instance, by what mechanism are the actions of the government to be evaluated? Who will judge if the legislative or executive act contrary to their trust? At what point do infringements of the trust, in abuses and mismanagements of power, become sufficient to warrant revolt and dissolution? Locke makes the enigmatic assertion that the people will judge. The ambiguity of this answer lies in the problematic relationship, for Locke's theory, between the people and the individual. Although all the people as a whole, or the majority, must rise up in order to make the right of resistance effective, nevertheless ultimately every man must judge for himself, Locke contends, because the right of resistance is in the final analysis a right carried by individuals, not by a group. Furthermore, to overcome the tension between a collective evaluation to resist and individual judgment, Locke relies on an unsubstantial argument. He maintains that the people have common sense and will be able to discriminate and thus judge when acts amount to persistent and serious infringements, and thus when they deserve to be recognised as forfeiting the trust. Locke also says that if only a minority is in dispute with the executive, then the majority decision should hold.

The tension between 'the people' and 'the individual' that leads to an uneasy majoritarianism is inherent in Locke's key 'supremacy of the people' principle. His version of the 'supremacy of the people' falls far short, by comparison, of the robust affirmation of the common good that it represents for instance in Rousseau's work. The spiritlessness of Locke's argument here can be accounted for in different ways. Two of the most plausible explanations are that Locke was afraid to spell out any more explicitly the terms of revolution in case his work was regarded as inciting treason, and that Locke was elitist enough to hold privately that it would be leading figures in politics, law and business who would decide the matter. Certainly, Locke was no democrat. Locke makes explicit in section 149 that the supremacy of the people is not to be translated into a principle of extended or universal suffrage, for their supremacy is 'not as considered under any Form of Government, because this Power of the People can never take place till the Government be dissolved'. As Barker notes, Locke 'stands on the whole for the Whig grandees, entrenched in the House of Lords and influencing the House of Commons' (Barker 1971, xxvi). Franklin confirms that Locke's theory 'did not originate in any particular zeal for political democracy' (Franklin 1981, 1). He observes that 'in Locke by clear implication, the test of membership [for citizenship with the franchise in the political community] is roughly equivalent to the forty shilling [property] freehold as it existed' at the time (Franklin 1981, 125).

In his chapter in the *Second Treatise* on the Dissolution of Government, Locke lists a number of scenarios that set out the conditions for the termination of government. These come down to two grounds on which the government can be dissolved. According to Locke, on the people's side, the government is abolished if limits were placed on it, such as on its duration, which have now been reached. On the government's side, power is rescinded if by miscarriages of its authority, either by the legislative or the executive, it's trust is forfeited.

Along with the notion of trust and the right of resistance, the third feature of Locke's theory of popular sovereignty is the separation of powers. For Locke, government is conditional upon its maintaining the trust, and is limited by the specific right of resistance. The rights of the people are further safeguarded by the separation of powers. Locke comprehends the organisation of political life as a system of powers. He specifies the government powers that are separated as three in number: the legislative, the executive and the federative.

The legislative is the primary form of government power of the separated powers. It is the 'supreme power'. Its supremacy lies in its power to make laws, for as Locke says, 'for what can give laws to another, must needs be superior to him'. The executive and federative powers are only powers to execute, implement and administer laws, but not to make laws. The legislative has an ethical authority based on our right to entrust it. According to Locke's theory we set up and take upon ourselves an obligation to obey the legislative power. When it is functioning properly — according to trust — we owe it legitimate obedience. So the legislative is 'supreme' within the terms of the trust, but if it forfeits that trust, it loses its supremacy and that supremacy reverts back to the people. As Locke precisely formulates, 'while government subsists, the legislative is the supreme power'. Indeed Locke goes so far as to argue, in section 212 of the *Second Treatise*, that the legislative is the soul that gives unity to the commonwealth and represents the one will of all. But Locke is not, thereby, a general will theorist like Rousseau. He is simply observing that when individuals come together politically they create a power which is available to them in institutional form for the purposes of their association, and which finds its first and highest form in the making of law.

While Locke describes the legislative branch of government as the 'supreme power', this legislative branch is disqualified from being a candidate for comprehensively holding sovereignty, in Locke's system, for several reasons. First, the 'supreme power' of the legislative is so heavily conditional on the fulfilment of the trust placed in it, 'being but a delegated Power from the People' (section 141) and 'only a Fiduciary Power to act for certain ends' (section 149), that it has a derivative rather than independent status. The emphasis in Locke's argument is on the liability and limitations of the legislative rather than on its positive features. Secondly, the legislative is a law-making body under the public rule of law to make 'promulgated standing laws' in line with its obligation to natural law, and has no other role. As Gough notes, Locke 'reserved the word "arbitrary" for power that contravened the law of nature, and avoided calling the legislature "sovereign"' (Gough 1973, 120). Thirdly, to insist on calling the legislative branch of government the location of sovereignty would be to invite the retort that, then, sovereignty is divided between the legislative and the people, which is impossible according to Locke.

Fourthly, the legislative branch, while 'supreme' is nevertheless only one of the three separated powers, and so cannot be the undisputed location of sovereignty. Locke is adamant that the logic of the theory is that the three powers are separated and not united. Fifthly, the supreme power of the legislative is merely functional, and is trumped by the moral status of individual pre-political rights, according to which revolt can be morally justifiable. Barker argues succinctly that '[w]e are generally prone to think of Locke as the exponent of the Social contract. It would be more just to think of him as the exponent of the sovereignty of Natural Law' (Barker 1971, xvi). In Locke's fudging of the term 'supreme power' — used to refer to both 'the people' and to the legislative's law-making power — it is clear that, taking a step back, the underlying and indispensable source of sovereignty is the rights accorded to individuals by natural law. As Gough notes, for the legislative to carry sovereign status would mean both that 'the validity of its enactments is unchallengeable' and that 'it can change the constitution itself by ordinary legislative process' (Gough 1963, 126), and Locke is perfectly clear that this is not the case.

Franklin usefully presents Locke's theory of sovereignty as the intricate solution to a contemporary dilemma in constitutionalism. Leaders of the opposition in 1642 had trapped themselves into asserting the validity of overthrowing a king while at the same time accepting that the king had independent powers from which he could not be deposed. The 'constituent power of the people' had been identified with Parliament (as an Estates assembly) as a representative institution while the king, seen as the executive branch in a mixed constitution, was agreed to hold independent powers. The tension in the inherited theory of sovereignty between 'the ultimate supremacy of the people's representative and the independence of the king' (Franklin 1981, 7) could not be resolved. Locke adopted the position that there could, after all, be a 'coherent justification of resistance in a mixed constitution' (Franklin 1981, 123), if the constituent power of the people was separated from the legislative branch of government, and if the executive power of the king was made subject to the supreme power of the legislature. In this way Parliament lost its equivalence with the people but gained a pre-eminence over the executive branch of government. At the same time the supreme power of the people as sovereign, to dissolve an illegitimate government, was clarified. Franklin argues that Locke's 'clear and consistent distinction between constituent and ordinary power', served to establish the key tenet underlying the modern tradition of constitutionalism. It provides a limit not just on kings overstepping their executive powers, but also on parliaments acting beyond their remit.

For it 'establishes the principle that no ordinary representative, no matter how democratically elected, may alter constitutional procedures, or freedoms peculiar to the system that are constitutionally reserved to individuals, without the consent of the general community' (Franklin 1981, 124). While Franklin's reading of Locke through this distinction between constituent and ordinary power is helpful, it still leaves exposed the tension between them which lies at the heart of Locke's theory.

However, in day-to-day terms for Locke, popular sovereignty is represented, in effect, in the 'supreme power' of the legislative body. In practical terms in the commonwealth, Locke is claiming the priority of Parliament over a monarch and over the possibility of royal absolutism. In this weak sense Locke's conception of sovereignty does specify unity in an abstract way as in Hobbes. But Hobbes places much greater emphasis on that abstract, analytical account of sovereignty. Locke is much more interested in the negative point of ensuring that government does not overstep its brief of protecting the liberties and property of individuals as individuals. According to Locke, the legislative body should be representative, though not necessarily with a very wide franchise. Moreover, he does not think that the legislative body needs to be in continuous existence. Notwithstanding his antipathy to a powerful executive, Locke allows that the executive can often carry on normal business and provide continuity.

The executive power is a lesser power because it cannot make law. It acts on prerogative or discretionary powers, deciding how the laws of the legislative apply to particular cases, and making urgent decisions when the cumbersome machinery of the legislative is too slow and clumsy to act quickly. There is a double trust involved in this branch of government — the trust imparted to agree to government in general (in the legislative), and the trust bestowed from the legislative to the executive branch of government.

In specifying the federative as a separate power, Locke indicates — without implying the modern fully-fledged internal/external dichotomy — that he thought that the external aspect of sovereignty was important enough to be highlighted in its own right. Indeed, he shows a clearer awareness of the value of external sovereignty than he does of internal sovereignty. Nevertheless he makes it plain that external sovereignty is subordinate to the legislative power, that is to internal sovereignty. The federative power is the power of the community directed outwards, both in amicable relations with other political communities and in protection of the commonwealth against aggression. Locke does not, however, set out a clear moral imperative to seek peace. Like the executive, it operates on prerogative powers. The federative power is responsible to, entirely accountable to, fully answerable to the legislative. But in practice the federative power is in the hands of the executive branch of government to allow for quick decisions, and because it is less capable than is the executive of being directed by antecedent laws of the commonwealth. The specific responsibilities of the federative power concern international relations and diplomacy — in practical terms, the power to make war and peace, leagues and alliances and all other transactions, with all persons and communities outside the commonwealth.

A brief comparison of Locke's theory of the separation of powers with the system established in the USA (perhaps the clearest case of a modern liberal constitution) highlights the distinctiveness of Locke's understanding. In the American example of the separation of powers, there is a more systematic arrangement of disaggregated powers than is found in Locke. Overall, in the American system the separated powers must be in different hands, whereas in Locke's system of separated powers, all three powers could in practice rest in the same hands. In the American system the doctrine of the necessary separation of powers in practice as well as in theory, along with the written constitution, becomes the key principle in its own right. In contrast, in Locke the proper functioning and just exercise of these powers derives directly from the primacy of the notions of trust, fiduciary powers, and the law of nature.

Moreover, in the American system the separated powers are balanced against each other horizontally, whereas in Locke's system, the legislative is superior to the executive, which is in turn superior to the federative, in a hierarchical ranking, and the powers do not operate as a check upon each other. In the US arrangement, the separated powers cannot operate effectively without the cooperation of other powers, and if one branch of government is corrupt other branches act to counterpose its influence. In Locke, the whole government could fall if one branch fails its trust. In addition in the American system the federative power is not a separate power but is part of the president's executive power, and the judiciary is the third separated power. For Locke, although the judiciary must be impartial and its pronouncements known and authorised, it is not a separate power and falls under the remit of the executive. In sum, the American system denies sovereignty to any one branch of government, while in Locke's schema sovereignty in the sense of the 'highest', law-making, power is functionally held by the legislative branch, but only on trust, and ultimately and meaningfuly in the 'individual rights under natural law'.

To conclude, sovereignty finally lies in Locke's system in an ingenious piece of logic. Ultimately sovereignty rests with the residual powers held by the people in perpetuity, and so which they never give up. But they hold this power individually, unless it is triggered by a resistance to government and a dissolution of government. In this way Locke's sovereignty is 'popular' only in a formal and foreshortened sense. Locke has a profound distaste for individuals taking on a collective, group persona as a strong part of their identity, and so only legitimises the utilisation of this perpetual residual power as an extreme measure. Sovereignty, for Locke, certainly does not function as a collective political identity. For the most part Locke's persons in civil society operate as individuals in the 'private' sphere. Because of his individualist stance, Locke is reluctant to discuss either obligation or sovereignty, because he does not want to emphasise duties but rather rights, and because sovereignty implies a unified group identity in which individuals are subordinate to the group. However, he does consider that one's legitimate obedience is owed to the legislative so long as that branch of government operates within the trust, and he does have a strong though reluctant and largely implicit sense of popular sovereignty in the notion of the right of resistance specifying a rigorous limit on the scope and actions of government.

The residual power of the people (understood as a collection of individuals and deriving from natural law) to abolish the government is what Locke's conception of popular sovereignty ultimately amounts to. This minimalist and weak conception stands beside Locke's fierce and positive championing of pre-political individual rights. Furthermore, while Hobbes's conception of sovereignty results in individuals being radically equal as 'subjects', in Locke's conception individuals in a sense become citizens (or at least some of them — propertied males — do), but more meaningfully they remain individuals. In sum then, while Locke does have a conception of sovereignty as a unity, a whole, he denies a notion of sovereignty as a collectivity. For Locke we are individuals first and foremost, and sovereignty exists only in order to further the rights of individuals. Locke's championing of individualism is necessarily a stronger element in his political theory than the notion of sovereignty. Indeed, Locke's individualism sits uneasily with his majoritarianism and with the principle of right of resistance as a group, and his inclinations are not towards democracy. The upshot of Locke's theory is that the collectivist resonances of the conception of popular sovereignty are the cost he is grudgingly prepared to bear in order to be able to reinforce the rights of the individual with a right of resistance.

Locke utilises two general features of sovereignty in his conception. In order to confirm the ultimate and performative 'supremacy of the people' over government, Locke reluctantly takes on the idea of a weak popular sovereignty designating the unity of the political community. As Laslett circumspectly observes, 'this residual power must be called Locke's idea of what we now think of as popular sovereignty' (Laslett 1965, 134). The 'supreme power' of the people is exercised, under strict limits and on a conditional basis, by the legislative branch of government. Sovereignty also serves to seal the relationship between rulers and ruled, but only on the proviso that the relationship is established through the trust extended in a one-way direction from the latter to the former. It is a conception of sovereignty that is wholly negative, in that its only purpose is to confirm the pre-eminence in political society of something else, namely pre-political individual rights. Indeed, Locke turns the concept of sovereignty on its head, by positing the sovereignty of (necessarily disaggregated) individual natural rights and so rejecting the idea of sovereignty as a *political* concept. Locke's grudging acceptance of the role played by sovereignty in his theory is consistent with his approach to all such political concepts and derives from the suspicion he has for any positive outline of the terms of government and political society.

Like Hobbes, Locke is not keen to allow for a political realm of debate about the conditions or moral standing of public policy. Hobbes regarded politics as too unruly and disruptive to be tolerated and all that is left is the public law-making of the sovereign and court politics. For Locke, a vigorous political realm would jeopardise the primacy of individuals pursuing their business and other interests in the 'private' realm, and politics in terms of regulating the competition between those interests is left to the political elite to manage. The strength of Locke's theory of sovereignty is that it places individual rights squarely at the centre of politics. The weaknesses are that it dismisses any positive sense that sovereignty can play in expressing a shared political world, and that its individualism conceals a strongly elitist commitment.

ROUSSEAU

Rousseau was born in Geneva in 1712 but left at the age of fifteen and spent much of his life unsettled, a citizen of no country, and wandering around Europe. The *Social Contract* was published in 1762, against the background of political despotism and inequality that led, less than thirty years later to the French Revolution. Dent, for instance, cites Louis XV's declaration of absolute sovereignty in 1766, that '[i]t is in my person alone that sovereign power resides ... it is from me alone that my courts hold their existence and their authority' (Dent 2005, 135). The intellectual context of the *Social Contract* was informed in part by Rousseau's falling out with Voltaire and the French Encyclopedist, Diderot. He took issue with the *philosophes* and with Enlightenment ideas such as the sweeping away of superstition, and progress and mastery through the development of empirical knowledge about the natural world. As well as being an early critic of Enlightenment rationalism, Rousseau also had no sympathy with the atheism of Diderot and the *philosophes* (Cranston 1968, 40).

Rousseau's philosophical perspective expressed his general conviction that, on the contrary, progress was illusory, the development of civilisation was directly responsible for the corruption of natural goodness and for moral ruin, as well as for the widening of inequality in private property between people. Simple society, freedom and innocence in the state of nature represented the ideal way of life. He also admired the political structure of the Swiss cantons, each of which was a sovereign body in which the male population came together periodically to deliberate and make law, and which together were loosely arranged into a confederation. Contemporary radical ideas of liberal representative democracy were regarded by Rousseau as hostile to the preferred 'unrepresentative' direct democracy practised in Switzerland. He also radically opposed the despotic political prescription favoured by the *philosophes* of appealing to European monarchs as strong rulers who could, in a *despotisme eclaire*, put Enlightenment principles into practice.

Cranston notes that by the mid-1760s Rousseau 'had offended almost everyone: Catholics, Protestants, materialists'. In this last phase of his life, 'as the victim of political and religious intolerance, he was harried from place to place in search of refuge' (Cranston 1968, 24–5). Gourevitch goes further and describes how, after the publication of the *Social Contract* Rousseau 'was forced to flee, and spent much of the next decade on the run or living under an assumed name' (Gourevitch 1997, ix). The *Social Contract* on its publication was regarded as a scandalous text, in part on account of its treatment of a civil religion, and was condemned by civil and religious bodies in Geneva and France. Rousseau died in Paris in 1778. Politically, he had an affinity neither with contemporary French despotism, nor with either of the two current progressive strands of thought — identified with the *philosophes* on the one hand and those in favour of liberal representative democracy on the other. Neither would Rousseau have been in sympathy with the revolutionaries in France who, eleven years after his death used his political theory to provide a vocabulary for their cause.

Like Locke, Rousseau crucially regards the right of the people to be a principle that is prior to the establishment of government. Both also develop the logic that the right of the people, and their freedom, is therefore superior to government. For both theorists popular sovereignty derives from a source outside the state. In Locke the ultimate source of popular sovereignty was the natural rights of individuals that come directly from God. Whether he was a sincere believer or not does not affect the political effect of his claim. In Rousseau the foundation of popular sovereignty is deduced from the unity of the people themselves. In some ways then, Locke and Rousseau are very similar, having an extremely functional attitude toward government, and giving it a purely subordinate and instrumental, limited and circumscribed role in the commonwealth.

But in others ways, the theories of these two thinkers are resolutely opposed. For Locke the most important thing about an individual remains his individuality, whereas for Rousseau the individual is morally redeemed only by taking on a performative role in the sovereign body, participating in the formation of the general will, the definition of the common good in general laws. Indeed for Gourevitch, Rousseau's status as a political theorist lies in the argument that 'we are moral agents by virtue of being citizens, or at least members of political societies; we are not moral agents first who then may or may not become political agents' (Gourevitch 1997, xv). For Locke, freedom is maximised by curtailing government and keeping it at arm's length, whereas for Rousseau freedom is redeemed positively in society through embracing sovereignty. Locke would regard with horror the vision that Rousseau puts before us, of a transformative public sphere of citizens actively engaged in popular sovereignty by collectively enacting the general will in the name of the common good. Moreover, Rousseau holds that his notion of the common good is not mystical but is plainly intelligible. He contends that, 'the common good makes itself so manifestly evident that only common sense is needed to discern it' (Rousseau, 1968, 149). What is distinctive about Rousseau's conception is that he provides us with the classic statement of a radically popular sovereignty.

Like Hobbes, Rousseau has a robust conception of sovereignty. Both emphasise the benefits of the state as an artificial body, made by the skill of men, not a natural consequence of human life, within which mankind can flourish. The radical nature of theories of sovereignty which sweep away the traditional rights of the priest and the vicar, monarchical divine right, and aristocratic privileges, scandalised readers in both countries. But whereas for Hobbes sovereignty is held by the ruler on the authority, the act of authorising, of the people who compose the sovereign body, for Rousseau the sovereign body and the government are strictly separate concepts. And whereas for Hobbes, sovereignty is most fittingly represented in one man, probably a king, for Rousseau sovereignty must comprise all citizens directly. It cannot be 'represented'. Moreover, returning to Locke and Rousseau, while Rousseau has a very strong sense of the importance of all citizens having an active public duty, for Locke active public duty does not figure at all in the harmonious running of a civil society. Modern participatory, deliberative or direct democrats draw upon Rousseau, while modern representative democrats draw on Locke.

Rousseau's conception of popular sovereignty is a very strong and prominent part of his political theory. Gourevitch considers indeed that popular sovereignty is so much the heart of the *Social Contract* that 'every issue and argument which Rousseau takes up in the course of the work seeks either to strengthen the case for it, or to ward off possible challenges to it' (Gourevitch 1997, xxiii). Rousseau has several central chapters in the *Social Contract* explicitly devoted to sovereignty. The key terms in his theory of sovereignty are sovereignty itself, the act of association (which is the social contract), government, the general and particular wills, general and particular laws, and the lawgiver. The meaning of these terms rests upon the more general importance of right, freedom, equality, morality and will in his political theory, so it is to these notions that we turn first.

The subtitle of Rousseau's text, *Principes du droit politique*, indicates the importance for him of the concept of right, and the difference between natural and political right. Cranston notes that Rousseau uses the term 'right' in a 'semi-technical' sense, 'to designate the general abstract study of law and government' (Cranston 1968, 26). The meaning of right in Rousseau also derives from his purpose, in The *Social Contract*, of writing in a normative and hypothetical vein about what is right rather than simply describing what is (Cranston 1968, 27). The force of this notion of rights in Rousseau's theory, as law and as normative, lies in the transformative exchange of rights that takes place with the move from the state of nature to civil society. As Cranston sums up, the rights people 'alienate are rights based on might; the rights they acquire are rights based on law' (Cranston 1968, 33).

Rousseau regards freedom as meaning political liberty as well as personal liberty. Also, whereas in the subsequent liberal tradition freedom and equality are in tension, in Rousseau's theory these concepts work hand in hand. For Rousseau, a person can only be properly free if they are participating in public life. As Cranston notes, for Rousseau, 'to be free means to live under a law of one's own enactment' (Cranston 1968, 42). In a line of argument also found in Spinoza, Kant and Hegel, Rousseau maintains that freedom means not just personal freedom to do whatever you want, and indeed he holds that just following one's appetites does not make you free, it makes you a slave. As Cranston succinctly puts it, for Rousseau, 'to be free is not to be left to do what you want to do but to be enabled to do what you ought to do' (Cranston 1968, 41). It follows for Rousseau that freedom entails political as well as personal liberty, and even personal liberty is much greater in the context of laws than in the state of nature. As Cranston observes, for Rousseau '[m]en can be both ruled and free if they rule themselves. For what is a free man but a man who rules himself? A people can be free if it retains sovereignty over itself' (Cranston 1968, 29).

Wokler identifies another important dimension of freedom in Rousseau's theory. He observes that, '[p]erhaps the most tenaciously held theme throughout all of his political writings, and indeed his personal life as well, was Rousseau's anxiety to avert or escape from ties of domination and subservience, which harnessed persons to their respective stations in life, destroying their liberty. Dependence on men ... as distinct from dependence on things, engenders all vices' (Wokler 1995, 62). Cranston agrees that there is also this meaning of freedom in Rousseau, 'that free-dom is not being subject to any other *man*' (Cranston 1968, 41).

Equality is also a key concept underlying Rousseau's notion of sover-eignty. Instead of the sovereign holding power over the ruled, sovereignty consists precisely in the equality between all citizens and of their will and right. As Rousseau puts it, 'the social pact establishes equality among the citizens in that they all pledge themselves under the same conditions and must all enjoy the same rights' (Rousseau 1968, 76). Gourevitch signals that, for Rousseau, equality is not simply an end in itself but is a means to establishing political freedom. The purpose of 'the conventional equality established by all of the parties pooling all of their resources is to render all unearned inequalities irrelevant before the law' (Gourevitch 1997, xix).

In addition the importance of morality and will and of refuting slavery are very noteworthy in the construction of Rousseau's early argument in the *Social Contract*. Rousseau values the will very highly. For him only morality (and only in the context of the state can awareness of morality lead to virtue) can be the legitimate basis of willing something to happen in soci-ety. As Strong puts it, in 'the act of association is created a moral body' (Strong 1994, 80). In these circumstances, willing leads to an obedience —rather than a bondage—to justice. Indicating the close connection between morality, obligation, and equality, and the transformative nature of the move to civil society, Rousseau maintains that the 'commitments which bind us to the social body are obligatory because they are mutual' (Rousseau 1968, 75). In contrast, when obedience is only due to the exer-cise of force over someone, it is only prudential compliance and has no moral dimension. For Rousseau it is profoundly true that the 'words "slav-ery" and "right" are contradictory, they cancel each other out' (Rousseau 1968, 58).

Coming now to the key terms in Rousseau's theory of sovereignty, the term sovereignty itself is central to Rousseau's political theory and it func-tions for Rousseau, as Dugan and Strong indicate, 'both normatively and descriptively' (Dugan and Strong 2001, 331). Again without eliciting a modern internal/external dichotomy, we can see that Rousseau is princi-pally and explicitly concerned with the nature of internal sovereignty. While he does mention foreign relations a couple of times, he explicitly notes in his Conclusion that he has not attempted to comprehensively cover the issues of external sovereignty in The *Social Contract*. According to Rousseau's conception, then, sovereignty is enormously positive because it enhances individuals. They remain individuals, but lose the right to all natural liberty in return for civil law and civil liberty. For Rous-seau, the benefits of this arrangement far outweigh its disadvantages. He reasons that 'since each man gives himself to all, he gives himself to no one', and 'each man recovers the equivalent of everything he loses, and in the bargain he acquires more power to preserve what he has' (Rousseau 1968, 61). Moreover, individuals are transformed and enriched by this conversion they undertake. Sovereignty also gives one an identification in the whole. As Strong observes, '[s]overeignty is how Rousseau legitimates the use of the first person plural', the 'we' (Strong 1994, 89). Sovereignty also establishes moral relationships between persons, and creates property based on right. That is, sovereignty transforms possession based on force into property based on right. This distinction between force and right is very important in Rousseau's political theory.

Rousseau also distinguishes between sovereignty as active and the state as passive, as two faces of the same entity, the public world. Thus individuals are citizens when taking part in the sovereignty, and they are subjects when implementing and obeying the particular laws of the government. He argues that 'the essence of the political body lies in the union of freedom and obedience so that the words *subject* and *sovereign* are identical correlatives, the meaning of which is brought together in the single word *citizen*' (Rousseau 1968, 138). Rousseau is the first of the theorists studied in this book to offer a full-blooded notion of citizenship, and to see citizenship and sovereignty as intimately linked. As Strong notes, the term 'citizen' does not 'designate only for Rousseau the member of a society or political system', but comprehends also and 'more importantly, a being in whom the thought of the common is realised' (Strong 1994, 76).

Rousseau makes it clear that external sovereignty is subordinate to internal sovereignty. The sovereign body, he says, is not constrained by any fundamental law, not even the social contract itself. But the sovereign body can take on obligations to other nations so long as they do not infringe the contract. Rousseau says, 'for in relation to foreign powers, the body politic is a simple entity, an individual' (Rousseau 1968, 63). Controversially, Rousseau holds that acts of declaring war and making peace, the instruments of external sovereignty, are not 'acts of sovereignty'. Such things are not laws themselves but applications of law, so are subordinate to the prior sovereignty and to the sovereign authority (Rousseau 1968, 71). This is an example, for Rousseau, of how sovereignty has not been divided, of how one implementation of it is inferior to the whole. In practical terms, Rousseau asserts that there must be fixed and periodic assemblies as well as special ones to deal with unforeseen events.

Rousseau emphasises very strongly that sovereignty is inalienable and indivisible. The general will alone can direct the forces of the state in accordance with its appointed end, which is the common good. Rousseau argues that 'sovereignty, being nothing other than the exercise of the general will, can never be alienated' (Rousseau 1968, 69). That is, the sovereign, a collective being, cannot be represented by anyone but itself. As O'Hagan notes, one of Rousseau's reasons against the representation of sovereignty lies in his criticism that in Ancient Greece, 'popular sovereignty was based on slavery'. The general point is that, for Rousseau, 'a "pact of submission" between people and rulers' would be 'incompatible with the doctrine of the subordination of government to sovereign' (O'Hagan 1999, 150). Strong notes that Rousseau's antipathy to representation is not just that it induces passivity. His antipathy derives 'from the particular nontemporal quality of sovereignty' (Strong 1994, 91), from its character as an activity rather than a thing. Power may be delegated, but the will cannot be. Because sovereignty cannot be alienated, Rousseau is very much against any notion of representative sovereignty, that is, deputies acting for citizens. Citizens themselves must participate in the public interest. In a true republic, citizens put public duty first. As he says, 'Sovereignty cannot be represented, for the same reason that it cannot be alienated; its essence is the general will, and will cannot be represented — either it is the general will or it is something else; there is no intermediate possibility' (Rousseau 1968, 141). For Rousseau, 'the moment a people adopts representatives [deputies] it is no longer free; it no longer exists' (Rousseau 1968, 143).

Dugan and Strong also observe that sovereignty cannot be represented because for Rousseau it 'does not exist in time' (Dugan and Strong 2001, 331). Dugan and Strong contrast sovereignty in Hobbes to emphasise these active features of Rousseau's conception. They note that the usual image we have of sovereignty is from Hobbes, 'a picture of the great benevolent giant severely but gently encompassing the land with the embodiment of regularity'. For Rousseau, however, 'sovereignty is designed to show precisely the contingent and yet atemporal nature of our relation to a political body'. The crux of the matter is that, for Rousseau, sovereignty cannot be represented because representation 'gives a temporal dimension to sovereignty', and so in 'this sense sovereignty has the quality of an aesthetic object'. Dugan and Strong develop the argument that this aesthetic quality indeed provides the answer to the dilemma of bridging the abstract and the particular in political theory. They pose the question of how political theory is possible, since it is 'a representation of a generalised political context or set of issues, but this generality removes individuals from the present'. Their answer lies in the notion that an 'aesthetic object, on the other hand, is at once fully present and particular, but also universal in scope' (Dugan and Strong 2001, 332). In answer to the further question of how this relation can be established in the political realm, they contend that it is precisely that the question of sovereignty is, 'how is creativity possible in the political realm' (Dugan and Strong 2001, 333).

Reinforcing again the performative and active character of Rousseau's conception of sovereignty Dugan and Strong also raise the question of language as crucial to the exercise of sovereignty. They argue that a 'society that has a language for political life will value eloquence over the use of public force', and they distinguish between the 'language of decree' and the language in politics that acknowledges others (Dugan and Strong 2001, 353). In Rousseau's sovereign deliberative assembly they see the operation of a crucial interplay of reciprocity. They argue that 'without the possibility of recognising others in one's own practice of judgment, one's human potential as a social creature is unfulfilled' (Dugan and Strong 2001, 354). It is this line of argument that leads Cranston persuasively to conclude that Rousseau is more accurately described as a republican, a champion of popular sovereignty, than as a democrat (Cranston 1968, 31).

Sovereignty is indivisible for Rousseau in the sense that the general will is not necessarily unanimous, but in order to be universal, all votes must be counted. Nevertheless in practice the majority vote can then hold for all. Cobban usefully distinguishes between the kind of indivisibility that sovereignty has in Rousseau's theory from that found in Hobbes. He argues that 'Rousseau appeals to the nature of sovereignty' whereas 'Hobbes depends on the result of dividing it'. Sovereignty in Rousseau is indivisible for the positive reason that it is the expression of the general will, while for Hobbes sovereignty is indivisible for the negative reason that, if divided, its unity is dissolved (Cobban 1964, 73).

Wokler notes the direct connection between Rousseau's conceptions of liberty and equality, and his idea of sovereignty. He says, '[t]ogether with modern advocates of participatory democracy who so often turn to him for inspiration, Rousseau supposed that the authority of every sovereign — which like Grotius, Hobbes, and Pufendorf he held must be absolute — was legitimate only if each citizen took a fully active role within it'. He continues that '[h]erein lies the kernel of his notion of popular sovereignty, whose links especially with his ideal of liberty in the state, form the corner-stone of his political doctrine'. Wokler concludes that 'Rousseau's conjunction of both liberty and equality with sovereignty comprises a strikingly original element in his writings' (Wokler 1995, 63).

Rousseau also explores the limits of sovereign power. He holds that sovereign power is restricted to matters that are the concern of the whole community. Therefore the sovereign body cannot impose a burden which is, by its own definition, not necessary to the community. Commitments to the social body are obligatory because mutual, and the general will must be general in purpose as well as in nature. However, the sovereign body alone is judge of what is of such concern. Underlying this line of argument is the sense, as Bertram explores, the notion that 'sovereign power is, in its essence, self-limiting'. There is for Rousseau 'a mutuality and a reciprocity about sovereign acts' in that 'I impose no condition on you that I am not also prepared to accept for myself'. Moreover, there is no 'pre-established restriction in principle, to what the citizens may legislate on'. Bertram concludes that 'sovereignty — properly constituted — poses no threat (and indeed is essential to) individual autonomy' (Bertram 2004, 110-11).

The second of Rousseau's key terms is the act of association in the social pact that establishes equality among citizens, and gives them all the same rights. Political society and rule are for Rousseau conventional, not natural. Every act of sovereignty, that is, every authentic act of the general will, binds and favours all the citizens equally, so that the sovereign recognises only the whole body of the nation and makes no distinction between any of the members who compose it. As Wokler notes, '[w]hile for Hobbes liberty is exchanged for authority in men's transfer of their natural rights to their ruler, for Rousseau, provided that citizens rule themselves, liberty is won within the state rather than protected by it' (Wokler 1995, 62).

The transition from the state of nature to the body politic entails a 'civil act' that Rousseau says 'presupposes public deliberation' (Rousseau 1968, 59). This is the social contact. Far from destroying natural equality, the social pact substitutes a moral, lawful equality for the physical inequality imposed on mankind by nature. From being unequal in strength and intelligence, men become equal by covenant and by right, says Rousseau. By this act of association, each puts into the community his person and all his powers under the direction of the general will. Cranston highlights the significance of this act when he says, 'by the deed of the social contract itself, to which *everyone* subscribes and pledges (there is no question of a majority here; you either subscribe or you are not in civil society at all) everyone agrees to accept the decision of the majority in the formulation of the law' (Cranston 1968, 37-8). Gourevitch reinforces the role of human agency here in identifying that the meaning of the social contract for Rousseau rests in its provision that 'legitimate political rule is not based directly on either a divine or a natural title to rule, but must be ratified — "authorised" — by the consent of the ruled' (Gourevitch 1997, xv).

Thus three consequences follow from the 'civil act'. First this act creates an artificial and collective body, composed entirely of the individuals who make it up, who can then 'act in concert' (Rousseau 1968, 60) to use their collective powers. In this way Rousseau's social contract is not a deed that stands for the one and only political act of the people, as in Locke (apart, for Locke, in the eventuality of resistance and deposition). For Rousseau the 'civil act' triggers an on-going process by an active citizenry. The sovereign body is not always in existence but comes together periodically to perform its role. Sovereignty for Rousseau is an activity and a performance, not a 'thing', while for Locke sovereignty is primarily a technical requirement. Second the 'act of association' assures the unity of that body, that public person, that republic, that city, that body politic. And third the act creates a relationship between being a member of the state and the sovereign. Rousseau says, 'There is only one [public] contract in the state — that of the association itself, and this excludes all others' (Rousseau 1968, 145). Therefore the relationship between the people and government (the second stage of the two-stage process) is not formed by contract. It is an act of the sovereign body that establishes it. Initially, this act establishes a law enacting government of a certain type. Then the law is executed through the magistrates nominated by the people.

Rousseau identifies a potential problem in his logic so far, in that the sovereign body is making an act of government before government exists. People in this circumstance are acting as a prince or as magistrates, confusing the strict dichotomy between sovereign body and government. Rousseau's solution to this problem is to say that in order to be able to set up government, the sovereign transforms itself just for a moment into a democracy. In a founding myth it breaches the dualism. This act of association, the social contract, only happens once. After the state is institutionalised, residence implies consent, Rousseau maintains. To inhabit the territory is to submit to the sovereign. And after the act of association the majority votes holds for all.

'Government' is another of Rousseau's key terms. Acts of popular sovereignty that produce general laws are distinguished from the role of government in administration and executive management. As Cole notes, governments, 'including representative assemblies … can enact only decrees' and 'cannot ever make laws' (Cole 1973, xxviii). Locke had a two-stage contract process, the contract of the consent of each to transform the state of nature into civil society, and the contract of trust to create government within civil society. Rousseau also has a two-stage process, but he is insistent that only the first part, the transition from state of nature to the republic entails a contract. He states that 'the act which institutes the government is not a contract but a law' (Rousseau 1968, 146). Government exists only through the sovereign — it does not exist independently. As Rousseau puts it, the government 'has only a kind of borrowed and subordinate life' (Rousseau 1968, 106). Gourevitch highlights the difference between the sovereign body and government, observing that 'government is merely the minister of the sovereign people' and so 'it clearly follows that every government is provisional'. Gourevitch surmises that 'the sovereign people may, and, Rousseau argues, should regularly call it to accounts and renew its mandate'. Gourevitch notes that it 'is easy to see how this doctrine … caused the *Social Contract* to be condemned by the Genevan as well as by the French political authorities' (Gourevitch 1997, xxiv).

Government is established by nomination. As noted, the sovereign body, for this one exception only, give up their character as dealing in purely general laws as a collectivity, and settle on particular people to act as prince or magistrates. Both legislative and executive powers are necessary to the body politic, says Rousseau. The legislative power belongs solely to the people. Executive power cannot belong to the generality, since it involves the exercise of particular acts with reference to particular people. It executes, implements and administers the laws and maintains civil and political freedoms. Like Locke, Rousseau asserts the pre-eminence of the legislative power over the executive. These executive powers are undertaken in Rousseau's schema by a 'prince' or by 'magistrates' or by 'governors'. This executive power mediates between the sovereign generality and the people as individuals, that is between citizens and subjects.

According to Rousseau, and as with Spinoza, no one kind of government is best suited to all nations and communities. He says we 'must assign to each people the particular form of constitution which is best, not perhaps in itself, but for that state for which it is destined' (Rousseau 1968, 97). Rousseau argues that the preeminent form of political community, however, is a republic, a state in which all citizens partake of active citizenship. He holds the view, unusual to modern readers, that republics can be monarchies, aristocracies or democracies or mixed types. These different types simply refer to how many hands the sovereign collectivity puts the government into. Therefore all forms of government are subordinate to the sovereign body. Rousseau thus holds that the sovereign body is not a democracy. It is a unity of all, whereas democracy is only a form of government. Therefore, prior to the establishment of any government, there must be an act of association by the sovereign collective, the general body, which establishes a unity and legitimises the particular form of government. The sovereign and government are two distinct artificial persons, says Rousseau.

Gourevitch makes a case that looking at the political work as a whole, Rousseau rejected both pure or direct democracy and absolute monarchy, because both distort the necessary balance between sovereignty and government. The first expresses a usurpation by the people while the second results from an encroachment from the government side. Gourevitch argues that Rousseau's preferred form of government was an elective aristocracy, 'because it combines the strictest requirement of legitimate political rule, election, with the most natural claim to rule, widom in the service of the common good' (Gourevitch 1997, xxiv-xxv).

The idea of the tendency towards degeneration and decay in the body politic plays an important part in Rousseau's theory, as it did in Machiavelli's, whose work Rousseau admired. Just as the particular will acts unceasingly against the general will, so does the government continually exert itself against the sovereign. It is natural and inevitable that all political communities become corrupted and degenerate. As Gourevitch notes, for Rousseau there is 'a tension between the good of the whole and the good of its parts, and even the most satisfactory resolutions of these tensions are fragile' (Gourevitch 1997, xxxi). Rousseau argues that it 'is not only through the law that the state keeps alive; it is through the legislative power', that is, through the common good freshly enacted by the sovereign body (Rousseau 1968, 135). The contrast between Locke and Rousseau is instructive here. As Cranston notes, 'Locke is not worried, as Rousseau is, by corruption; and he does not hanker after virtue' (Cranston 1968, 36). For Locke the public sphere is certainly not a realm of moral action as it is for Rousseau. According to Rousseau, corruption and degeneration happen in two ways — either by the natural tendency of democracies to become aristocracies to become monarchies, or when the state dissolves because the prince or group of magistrates usurps the sovereign power. In either of these two ways, the social pact is broken. In this case, citizens recover their natural freedom, and may be compelled by force to obey, but are no longer under a moral obligation to do so. There is a strong link here between obligation and sovereignty. This process of decay cannot be prevented, but it can be delayed as noted above by a properly-working sovereign authority, when the legislative power operates effectively.

The next of Rousseau's key terms is the distinction between general and particular wills. As Gourevitch notes the general will — that which 'wills the general good' — expresses 'the guiding principle of the sovereign body established by the social contract'. The general will is the will of the members of political society *qua* citizens, and refers only to general cases or types. It ensures Rousseau's aim of advocating 'freedom under self-imposed law' (Gourevitch 1997, xx). Rousseau states that 'the general will alone can direct the forces of the state in accordance with that end which the state has been established to achieve — the common good' (Rousseau 1968, 69), while particular wills are held by each person as a private individual. Cole argues that Rousseau's conception of the general will means that it is, 'above all a universal and, in the Kantian sense, a "rational" will' (Cole 1973, xliii). As Wokler describes, the 'general will was Rousseau's term for the exercise of popular sovereignty' (Wokler 1995, 67), and O'Hagan emphasises that, according to Rousseau, 'sovereignty and the general will are tied conceptually to one another. When a people exercises its sovereignty it is expressing its general will'. Indeed, Rousseau criticised 'other theories which would make sovereignty a bundle of powers, condensed and bestowed on a single bearer, the sovereign'. For Rousseau, such theories 'can never explain the absolute unity and indivisibility of sovereignty'. O'Hagan sums up that Rousseau replaces 'an ontology of "parts" by an ontology of "emanations"' (O'Hagan 1999, 114). Cranston notes another feature, that the general will 'is a normative concept, its connection with right is a matter of definition'. By contrast, the will of all 'is an empirical concept; the only test of the will of all is what, in fact, all will' (Cranston 1968, 37). Strong highlights the moral character of the general will when he notes that it is 'Rousseau's formulation of the recognition of what it means ... to be capable of living with other human beings as human beings and as a human being (rather than as, say, a beast or a god)' (Strong 1994, 88).

Wokler points out the dual character of the general will. Rousseau ascribes the general will 'both to the public interest or common good which the sovereign of every state ought to promote, and to the individual will of each citizen to achieve that good, often contrary to the same person's particular interest as a man or member of other associations within the state' (Wokler 1995, 67). It follows that the private will of an individual is different from their general will as a citizen. Private interest is acknowledged by Rousseau as a necessary part of human life, but he says that it leads to partiality, whereas the public interest leads to equality. The common interest of the general will is a harmony of interest and of justice (and so has a moral character) which 'gives to social deliberations a quality of equity' (Rousseau 1968, 76). But as Wokler makes clear, 'the general will, in its focus upon the common interest, should not be confused with the will of all, which was merely the sum of private and thus necessarily conflicting interests' (Wokler 1995, 67).

Rousseau maintains that the general will is indestructible, unchanging, incorruptible and pure. Because the 'civil act' was based on unanimity, the general will can operate according to majority decisions. As noted earlier, Rousseau argues that for 'the will to be general, it does not always have to be unanimous; but all the votes must be counted. Any formal exclusion destroys its universality' (Rousseau 1968, 70). Cranston illuminates Rousseau's theory when he says it is 'understood that the members of the majority whose decision is accepted do not ask themselves what do I, as an individual, demand, but what does the general will demand'. In this way, 'it is the majority *interpretation* of the general will which is binding and not the majority will. This is how it can be morally obligatory for the minority to accept' (Cranston 1968, 38). However, the general will can be annihilated when other, particular, wills prevail over it by force. Nevertheless, the more that public deliberations result in public opinion that approaches unanimity, the more the general will is dominant, says Rousseau.

The distinction between general and particular laws is also a key term for Rousseau. If the will is general, its declaration is an act of sovereignty and constitutes a general law. The general will can only issue in general laws, which do not single out any particular person, whereas government can only make particular laws. It is general laws alone which carry the relationship with sovereignty. Rousseau maintains that such laws are related to the general will in that 'the laws are nothing other than the authentic acts of the general will' (Rousseau 1968, 136). As Dugan and Strong note, generality is 'the object of law. That is, any act of the sovereign

— thus any element of the general will — must have the quality of applying to each member of the body politic in exactly the same way' (Dugan and Strong 2001, 331). Acts of sovereignty are laws, and sometimes Rousseau calls them covenants. Cobban registers the significance of general laws for Rousseau when he notes that, 'while for Locke the sovereignty of the people is only operative in the last resort, for Rousseau the sovereign people is the actual legislative authority of the community' (Cobban 1964, 72).

The object of law in this sense, for Rousseau, is freedom and equality. They are laws, not between a superior and an inferior, but of a body with each of its members. Such covenants are legitimate because based on social contract, equitable because common to all, useful because they have no aim or object but the common good, and durable because they are guaranteed by the armed forces and supreme power. Cranston argues that Rousseau had two conceptions of law. According to the logic of his theory, the law as right and the general laws enacted by popular sovereignty, are by definition just. But the instantiations of law that Rousseau observes in the world are often unjust and benefit the stronger over the weaker. Cranston concludes that there is 'for Rousseau a radical dichotomy between true law and actual law, between law as it should be and law as it is seen in the existing world' (Cranston 1968, 37).

Rousseau outlines a classification of laws, with moral laws playing an influential but distant role, then fundamental or political laws at the top of the political structure, then civil laws, and then criminal law. Schwartzberg's argument about the importance of 'fundamental law' to Rousseau only goes to reinforce the way that for him law, properly speaking, enables sovereignty to function. Fundamental law 'does not constrain the sovereign will, but is constitutive of the sovereign or transforms its operation with respect to morality and justice' (Schwartzberg 2003, 387). Rousseau makes it clear that, of 'these various classes of law, it is only Political Laws, which constitute the form of government, that are relevant to my subject' (Rousseau 1968, 100). Nevertheless, Gourevitch argues that potentially, according to the logic of Rousseau's position, 'nothing prevents equals from instituting laws that recognise inequalities earned by contributions to the public good'. Because conventional equality is 'inherently unstable', since 'men's natural inequalities will repeatedly reassert themselves', conventional equality 'has to be repeatedly restored' (Gourevitch 1997, xix).

According to Cranston, while Rousseau takes from Hobbes the notion of indivisible sovereignty he also borrows from Locke the idea of limited sovereignty — a coupling which would have pleased neither Hobbes nor Locke, and which neither would have thought possible. Rousseau agrees with Hobbes 'that sovereignty is an absolute power; it cannot be divided and remain sovereign; and it cannot be subject to "fundamental laws" and remain sovereign'. But Rousseau concurs with Locke, as Cranston notes, that sovereignty 'is absolute but not unlimited. The limits are those imposed by natural law and by the considerations of public good' (Cranston 1968, 38). Rousseau does make it clear that the 'right which the social pact gives the sovereign over the subjects does not…go beyond the boundaries of public utility' (Rousseau 1968, 185). Nevertheless, Rousseau does not allow, as Locke does, an independent appeal to natural law by individuals, overriding the sovereign, in the case for instance of an invalid agreement to enter into slavery (Cranston 1968, 39). Cranston notes that 'Rousseau takes up the position of Hobbes, namely, that the citizen can have no other guide but the civil law and the public conscience. The general will is itself the arbiter of just and unjust' (Cranston 1968, 39). Wokler takes a different view, noting that '[e]arlier political thinkers had frequently sought to provide safeguards against threats of despotism by invoking principles of natural law which rulers could transgress only at the peril of their soul or even their lives, risking regicide or revolution'. According to Rousseau however, Wokler continues, only 'the vigilant exercise of those powers [of sovereignty] by the people themselves was the only safeguard against despotism' (Wokler 1995, 71).

Moreover, it remains open whether Rousseau intended to give a substantive meaning to natural law or whether it is simply immediately identified with reason as when he says, '[t]hese principles … are derived from the nature of things; they are based on reason' (Rousseau 1968, 57). Whether we read Rousseau through Cranston's interpretation of the role of natural law in Rousseau's theory, or see natural law as playing only a nominal part, Rousseau is clear that 'the social pact gives the body politic an absolute power over all its members' (Rousseau 1968, 74). The role of the lawgiver provides the only practical opportunity to make a corrective, to ensure that the general will coincides with the public good.

The lawgiver is the last of Rousseau's key terms to be considered. For Rousseau, the general will cannot be wrong but it can be misguided. He argued that, by definition in a properly constructed republic where the people as sovereign make the law, the 'people is never corrupted, but it is often misled' (Rousseau 1968, 72). However, he says, '[i]ndividuals must be obliged to subordinate their will to their reason; the public must be taught to recognise what it desires' (Rousseau 1968, 83). Gourevitch notes that for Rousseau the 'great problem for the doctrine of popular sovereignty is that achieving the willed good requires wisdom' (Gourevitch 1997, xxi). Therefore it needs a lawgiver to teach, to give public enlightenment to produce the union of understanding and will in the social body, and to bring the parts into perfect harmony and lift the whole to its fullest strength. The office of the lawgiver is neither that of government nor of the sovereign. This is the office that provides the republic with a constitution.

But it has no place in that constitution. It is a special and superior function, deals only with laws and not with the direct enforcement of the laws on particular men. Nevertheless the legislative right remains with the people — the lawgiver can only advise. The role of the lawgiver enters after a people have bound themselves together by some original association, and before they have borne the yoke of law — before deep-rooted customs and superstitions have taken hold. Gourevitch presents an alternative interpretation, arguing that the lawgiver represents an on-going process. He says that just 'as "contract" in part stands for the ongoing *civil*ising process in which all of us are in varying degrees involved throughout our lives, as were our forebears, and as our descendants will be, so "Lawgiver" in part stands for the activities of every generation of public-spirited citizens' (Gourevitch 1997, xxiii).

Connolly describes how Rousseau 'resolved' the paradox of sovereignty — how self-rule can be established in the absence of a 'prior ethos of community already infused into the populace' — through 'recourse to the fiction of a wise legislator who imbues people with the spirit of self-rule before they begin to rule themselves' (Connolly 2004, 24).

Rousseau also allows that in an exceptional situation, a 'dictator' can be nominated, who can suspend the current body of law, if 'the inflexibility of the laws … prevents then from bending to circumstances' (Rousseau 1968, 170). But even in this case the general will remains supreme, and remains the only body capable of making law. In this way then, and whatever our modern scepticism, the function of the lawgiver and the role accorded to a dictator do not for Rousseau constitute measures that could undermine the argument for popular sovereignty that he is at pains to develop.

Having explored the key terms in Rousseau's conception of sovereignty, we come back to the understanding which sees as central to Locke's conception of sovereignty the distinction between the constitutive power of the people and the 'supreme power' of the legislative branch. The difference between constitutive and ordinary power here can be mapped onto one of the meanings of the distinction between political and legal sovereignty. The comparison between Locke and Rousseau raises here the question of whether it is a necessary part of the concept of sovereignty that a distinction be made between legal and political sovereignty in this sense. Gough takes the view that 'Locke … avoids the confusion in which Rousseau became involved, when in the attempt to make the political and the legal sovereign correspond, he ascribed sovereignty to the general will and thought it could only be ascertained in small communities' (Gough 1973, 128). Franklin makes a similar point, in effect praising Locke's adoption of a division between the constitutive principle and the location of legal authority. In defence of Rousseau, Cole argues that the 'most he did was to insist on the paramountcy of the general interest over all particular interests' (Cole 1973, xxxix).

There are several lines of argument that can be developed here. The first is to see the merits of the distinction between political (constitutive) and legal sovereignty. There is a widespread consensus that it is important to identify the source of the authority to exert political power as separate from the role of legislators and judges. This division was invoked in criticising the government in Britain's incarceration and treatment of suspected terrorists outside the normal rule of law was subject to a challenge in the courts early in 2005, and the government was forced to make another law to cover these cases. Moreover, in the Soviet Union and Nazi Germany for instance, government (to a large extent) acted according to a legal code, under the rule of law, but that did not offer sufficient safeguard against oppression and tyranny. The lesson that is often taken from such cases is that, in terms of sovereignty, it is best if political authority is not aligned or integrated with legal authority. This distinction also allows for the possibility of a right of resistance. While Rousseau grants that the social pact is dissolved if the state degenerates, he does not reserve to individuals a natural 'right to judge the actions of the sovereign' (Dent 1999, 189), and so to resist them. For Rousseau, as for Hobbes, the pronouncements of the sovereign can by definition never be unfair or unjust.

The second line of argument begins by identifying that distinction as central to the liberal tradition rather than as necessary to the concept of sovereignty. The very distinction is a liberal conception, inflating one conception of sovereignty into the concept, and writers like Gough and Franklin fall into the trap of equating a liberal conception with the concept itself. The distinction marks the particularity of the liberal model. Indeed the distinction does not clarify and provide a solution to a problem, it simply extends the problem. For if *political* sovereignty, as in Rousseau, is the power to make general *laws*, then what does the distinction between legal and political consist of? It becomes a distinction between the power to make law on the one hand, and the power to scrutinise and cast down law and so hold law-makers accountable on the other. This is one step removed from the idea of legal sovereignty contrasted with political sovereignty as a constitutive principle. Moreover, notwithstanding the separation between political and legal authority in the case of the suspected terrorists, in Britain there is a fusion of political and legal sovereignty at the top, the House of Lords containing the highest legal authority and part of the Parliament which is the highest political authority. Furthermore, a separation between political and legal sovereignty cannot altogether hold, because the organisation, norms, and conventions of the legal system help to shape the expression of political sovereignty.

The third line of argument is to defend Rousseau's conception on the grounds that, if you are going to have a robust conception of sovereignty you may as well see how far the logic of it can be developed. In addition, Rousseau is advancing a different conception that offers certain advantages. His conception of popular sovereignty as constituting all citizens together making laws in the common good, is genuinely egalitarian. It also fulfils a need for political sovereignty to be enacted by the populace. Against the accusation that Rousseau's conception fails to provide sufficient safeguards against despotism it could be argued that an important protection is secured in the way Rousseau's general will enacts only laws that are perfectly general. As Strong puts it, the 'general will...cannot as general will have anything to say about that which is particular' (Strong 1994, 84). Such laws are designed to apply universally to all citizens, such that neither individuals nor minorities can be singled out. Wokler highlights the value of Rousseau's vigorous notion of sovereignty. He argues that '[n]o major political thinker before Rousseau had ever shown so much devotion to the idea of collective self-expression or popular self-rule. Although he allowed that the common people could be deceived or misled, he believed that the only possible safeguard against despotism was popular sovereignty itself. Only when the people all took part in legislation could they check the abuse of power which some of them might seek to wield' (Wokler 1995, 65).

Having opened up the question of the plausibility of the different connections in Locke and Rousseau on the complex issue of the relation between political and legal sovereignty in this sense, we turn now to an overall assessment of Rousseau's theory of sovereignty. Looking at Rousseau's logic of reasoning on sovereignty as a whole we can see that it is framed by three great dualisms, which act as another safeguard against tyrannical abuse of the system, either by government or powerful individuals or groups. A dualism constitutes much more than a distinction. It contains a hierarchy of value between the two parts, and an opposition between them, and in this case also an inter-dependence between them. The over-arching dualism in Rousseau's system is between sovereignty and government. The theory is set up in such a way as to insulate the political and civic realm of the enactment of popular sovereignty from the public realm of government and administration. Following logically from this framework of a separation between politics and government there is the dualism between general and particular laws. These two separations are primarily designed to ensure that administrators and magistrates do not encroach on the territory of legislation reserved for the sovereign body. In the third place, these two dualisms rest on a binary between the general and particular wills. The first two dualisms refer to a dichotomy between the political and public realms, while that between general and particular wills refers to a dichotomy between the political and private realms, the proper spheres of public (common good) and private interest. Such dualisms are a distinctive feature of Rousseau's manner of theorising. Others that also occur in his work are between natural independence and freedom, force and right, freedom and bondage, possession and property, and subject and citizen. As well as protecting the individual and the common good, these dualisms work to mark out the strong sense of the transformative power of sovereignty, enabling mankind to benefit from a richer conception of liberty and from a moral framework for action.

The idea of popular sovereignty, of which Rousseau stands as the exemplar, also raises the question of how far it can be stretched and who can be excluded from the list of its proponents. Hobbes represents a test case here. Hobbes is often regarded as setting out the exemplary form of absolute sovereignty, in the sense of the very opposite of its popular form, investing the sovereign with unlimited and absolute powers over the people. However, he can also very plausibly be read as a genuine popular sovereigntist, since his theory hinges on the act of authorising of the sovereign by all persons as equals, and on the representation by the sovereign of the people, literally expressed in the frontespiece of *Leviathan*. In contrast, Locke's form of popular sovereignty does not contain the spirit of the popular form. It prevents the government from acting in the common good, for instance for the benefit of the poor or disadvantaged minorities, because its role is restricted in effect to protecting individual property rights. It also, for instance, prohibits suicide because that right (to life) is not popular (indeed there are no popular rights for Locke) but derives from God. The net effect of the strict limits Locke places on the portrayal of popular sovereignty is to prevent any progressive potential for government.

The key general features of sovereignty that preoccupy Rousseau are the relationship between rulers and ruled, sovereignty as self-government within a moral framework, and sovereignty specifying the highest legal authority. Wokler points to one of the strengths of his theory when he notes that, '[p]rior to the meaning he ascribes to it in the *Social Contract*, the concept of sovereignty had been connected by its interpreters to the idea of force, power, or empire'. Moreover, 'it had generally pertained to the dominion of kings over their subjects, however that had been acquired, rather than to citizens' freedom'. Wokler argues that for 'both Bodin and Hobbes in particular — the best-known advocates of absolute sovereignty before him ... [sovereignty meant the] unequalled power of the ruler'. In contrast, for Rousseau 'the idea of sovereignty is essentially a principle of equality, identified with the ruled element, or the subjects themselves, as the supreme authority, and it is connected with the concepts of will or right, as he defines them, rather than force or power' (Wokler 1995, 64). Of all the conceptions of sovereignty in the mainstream political theory tradition, Rousseau's is one of the ones that has the strongest sense of politics as a positive realm of deliberation and contestation in pursuit of the common good. Thus, in answer to Strong's question, 'what claim [does] the common ... have on me'? (Strong 1994, 78), Rousseau would reply 'a great deal' while Locke would respond, 'a minimal amount'.

Gourevitch highlights even more starkly the importance of politics for Rousseau. He notes that there are 'three basic principles of his politics, that man is by nature good, that political society corrupts him, and that everything is radically dependent on politics'. In Gourevitch's insightful reading, 'Rousseau categorically denies that any political solution can transform "men as they are" into "men as they ought to be"'. Rousseau 'holds out no prospect whatsoever of an end to politics, be it by men's rationally choosing what is in their enlightened self-interest, or by their becoming "moralised", or by the "withering away of the state"'. In Rousseau's nuanced understanding of politics there is both 'no alternative to politics' and no political solution can be definitive (Gourevitch 1997, xxxi). The tensions are at best held in place by the workings of politics.

Despite its evident strengths, the major weakness of Rousseau's conception remains the threat of degeneration into tyranny, notwithstanding the nobility of his ideal and the safeguards he puts in place. The energetic vigilance of the sovereign body, the set of dualistic prescriptions in which the theory is couched, the generality of the law enacted by the sovereign body, the limits placed on the institutions of lawgiver and dictator, the mechanism by which citizens recover their natural freedom if the social pact is broken through the degeneration or corruption of the state, are yet insufficient to overcome that threat. The problems of preventing the merger of political and public interest (in the form of government despotism), or the fusion of political and private interest (and the dominance of certain particular interests), or of majoritarian tyranny, persist.

Chapter Four

KANT AND HEGEL

KANT

Kant lived in Konigsberg in East Prussia from his birth in 1724 until his death in 1804. The fragmentary condition of the patchwork of German states at this time, without a metropolitan culture and political centre were, as Reiss points out, 'not conducive to the rise of lively political discussion' and provided 'virtually no opportunities for ... intellectuals to take part in politics' (Reiss 1997a, 7). Kant argued against the patriarchal 'benevolent despotism' or 'enlightened autocracy' of the Prussian king, Frederick the Great (while admiring his enlightened attitudes) and disagreed even more with the subsequent and more repressive regime of Frederick William II.

Kant's political theory is not found in a single work but in a number of scattered writings from the later part of his career, in the period around and immediately after the American Revolution of 1776. Reiss makes a strong case (1997a, 4) that Kant's political views were already formed well before the beginning of the French Revolution in 1789 and cannot be regarded, therefore, as a response to those events. Kant's political works were therefore published about twenty-five years after Rousseau's *Social Contract*, whose moral aspect Kant admired. Kant's political theory, as a dynamic form of progressive rational self-emancipation, was also developed against the intellectual background of the Enlightenment movement, and his criticisms of it. His political writings appeared after his philosophical perspective and reputation were already well-established. The most significant source as far as Kant's conception of sovereignty is concerned is *The Metaphysics of Morals* of 1797. *Perpetual Peace* of 1795, *Theory and Practice* of 1792 and *What is Enlightenment?* of 1784 are also important. Unless otherwise stated, references are to *The Metaphysics of Morals*. Hegel's most notable political writing is the *Philosophy of Right* of 1821, though his great interest in political matters was also expressed in pamphlets and newspaper articles.

Kant's and Hegel's conceptions of sovereignty pose a useful comparison. Kant and Hegel were both explicitly concerned with the notion of sovereignty in the context of the *Rechtstaat*. This crucial concept refers not just to the rule of law, but to the idea of the rule of law in a constitutional state as a moral principle governing social and political order. Amorphous nationalism and cultural Germanicism are both rejected in the *Rechtstaat* ideal. In contrast with some of the other writers studied here, for both Kant and Hegel the conception of external sovereignty (now taking on its modern form, with internal sovereignty as identified in the context of the modern state form) was a significant part of their political concerns. In some respects both Kant and Hegel, working in the tradition of German philosophy and political theory, were exercised by contextual factors such as the power of nation-states in Europe, notably in France and England, by the dominance of Prussia amongst the German states, and by the absence of a unified German state. However, this contextualisation does not provide grounds for a deterministic interpretation, in simply reading off their political theories as simple responses to issues in the politics of the day. This caution is especially pertinent here, since both were thinkers whose philosophical precepts deeply affected their approach to and conclusions about political theory and practice. Nevertheless it is clear that both philosophers were keen to bring (in different, though overlapping ways) a philosophical perspective to bear on the nature of *politics* in the context of an emerging system of nation states. In this way there is a direct connection with the prominence of a concern with external sovereignty in their works. With our familiarity of living in nation states and an international order of nation states, it is not easy to capture the genesis and contingency of that formation and how it appeared to Kant and Hegel.

In both writers the specific meaning of law, deriving from a metaphysics of morals, and the value placed on it meant that a strong conception of state sovereignty had to accompany it. With Kant and Hegel, for the first time unequivocally in this book, the modern state — as a moral and political agent — is an inherent part of what it means to conceptualise sovereignty. In both writers, in different ways, a robust form of sovereignty explicitly attached to the state, necessarily followed from the power, scope and reach of law as ordering the lives of individuals. This rule of law contains a cluster of features — publicly-known laws (rather than sheer power, customary privilege, or particular interest) governing the relations between persons, law as a civilising influence, the rule of law as a moral norm, law as the intermediary translating moral principles to apply to concrete cases, the state as a law-giving state, and law articulating right (justice and rightness). The pre-eminence and wide coverage of such law in their sense demands the political form of a *Rechtstaat* and this idea of the constitutional state demands a sturdy and vigorous state sovereignty. Law, state and sovereignty are all absolute in the same way.

In terms of their responses to the issue of external sovereignty, Kant and Hegel took radically opposed positions. Kant mostly but not always draws cosmopolitan conclusions (although, as we shall see, his position was a complex one) about the importance of inter-state harmony between likeminded republics as a means to ensure global peace and mediate to seek to prevent wars between nations. Hegel has a communitarian temperament that emphasises the importance of developing a political identity and patriotism within the framework of a nation state. Indeed Kant is best known for arguing that the nature of freedom for persons requires peace and cannot co-exist with a condition of war, while Hegel argues that individuals can only achieve real freedom within the identity of a state that has experienced war.

Both Kant and Hegel are concerned, like Rousseau, with the problem of establishing the conditions for legitimate government, founded on right rather than power. In this way, Kant and Hegel, along with Rousseau, Spinoza and even Hobbes, also wanted to see sovereignty as beneficial to citizens, setting out the conditions of political life in which individuals (and for some of these writers, the collective) could flourish. In addition, society is a civilising influence for Kant and Hegel, as it was for Hobbes and Rousseau. In articulating the idea of legitimate government being founded on right rather than power, the views of Kant and Hegel are influential in the development of the powerful notion of the specifically German *Rechtstaat* or state governed by moral right. Both were concerned with how right could be translated into law, with how moral principles could be implemented in the state through a system of law.

What is most distinctive about Kant's conception of sovereignty is the tension in his theory around the sovereign state. According to Kant the logic of politics as a metaphysics of morals requires that the sovereign state and its laws is the locus for the realisation of individual freedom. At the same time Kant is attracted to extrapolating his logic, which includes the recognition of politics as a realm of practical and contingent activity in which principles can guide but not dictate, into the international realm. However, he is prevented from fully doing so by the obstacle of the sovereign state he has constructed. The relationship between morality and politics leads for Kant to two contradictory conclusions — the sovereignty of the state as the focus for right and law, and the sovereignty of moral principle in the international sphere leading to peace — and for Kant it is ultimately but not at all satisfactorily the first that must take priority.

Four aspects of Kant's philosophical framework are crucial to the meaning of his political theory. The first is the importance of the individual's capacity for reason, morality and freedom, from which the categorical imperative derives. The second is the significance of deontological obligations—of duty. The priority of duty over self-interest is central to Kant, even if duty is directly against self-interest or leads to unpalatable consequences. From these first two aspects it follows for Kant that the object of politics is not to promote happiness, and he strongly disapproves of utilitarian theories of politics. This view is confirmed by Kant by another argument about the subjective nature of individual happiness. In *Theory and Practice* he maintains that '[m]en have different views on the empirical end of happiness and what it consists of'. Articulating what later became a key liberal principle, Kant says that '[n]o-one can compel me to be happy in accordance with his conception of the welfare of others' (Kant 1997, 73, 74). The third aspect is the key distinction Kant draws between theoretical knowledge, which is universal, and empirical knowledge, gained from experience and always particular. The fourth aspect is a paradox Kant perceived, namely the tension between duty, which is universal, and the demands arising from the messy, particular, and contingent world of politics.

Kant saw his political theory as an extension of his moral philosophy. As Franceschet explains, politics 'cannot be (entirely) sovereign for Kant', because 'the political world is essentially one of contingent, not formal-universal, causes'. Within 'the mechanism of nature and the political relations that emerge from it, there is no inherent respect for humanity' (Franceschet 2002, 32). For Kant, the distinctive ground of moral philosophy was, in turn, aimed at specifying a space protected from the new scientific temper and empiricist approach to knowledge, which regarded human beings as simply part of nature. Franceschet underlines the radical and innovative step that Kant took in proposing that the autonomy of morality is an autonomy 'from nature and animal instinct' (Franceschet 2002, 20). Kant posits a form of subjectivity that provides for freedom from nature and for human dignity, based on an autonomous morality rather than (as previous thinkers had done) on our capacity to know the world or to 'will upon maxims of expediency' (Franceschet 2002, 22). However, the dualism that Kant thereby instantiated, along with the unresolved tension in his thinking that followed from it, together with the varied and dispersed character of his political writings, without a single definitive text, results in a very wide interpretive openness that invites commentators to draw conclusions from selective readings. Kant has thus been seen as both subversive and authoritarian, both moralistic and Machiavellian.

Kant's view of philosophy as explicating the nature of morality, dictates that philosophy must be used to understand politics, and that the same logic must be used to understand international relations. According to Kant, we are all citizens of a single moral order. This is because of our shared rationality. Kant's view of philosophy, and so his approach to politics, is agent-centred, places emphasis on moral motives, and allows principles to trump considerations of consequences. The way to evaluate an act, says Kant, is to examine the motive. Kant distinguished sharply between acts merely done in accordance with obligation and those done for the sake of obligation. It is only the second kind that have moral worth. To act because something is the right thing to do, even if it against one's self-interest, and regardless of the likely consequences of the action, is to act according to reason, to be free, to be moral. This is his deontological moral theory. Franceschet identifies the importance of duty for Kant when he notes that it 'is only because the subject is so divided by his rational capacity to obey laws and his natural inclinations to make an exception for his self that duty is a meaningful moral concept'. Moreover, duty separates human beings from both God and animals — the former is exempt because God is not subject to instinct while the latter 'lack a rational will that could intervene with and subordinate inclinations' (Franceschet 2002, 20).

Reason, according to Kant, is 'our innate capacity … to transcend human nature and obey formal causes and universal laws' (Franceschet 2002, 64). It is also the faculty that discovers moral principles, for Kant. Reason, not inclination or interests (including state interests) certifies right action. It follows, as Nussbaum makes clear, that Kant 'defended a politics based upon reason rather than patriotism or group sentiment, a politics that was truly universal rather than communitarian' (Nussbaum 1997, 27). When reason guides action, the behaviour is motivated by duty. Reason is the faculty that seeks the unconditional, that which has no further cause or explanation. But reason cannot find the unconditional in theoretical reflection, because reason there is always doomed to seek a further cause or explanation. Reason can find the unconditional in practical activity. The essence of acting morally for Kant lies in responding to a demand of reason — not in achieving self-interest (even when it is 'enlightened self-interest' or national interest), nor as Aristotle believed in actualising human potential. This demand, of responding to reason, is the categorical imperative. It requires that we treat others not as a means to our ends, but as ends in themselves, as rational agents.

Kersting highlights the significance of reason for Kant, and sets out well the train of argument that leads, for Kant, to the view that '[w]e are subject to the laws of reason alone'. Kersting notes that in the previous history of practical philosophy, of which politics is a part, 'foundations and first principles were sought in objective ideas, in a normative constitution of the cosmos, in the will of God, in the nature of man, or in prudence in the service of self-interest'. Kant, however, 'was convinced that these starting-points were without exception inadequate for the foundation of unconditional practical laws'. For Kant, human reason alone could 'concede absolute practical necessity and obligatoriness to norms that arose from its own legislation'. Kersting concludes that with 'this recognition Kant frees us from the domination of theological absolutism and the bonds of teleological natural law, and likewise elevates us above the prosaic banalities of the doctrine of prudence'. It follows for Kant that human beings 'may and must obey only their own reason; in that lies their dignity as well as their exacting and burdensome moral vocation' (Kersting 1992, 342).

At the same time, as Onora O'Neill cautions, Kant's critique of the inflated claims for reason made by previous thinkers means that he 'rejects the rationalist claim that the principles of reason can provide a unique and integrated answer to all possible questions'. Indeed, O'Neill explains, 'any view of principles of reason as divinely inscribed axioms or rules of thought, that correspond to reality, leads to contradictions', as far as Kant is concerned. For him, 'human reason is quite simply incompetent for these illusory tasks' (O'Neill 1992, 283). It follows for Kant that no form of arbitrary power, whether it be 'state, church, majority, tradition, or dictator' could be accepted as a source of reason (O'Neill 1992, 305). The basis of Kant's critique of reason was a distinction between understanding and reason. As he says in the *Critique of Pure Reason*, understanding is 'the faculty which secures the unity of appearances by means of rules', whereas reason is 'the faculty which secures the unity of rules of understanding under principles'. The key point for Kant is that 'reason never applies itself directly to experience or to any object, but to understanding' (cited in O'Neill 1992, 282–3).

Kant's approach to politics, then, follows from his approach to all forms of enquiry, that, in Reiss's words, it is 'necessary to start ... not from objects of experience, but from the mind'. According to Kant, Reiss notes, we 'can never explain the world as it appears to us merely by reference to experience; to do so we need necessary principles logically prior to and independent of experience' (Reiss 1997a, 17). Thus for Kant there are two very different sources of knowledge — *a priori* knowledge that is the product of rational reflection and is not dependent on experience or the senses, and *a posteriori* knowledge that comes from experience. *A priori* knowledge is philosophical knowledge, because it is necessary, timeless and of universal application. As Ameriks observes of Kant's thinking, 'a priori concepts ... [are] pure concepts of reason, or transcendental ideas' (Ameriks 1992, 251). According to Kant the way the world is cannot be used to derive the way it ought to be. Put the other way around, as Franceschet sums up, it 'is because the human is the only creature that can set ends undetermined by the natural, phenomenal world and its material causes that he or she is capable of morality' (Franceschet 2002, 31). The categorical imperative, which is the essence of rational morality to choose to act in accordance with universal moral duty rather than in conformity with desire, and to treat others as ends in themselves rather than as a means to an end, is said by Kant to be *a priori*, and to contain no *a posteriori* or empirical elements.

A metaphysics of morals precisely sets out, for Kant, the relevant *a priori* principles of reason for that field of enquiry, and the study of politics belongs within the realm of moral action and conduct, not towards oneself (as in ethics) but to others. But as soon as the categorical imperative is applied to a practical context, Kant grants that empirical considerations come into play. This is because it is part of what it is to be human, to have purposes and aims that are particular. Kant's moral theory from the start implies a politics that puts law at centre stage, as the means to maximise freedom and moral choice, and highlights inter-personal relations on a basis of equality. It also presupposes within it a universalism across different individuals, but also right across different cultures and societies.

As far as politics and international relations are concerned, the concept of 'right' is central. By 'right' Kant means a moral right based on universal reason, translated into law, rather than our modern notions of 'justice' or 'human rights'. Kant argues that the connection between freedom, law, and right is as follows: '[e]very action which by itself or by its maxim enables the freedom of each individual's will to co-exist with the freedom of everyone else in accordance with a universal law is right' (Kant 1997, 133). At the same time, Kant's theory commits him to the position that whatever existing cooperation there is between people and between countries, considered as an empirical matter, is largely irrelevant for framing the responsibility of political and international actors. The basis of international morality must remain for Kant what it is for domestic morality: the moral demand of reason. Morality justifies cooperation, not the reverse. While international cooperation, as an empirical matter, may make it possible to create a league of nations, the reasons why we want a league must derive from our *a priori* concepts of morality. Kantian cosmopolitanism affirms for him the existence of cross-cultural moral truth.

For Kant, the way to think about international morality must be based not on any empirical fact or probability, but simply on the authority of the categorical imperative, the demand of practical reason that informs the activity of all rational agents. Whether or not a global moral consensus or cooperation actually emerges, Kant would defend the existence of international obligations. Even if there were no possibility of realising the outcomes prescribed by the categorical imperative, practical reason demands that we must act as if there were. Kant's theoretical radicalism must not be understated — for him the ideal cannot be dismissed simply by pointing out that it cannot be achieved at present.

Kant's political theory is in part a response to the problem he perceived, that an external fulfilment of the ends of reason is not a genuine fulfilment.

If the realm of right is one that deals with the sometimes self-interested will, then how can it be part of a metaphysics of morals? Kant gives three answers throughout his political writings, and commentators vary in their judgments about how successful Kant was in drawing together the realms of the legal and the moral. First, in the doctrine of 'right', the answer involves the deduction of pure principles of right from practical reason itself, so that the non-virtuous realm of legality is itself legitimated by reference to the moral law. Another answer is given in Kant's view of international relations, in which inter-state harmony may approximate more and more closely to the ideal of a kingdom of ends. Then, in Kant's writings on the kind of judgment that deserves publicity, a third answer is given, in which the philosopher's assessment of the course of history helps to steer the realm of right towards the realm of virtue. In all three answers, however, there are grounds for holding that the tension as Kant saw it between legality and morality is not fully resolved, and that the basis of the connection between right and reality is never genuinely secure and remains open. A strong case can be made that Kant is caught between an abstract principle that must condemn all actual practices as inadequate on the one hand, and the defence of the actual status quo on the faith that it instantiates the moral law on the other. In sovereignty, for Kant, an attempt is made to provide a location for both sides of this dilemma.

Having set out the four aspects of Kant's philosophical framework that inform his view of politics, we turn to sovereignty. The important concepts in Kant's theory of sovereignty are right, international relations, publicity, law, and representation. After looking at each in turn, some conclusions about his theory of sovereignty itself will be made.

Kant begins his enquiry into politics with the conception of the autonomous individual, that is, one who is self-governing and not acting on the basis of the natural inclinations and desires of the phenomenal self. Kant's logic dictates that we must start with autonomy, since without autonomy, morality would be impossible (Franceschet 2002, 30). The notion of 'right' is then introduced, which is his key principle for politics. At the end of *Theory and Practice* Kant says of his method, 'I put my trust in the theory of what the relationships between men and states ought to be according to the principle of right' (Kant 1997, 92). However, right conflicts with individual autonomy. Right is the capacity to obligate someone to a duty to respect the freedom of others, or the freedom of others to make choices that do not conflict with universal laws. In this way 'right' in general terms governs the translation from the internal freedom we all have, into the public world of being able to make claims on the external world, to interact with the external world, the world outside our own minds. With the idea of 'right' Kant seeks to negotiate the paradox, the tension between absolute, universal, theoretically-correct duty, and the demands of contingency, history, circumstances, interests and consequences. Moreover, it is important to remember that right sanctions both freedom and coercion. As Kersting puts it, the 'authorization of coercion as permission for the defense of universally compatible domains of freedom is a constituent of the concept of right' (Kersting 1992, 346).

Freedom is expressed in terms of power over something or someone. 'Right' guarantees that possession in theory. Men have inalienable equal rights to freedom in the state of nature. But the state of nature is not a state of innocence for Kant, and he regards society as a civilising construction. This view ties in with the priority Kant gives, as noted earlier, to the autonomy of morality over nature and animal instinct. So in practical terms, a social contract is needed, to guarantee that possession of freedom in practice. But the social contract is a necessary hypothesis, not a historical event. The social contract is thus the hypothetical but particular act of a group of people, the original universal validating act of will on the part of a particular group of people. The social contract discriminates between the state of nature, in which possessions can only be held provisionally, and the civil condition in which possessions can be guaranteed. Thus for Kant (as for Hegel) the necessity of politics, the contractual basis of politics and the role of law, as well as deriving from the primary moral argument, all come also in a secondary argument from the fact of private property, and private property is derived from the nature of freedom and the moral will. Private right depends upon public right.

In the 'rightful' civil condition, persons are related juridically with each other. In the move from the state of nature to the state, says Kant, 'we cannot say that men ... have sacrificed a part of their inborn external freedom for a specific purpose; they have in fact completely abandoned their wild and lawless freedom'. They have given up this disorderly freedom, 'in order to find again their entire and undiminished freedom in a state of lawful dependence (that is in a state of right), for this dependence is created by their own legislative will (Kant 1997, 140). Reiss affirms that for Kant, political freedom refers to 'those restraints which the individual must accept in order to avoid conflict with others so that he may enjoy the freedom of moral action' (Reiss 1997a, 39). Thus 'the state' is this condition of juridical relationship between persons, viewed as a whole in relation to its members. The purpose of the state is not to make people happy. Kant argues that '[o]n the contrary, the welfare of the state should be seen as that condition in which the constitution most closely approximates to the principles of right; and reason, by a categorical imperative, obliges us to strive for its realisation' (Kant 1997, 143). For Kant, legislative authority is only legitimate when it follows the universal principle of right.

Kant does not require that the sovereign body of the state take on any particular form, but insists that it should be in accord with the spirit of republicanism. Republics are defined as states that guarantee the separation of the legislative, executive and judicial powers in different hands. All other states, which do not separate powers, are despotic. The value that Kant places on republicanism is analogous to the value that we place on 'democracy' as the only legitimate form of political community. As we shall see Kant did not approve of democracy and this is why the relationship is only analogous. But the significance Kant placed on the separation of powers closely resembles a key part of what democracy symbolises for us. The differentiation of judicial power, legislative power and executive power, and a legally-sanctioned flourishing internal pluralism and public sphere are important to Kant. Other central aspects of democratic politics for us such as competing parties and especially the authenticity of political rule stemming from universal suffrage, are anathema for Kant. For him it is the separation of powers that preserves the formal legitimacy of sovereignty, which is always both inviolable and absolute. As Kant puts it, 'the universally united will is made up of three separate persons' (Kant 1997, 138).

Thus with Kant we move a step closer to the American system of a republican separation of powers, though Kant's system lacks the democratic impulse of the American system, and the role of the universal law of reason is taken on, in the US system, by the American Constitution. But in both the legislator, ruler (executive) and judiciary are in separate hands, and a separate court of law or jury is appointed to interpret the law. This is a long way from Hobbes, for whom the separation of powers necessarily registered the dissolution of sovereignty, but is a self-conscious development of Rousseau's notion of sovereignty. However, Kant agreed with Hobbes that democracies were dreadful, though for Hobbes this was because they were chaotic and lacking a location for sovereignty, whereas for Kant it was because they did not properly differentiate between branches of power.

Kant holds the view that whether citizens are active participants in legislation or not (and only those independent of another's control are allowed to be active citizens, and therefore to vote. This, in his schema, rules out everyone apart from self-employed men), all citizens *do* ground the law and are absolutely bound by it. This view is demonstrated in his approach to punishment—because the criminal as citizen is responsible for the law, he has the right to be punished by it. The way in which for Kant all citizens ground the law and are bound by it is also indicated in his attitude to revolution. Revolution can never be right, legally or morally, because there can be no legitimate contesting of the source of legitimacy and all legislative authority must be perceived as derived from that source. Citizens in revolution are a self-contradiction. Kant's view on revolution brings out clearly the absolutism of sovereign power for him, for the sovereign is the law. Change can only rightfully stem from the sovereign body itself, reforming the law in accordance with the demands of right. Again the problem arises with this conception in that it involves a tension between the legitimating power of the theoretical and abstract, and the legitimating power of actual practice. In this way, Kant's theory of 'right' is in serious danger of being caught between the originating power of pure practical reason, which is beyond comprehension, and a juridical ideal in which right is realised, but which is beyond attainment.

International relations is the next of Kant's key concepts. The role of sovereignty is to be the focus of legitimate public law. Any legislative authority that upholds intelligible possession must be treated as if it were legitimate. The notion of right depends on the existence of absolute sovereign authority in relation to a group of citizens. It follows from Kant's argument that any law is preferable to no law, since the demands of practical reason compel an end to the state of nature. But in relation to each other, states are in a lawless condition. They are in a state of nature with each other which is, he says, 'a condition of constant war' (Kant 1997, 165), even if actual fighting is not taking place.

A very significant feature of Kant's view of the relation between internal and external sovereignty is that Kant applies his logic directly from the domestic to the international stage, and regards a state 'as a moral person' (Kant 1997, 165) in the same sense as is an individual. He disregards the idea that any factor, such as the nature of particular communities, or the autonomy of international politics as a separate sphere of action or field of inquiry, might modify this direct application. It follows for Kant then (because the logic of the domestic is mapped onto the international), that internal sovereignty is superior to and dictates the terms of external sovereignty. The logic of Kant's internal prescription for the gradual approximation towards a republican state, leads also to his argument for states to work towards perpetual peace with each other. Moreover the analogy between moral persons and moral states is extended in that Kant's theory of sovereignty also significantly follows from his theory of modern subjectivity. The relationship between internal and external sovereignty in important respects mirrors that between the realms of morality (internal, within a person) and right (concerning the external effects of inter-subjective relations) with, as Franceschet appositely puts it, 'the sovereignty of morality over the political' (Franceschet 2002, 31) in both. Kant's conception of sovereignty is very much a part of his critical project which, as Franceschet observes, 'is at root designed to provide the principles by which individuals become truly sovereign and dignified by limiting and overriding the natural causality within' (Franceschet 2002, 20).

Indeed, Franceschet makes a strong case that the powerful analogy between individual and state in Kant's theory of sovereignty is underpinned by his basic commitment to the individual (and their freedom), rather than the state, as the primary subject of international justice (Franceschet 2002, 55). The consequence of the priority given to the individual is the limits of the mapping of the logic of internal sovereignty onto its external counterpart. As Ellis observes, 'the imperative to leave the state of nature cannot apply to states' because 'the need of individuals for a rule-governed sphere of action' is already fulfilled in the state (Ellis 2005, 91). This is a crucial step in the argument. It follows for Kant that the achieved autonomy of the individual corresponds to the achievement of state sovereignty, in contrast with the violent lawlessness of the state of nature. Moreover, the starting point of the autonomy (self-determining positive liberty) and freedom (to act independent of constraints from other wills, in negative liberty) of the modern subject corresponds, for Kant, to the internal and external sovereignty of the state (Franceschet 2002, 30). In his politics, in a crucial example of what we can recognise as a distinctive feature of liberal thinking, Kant takes his (specific cultural) notion of internal sovereignty to be abstract and universal, and extends it to apply both to relations with other states and the principles of relations between states.

The priority of individual freedom and limits of the analogy between individual and state, however, run counter to the *logic* of the demand of 'right', which moves from public domestic law to the necessity for an overarching authority to ensure perpetual peace between states. The universality of the demand of 'right' is only possible if war is abolished as a means of politics. Kant also regards war as invalid on the grounds that states must not, in this way, treat citizens as means for their own ends, namely the continued existence of the state. However, the analogy between individual and state that Kant employs in the logic of 'right' is apparent in the following quotation. He says, 'if a state believes that it has been injured by another state, it is entitled to resort to violence, for it cannot in the state of nature gain satisfaction through legal proceedings, [which is] the only means of settling disputes in a state governed by right' (Kant 1997, 167).

However, Kant also produces an argument in *The Critique of Judgement* of 1790, not only condoning the inevitability of war but also suggesting the utility of war in creating larger political units and other benefits. This is another example of the interpretive openness of Kant's political writings and leads again to the caution about too-selective readings of Kant. He makes the case that in the absence of a cosmopolitan 'system of all states', and taking into account the obstacles to such a system afforded by 'ambition, love of power, and avarice, especially on the part of those who hold the reins of authority', then 'war is inevitable'. While war is the 'thoughtless' produce of 'unbridled passion', it can also have the positive effect 'to prepare the way for a rule of law governing the freedom of states, and thus bring about their unity in a system established on a moral basis'. Indeed, says Kant, war 'is one further spur for developing to the highest pitch all talents that minister to culture' (Kant 1952, 96).

Franceschet also draws attention to the key role of sovereignty in placing limits on the analogical argument in Kant's political theory. He observes convincingly that, while Kant has been appropriated by the liberal tradition and his *Perpetual Peace* has been invoked as a foundational text for (the ultimately flawed project of) liberal internationalism seeking cosmopolitan solutions to the problem of war in international politics, the priority that Kant gives to state sovereignty as the touchstone for justice, frustrates attempts to use Kant's work as the basis of reform of the modern state system. Franceschet makes a strong case that Kant's 'dogmatic commitment to sovereignty' sets up 'the crippling limitations that his theory of justice imposes upon his relevance as an intellectual foundation'. More broadly he takes the view that Kant's 'legacy has been central and yet ambiguous within the context of an evolving liberal internationalist tradition', since 'contemporary liberals are divided on the very same political and ethical conundrums on which Kant's texts are … unable to render decisive judgements'. He argues clearly that Kant's ideas on international relations 'cannot be viewed independently of his larger "critical" system', whose 'paradoxes and dualities … do not necessarily cohere with existing approaches and paradigms in International Relations' (Franceschet 2002, ix-x). Ellis is allied to another, but less persuasive, interpretive position of Kant's theory when she follows the line of reasoning that, for Kant, 'to exercise any real sovereignty, that is, any real self-rule, states must embed themselves in a context of international security', and that 'since agents necessarily interact with one another, they must regulate these interactions if they are to enjoy any rights at all' (Ellis 2005, 87).

It is thus a distinctive feature of Kant's theory of sovereignty that he did not distinguish fundamentally between the moral agency of individuals and of states. States, like individuals must recognise specific moral problems and moral precepts. For him, the universalisable, timelessly valid and objective imperatives that rationality imposes remain the same for states as for individuals. This feature of the theory can be seen as either a strength or a weakness. It is a strength if one agrees that states are responsible for their actions in the same way as individuals are. It is a weakness if one holds that Kant is making a category mistake, on the grounds that states are not like individuals but are artificial constructs without any necessary moral character.

Kant presents two views on 'perpetual peace'. The logic of his metaphysics of morals for international politics leads to the formal ideal of enduring peace as ultimately an ideal of world government instituting a global harmony substantively regulated by international law, thus overcoming the tension between internal and external sovereignty from both the internal and external directions. But his theory of sovereignty leads to a very different and much more limited and conditional outcome, of a gradual, mutual and reciprocal working toward agreement over international laws that in no way undermines the sovereignty of any of the parties to the agreement. This more complex and indeed more prominent conclusion comes from not just relying on Kant's call for international reform in *Perpetual Peace* (the primary text for those engaged in the project of 'Kantian cosmopolitanism' (G W Brown 2005) in both its world government and 'Kantian federation' versions), but from also giving due weight to the theory of sovereignty in *The Metaphysics of Morals* (written two years later) and other writings. As Franceschet puts it, for Kant states are more likely — however imperfect — vehicles of international reform than a world state would be (Franceschet 2002, 45). Moreover, Kant says bluntly that 'perpetual peace ... is an idea incapable of realisation'. However, he holds that 'the political principles which ... encourage the formation of international alliances designed to approach the idea itself by a continual process, are not impracticable' (Kant 1997, 171). The line of argument that Kant traces in *Theory and Practice* is that states might well be led, 'even against their will' to 'enter into a cosmopolitan constitution' by the distress accompanying constant wars 'in which states try to subjugate or engulf each other'. But this 'state of universal peace', Kant underlines, can result in the 'most fearful despotism' that is 'even more dangerous to freedom'. The conclusion that this line of argument reaches is the desirability, instead, to form 'a lawful federation under a commonly accepted international right', rather than 'a cosmopolitan commonwealth under a single ruler' (Kant 1997, 90). It is a federation of states which are opposed to war.

Kant underlines his meaning of 'peace' at the beginning of *Perpetual Peace* when he remarks that it is not 'a mere truce, a suspension of hostilities' but 'an end to all hostilities' such that the term 'perpetual' is 'suspiciously close to pleonasm' or tautology (Kant 1997, 93). Bohman and Lutz-Bachmann note that the practical impetus for the writing of *Perpetual Peace* was the 1795 Treaty of Basel between Prussia and revolutionary France, by which Prussia gave up to France its territory west of the Rhine but gained the right to take part in the partition of Poland along with Russia and Austria. As Bohman and Lutz-Bachmann observe, it was 'just this sort of strategic treaty that Kant condemns as illegitimate' (1997, 1). The telling point about a real peace, for Kant, is that 'rights cannot be decided by military victory'. Reason sets up peace, and striving towards a 'pacific federation' — which 'does not aim to acquire any power like that of a state, but merely to preserve and secure the freedom of each state in itself' — is an 'immediate duty' (Kant 1997, 104). He adds that the 'concept of international right becomes meaningless if interpreted as a right to go to war'. Kant's reasoning is that '[j]ust like individual men', states 'must renounce their savage and lawless freedom, adapt themselves to public coercive laws, and thus form an international state'. But because this 'positive idea of a world republic cannot be realised', we must settle for 'a negative substitute in the shape of an enduring and gradually expanding federation likely to prevent war' (Kant 1997, 105).

The significance of the idea of federation is, as Kant puts it, that 'this association must not embody a sovereign power as in a civil constitution, but only a partnership or confederation ... an alliance which can be terminated at any time ... renewed periodically' (Kant 1997, 165). Not only would states not want to relinquish their sovereignty – they are innately unable to do so. In *Perpetual Peace* Kant underlines this view when he says that this federation 'would not be the same thing as an international state. For the idea of an international state is contradictory' (Kant 1997, 102). But the urgency, for Kant, of seeking to move towards enduring and perpetual peace is that 'rightful government' in any one state is jeopardised by threats from other states. As Reiss maintains, right 'cannot prevail among men within a state if their freedom is threatened by the action of other states'. Indeed, the 'law can prevail only if the rule of law prevails in all states and in international relations' (Reiss 1997a, 33).

With the idea of working towards an international federation of peaceful republics in mind, it perhaps strikes the reader as odd that Habermas should make the judgment that 'Kant was satisfied with a purely negative conception of peace' (Habermas 1997, 133). However, the assessment makes sense in the light of Habermas's much more muscular sense of cosmopolitanism. Habermas calls for consensus in three areas – 'a historical consciousness shared by all members concerning the nonsimultaneity of the societies simultaneously related by peaceful coexistence; a normative agreement concerning human rights, the interpretation of which remains disputed between the Europeans and the Asians and Africans; and a shared understanding concerning the meaning of the goal of peace' (Habermas 1997, 132–3).

Kant's prioritisation of peace over any other aim, such as the eradication of poverty, the end of slavery, or equality in gender relations (as proposed by Mary Wollstonecraft at around this time), indicates both the conservative element in Kant's political viewpoint and the extent to which his framework for thinking about politics is dominated by the importance of international relations.

Kant has a distinctive teleological view of history that is very important for his political theory and theory of sovereignty. Indeed, Franceschet uses Kant's theory of history to argue to good effect that it 'serves to bridge the sharp chasms between nature and moral freedom that he first posits', by showing that for Kant moral principles are not only regulative ideals but also have a material basis. Franceschet argues that the 'material principle of enlightenment is, most generally, that reason is promoted and advanced in the political world' (Franceschet 2002, 39). Whether or not this claim can be sustained, Kant does outline a story of progress proceeding from the 'unsocial sociability' of individuals, that is, their incapacity and yet need for coexistence with others. For Kant moreover, as Reiss puts it, 'the purpose of nature is to realise man's essence', that is his reason, and to 'advance the spread of rationality is a moral obligation' (Reiss 1997a, 36, 37). As well as his idea of international reform working through the intentional agency of sovereign states, Kant puts forward the view that, in terms of politics, the historical process can itself work towards the instantiation of the moral character of man in legal arrangements, in a republican constitution, and in a confederation of such states. Kant argues in *Theory and Practice* that 'since the human race is constantly progressing in cultural matters (in keeping with its natural purpose), it is also engaged in progressive improvement in relation to the moral end of its existence'. He is adamant that '[t]his progress may at times be interrupted but never broken off' (Kant 1997, 88). Progress is delivered initially through war (Kant 1997, 47), trade and culture, and potentially to the end of international law.

The third of Kant's key concepts is the complex notion of publicity, whose limit is the denial of a right of resistance. One important meaning of publicity for Kant is that all laws must be public laws, all citizens are equal under the law, and justice arises from the public character of laws. The origin of this view is the universal character of reason and its outcomes, for Kant. As he says in *Theory and Practice*, 'a public law which defines for everyone that which is permitted and prohibited by right, is the act of a public will, from which all right proceeds and which must not therefore itself be able to do an injustice to any one' (Kant 1997, 77). Another, not unrelated, meaning derives from the great emphasis Kant puts on the idea of enlightenment, which he defines as the courage to use your own reason. He argues for the desirability of freedom of thought as the essential prerequisite of a fully enlightened age. Kant is aware, however, that there are dangers in a blanket encouragement of independence of thought in a people used to close guardianship. Sudden access to freedom may result only in the embracing of a new range of prejudices. For Kant, private uses of reason, for instance when resulting in the disobedience of servants of the state such as government employees or soldiers, must not be allowed. Given the status accorded to legislative authority in all actual states, it is clear that Kant cannot endorse the direct contradiction of this authority through the use of private reason. All change must come from above.

However, Kant argues in *What is Enlightenment?* that private uses of reason can be distinguished from public uses, in informed public debate about political issues (Kant 1997, 55). As Reiss puts is (1997a 32), obedience does not have to mean silence. Scholarly, rational public debate is essential to the possibility of enlightenment in a way that civil disobedience is not, because the former can influence the government to reform existing legislation more into accord with the principles of right. Kant contends that the example of an enlightened head of state such as Frederick the Great shows that 'there is no danger even to his legislation if he allows his subjects to make public use of their own reason and to put before the public their thoughts on better ways of drawing up laws, even if this entails forthright criticism of the current legislation' (Kant 1997, 59). Kant's principle of publicity therefore implies a notion of tolerance – that all views which tolerate other views should be allowed a public hearing, that all views which do not attempt to subvert the constitution should be open to informed and rational public debate. It also follows for Kant that a republican constitution should guarantee the right to criticise in public, so long as that criticism is not designed to overthrow the constitution (Reiss 1997a, 32).

We can observe here two clear signs of Kant's Enlightenment optimism about a progressive rationality. Kant assumes that the principles of right do become progressively more enunciated over time (although states can also regress), and in *Perpetual Peace* that philosophers know best. Despite the intellectual status given to philosophers, however, Kant then argues that philosophers should not become kings because 'the possession of power inevitably corrupts the free judgment of reason' (Kant 1997, 115). His reasoning is that political judgment is a kind of reflective judgment and can only be genuinely exercised when uncontaminated by empirical interest. Thus the influence of the public use of reason is always dependent on the attitude of the sovereign. A second political role for the philosopher's judgment lies in keeping the ends of reason before the eyes of the public (for instance by interpreting events in history through the progressive morals that can be drawn from them) and thereby inspiring people to the possibility of their fulfilment.

We noted above Kant's view that citizens in revolution would necessarily be a contradiction. He advances a related argument when, because of his reliance on the idea of the primacy of law, Kant is adamant that no right of resistance, rebellion or revolution can exist. In a line of argument articulated in *Theory and Practice,* and spelling out the consequences of his notion of sovereignty as absolute, Kant maintains that a constitution setting up conditions under which citizens could rightfully rebel and depose the sovereign, would thereby set up a second sovereign. This confusion would then require a third sovereign to arbitrate, all of which is an absurd upset to the system of laws which the sovereign safeguards (Kant 1997, 84). Indeed, says Kant, the execution of a monarch, as in the cases of Charles I and Louis XVI, 'is an act of suicide by the state'. For such an act 'amounts to making the people, who owe their existence purely to the legislation of the sovereign, into rulers over the sovereign, thereby brazenly adopting violence as a deliberate principle and exalting it above the most sacred canons of right' (Kant 1997, 146).

Holtman regards Kant's prohibition on rebellion as quite distinct from that of Hobbes's, despite their initial similarity. She argues that for Hobbes, 'revolution is a threat to stability because it risks undermining the peace that only the state can secure' (Holtman 2002, 222). For Kant, however, most importantly 'we require the state in order to honour moral equality'. Holtman contends that since 'the demands of justice are inevitably underdetermined', because many significant disputes cannot be resolved by argument alone, it follows for Kant that 'we need some designated authority to settle on one just option' (Holtman 2002, 225). The state has a much more explicitly moral purpose for Kant than it did for Hobbes.

How does Kant's enthusiasm for the American Revolution and the French Revolution square with his denial of any right of resistance or revolution? On the one hand those events constituted, as Reiss puts it 'an open break with the political past', with which Kant did not sympathise. Kant's conservative disposition and his argument that rebelling against legitimate law was tantamount to rebelling against oneself, conflicted with the revolutionaries' Enlightenment belief in reconstructing political institutions on a rational basis. His scepticism about authority, as far as political arrangements were concerned, was not unlimited. But on the other hand the attraction of those events to Kant was that their proponents had appealed to 'a secular natural order and to the political rights of individuals' (Reiss 1997a, 4), as well as to a notion of progress — all principles in line with Kant's thinking. While Kant held that legal government could not legitimately be challenged, he also held that if a revolution takes place, then citizens are morally required to obey the new legal order. Kant may also have approved of the American Revolution on the grounds that the British colonial government had been despotic. He argued controversially, as well, that in the French case there was not, strictly speaking, a revolution for the king renounced his power to the Estates General. Moreover, Kant's view of the French Revolution was that, whatever illegal acts and atrocities were committed, the reflection by philosophers upon it had led to a valuable elucidation of the principles of enlightenment. Kant's enthusiasm for events in America and France may also have been due to a perception on his part of the limits to the revolutionary character of those events. As Reiss points out, the American revolution 'was essentially a revolution of landowners' and the French revolution was 'a revolution of the bourgeoisie' (Reiss 1997a, 27).

Law is the next key concept in Kant's theory of sovereignty and its immense importance in Kant's politics is described by Reiss in that, for Kant 'a theory of politics ... amounts in the main to a metaphysics of law' as 'part of a metaphysics of morality' (Reiss 1997a, 20). The *a priori* principles of reason for law set out the necessary hypotheses and universal framework within which politics ought to be conducted. Moreover, whereas morality is concerned with subjective motives, law inhabits the world of 'objective facts'. The value of law is, in part, that while '[m]oral actions can thus only be commanded; legal actions ... can be enforced' (Reiss 1997a 21), thus bridging the realms of moral theory and political practice. Reiss reinforces that the principles of politics are, for Kant, 'substantially the principles of right (*Recht*)'. The role of the philosophical enquiry into politics must, therefore, 'establish which political actions are just or unjust'. Justice, however, must 'be universal, but only law can bring it about'. It follows for Kant that, in a strong sense, a 'coherent political order must then be a legal order'. The logic for Kant is that, just as in ethics, 'actions ought to be based on maxims capable of being formulated as universal laws, so in politics political arrangements ought to be organised according to universally valid laws'. It is in this sense, then, as Reiss sums up, that 'Kant's principles of politics are normative. They are applications of principles of right to experience' (Reiss 1997a, 21).

With respect to law, Kant presents himself with a paradox—man's freedom can be safeguarded only by his submitting to coercion (for law presupposes coercion), and thus to an infringement of the individual's freedom. Kant wants to overcome this paradox through a notion of 'legitimate law'. According to legitimate law, we submit only to coercion that is legally exercised, on the basis of public law given by the sovereign authority. As Reiss notes, if 'coercion is exercised according to a universal principle, it is law ... Legality is therefore the decisive principle in the sphere of politics' (Reiss 1997a, 21-2). Kant's sovereign is therefore not above the law as Hobbes's was. The universal law of reason encompasses the sovereign as well as citizens. A comparison with Rousseau is also prompted here. For Rousseau the general will expresses the unity, the sovereignty of the people. While the general will can be misguided, it is the only possible basis for general laws, upon which government depends in order to administer and execute those laws. For Kant, in contrast, the universal law of reason, which is behind the act of social contract that establishes sovereignty, is therefore one step of abstraction removed from Rousseau's notion of the general will.

A fundamental feature of sovereignty for Kant is a respect for law. Sovereignty rests with the agent that has sole (and therefore absolute) legislative power, and the sovereign safeguards the operation of the system of law. In reflecting upon the activity of politics, Kant is caught between an abstract principle that must condemn all actual practices as inadequate, and the defence of the actual status quo on the faith that it instantiates the moral law. As already mentioned, his conception of sovereignty is crucial in his attempt to resolve the tension between the two, but is also decisive in demonstrating this tension. That is, in his notion of sovereignty, Kant attempts to provide the locus of the abstract principle of right and law, and the location of actual sovereigns who deserve to be acknowledged as legitimate.

Law is fundamental to Kant's notion of sovereignty but, moving on to the last of the key concepts in his theory of sovereignty, the idea of representation is also very important, though in a sense which is different from twenty-first century terms. The representative relationship between citizens and sovereign is central to the meaning of sovereignty for Kant, because it offers the conditions for individual freedom in a way that, for instance, a global state could not do. Kant does not believe in direct democracy but for the right of citizens (at least those who are economically independent, thus excepting women, servants, employees, criminals and the insane) to participate in government indirectly, through electing representatives to an assembly where rational debate can take place. At a deeper level Kant argues, in effect, that authority is granted in a one-way non-reversible process, from the people to their sovereign representative, who makes law and sets up a juridical relationship that cannot be challenged. For Kant, like Hobbes, this is the basis of the absolute nature of sovereignty. The value Kant places on the idea of representation is found in that he argues strongly that any form of government that 'is not representative is essentially an anomaly', on the grounds that 'one and the same person cannot at the same time be both the legislator and the executor of his own will' (Kant 1997, 191). According to Kant, the 'head of state (the sovereign) is only an abstraction (representing the entire people) so long as there is no physical person to represent the highest power in the state and to make this idea influence the will of the people' (Kant 1997, 161). Again he says, '[a]ny true republic ... is and cannot be anything other than a representative system of the people whereby the people's rights are looked after on their behalf by deputies who represent the united will of the citizens'. However, he holds that 'as soon as a head of state in person (whether this head of state be a king, a nobility, or the whole populace as a democratic association) also allows himself to be represented, the united people then does not merely represent the sovereign, but actually is the sovereign itself' (Kant 1997, 161).

Kant's argument here rests on the view that 'the supreme power originally rests with the people, and all the rights of individuals as mere subjects ... must be derived from this supreme power'. It follows, for Kant, and here we see Kant's crucial difference from the right of resistance given by Locke, that '[o]nce it has been established, the republic will therefore no longer need to release the reins of government from its own hands and to give them back to those who previously held them, for they then destroy all the new institutions again by their absolute and arbitrary will' (Kant 1997, 163). Kant reinforces in the appendix to the *Metaphysics of Morals* that 'even if the organisation of a state should be faulty by itself, no subordinate authority in it may actively resist its legislative supreme authority; the defects attached to it must instead by gradually removed by reforms the state itself carries out' (Kant 1999, 505). He goes on that to 'permit any resistance to this absolute power ... would be self-contradictory' (Kant 1999, 506). In this way, the idea of popular sovereignty plays a very small role in Kant's theory. Kant's philosophical position, that both individual freedom and that of states is best defended through a 'metaphysics of morals' and so through the principles of right and law, thus dovetails with his political preference for a narrow and limited role for representation and popular sovereignty. Furthermore, Kant contends, '[t]he right of the supreme legislation in the commonwealth is not alienable ... Whoever possesses it can only exercise control over the people through the people's collective will, but not over the collective will itself, the original foundation of all public contracts' (Kant 1997, 164).

For Kant, republican government has the opportunity to be 'rightful government', organised around a workable civil constitution. Republican government (grounded in a separation of powers) is counterposed by Kant in *Perpetual Peace* to despotic rule, and this distinction between forms of government is different from that between the three possible forms of sovereignty (monarchic, aristocratic, and democratic). Forms of government is thus quite distinct from 'the different persons who exercise supreme authority' (Kant 1997, 100-1). Kant is here seeing two things as unconnected in a way that is quite foreign to our approach to politics. In *Perpetual Peace*, moreover, Kant holds that democracy 'is necessarily a despotism', on the grounds that it 'establishes an executive power through which all the citizens may make decisions about (and indeed against) the single individual without his consent, so that decisions are made by all the people and yet not by all the people'. Kant's logic is that 'this means that the general will is in contradiction with itself, and thus also with freedom' (Kant 1997, 101). While Kant was never a populist, as Reiss notes, he holds that representatives are less likely to be swayed (than are the people as a whole) by 'demagogy, empty rhetoric and zealotry, let alone fanaticism, all of which Kant abhorred as the rule of unreason' (Reiss 1997b, 260).

This process of representation therefore makes sense, at least to some extent, of the rather confusing way in which Kant in different places refers to sovereignty as the abstract unity of the people, and as the actual legislative agent. That is, Kant sometimes identifies sovereignty as the 'universal sovereign (who, if considered in the light of laws of freedom, can be none other than the united people itself)' (Kant 1997, 140). At other times he sees sovereignty as the primary, legislative branch of power, 'the ruling power (or sovereignty) ... the person of the legislator' (Kant 1997, 138). In the *Critique of Practical Reason* Kant regards morality as that which 'gives authority and absolute sovereignty to the law' (quoted in Franceschet 2002, 37). He also refers to 'the sovereignty of the people (the legislator)' (Kant 1997, 141). A further consequence of this dual usage is that when Kant discusses the confusion between competing sovereigns that would result from an authorised right of resistance (Kant 1997, 145), it is again clear that he holds a conception of popular sovereignty of only the most abstract and tenuous kind. Here he regards the legislator's law-making powers as the crucial and inviolate mark of sovereignty. Kant's dual usage in some ways recalls Locke's similar ambiguity, and the liberal solution — of distinguishing between the residual constitutive power of the people and ordinary, legislative, power — offers a way of presenting both theories as coherent.

Kersting helps to clarify the attenuated popular sovereignty in Kant's theory by pointing to the severely qualified role played by the social contract in his political theory. For Kant the social contract can operate only as an idea and only to trigger the implementation of right, with the establishment of an ethical politics and the juridical state. Moreover, as Kersting notes, the 'application of the norm of a contract requires nothing more than a thought-experiment that is a variant of the test of universalizability' (Kersting 1992, 355). The voluntaristic element of social contract that is found in Hobbes, Locke and Rousseau, has no place in Kant's thinking because he cannot allow that any other motives — consequentalist, prudential, utilitarian, or self-interested — other than the deontological one can play a role in a politics governed by right, in 'the form of the rational state' (Kersting 1992, 354). The tenuous nature of popular sovereignty for Kant is not substantially improved by his argument that, as Kersting puts it, every actual 'legislator is bound by the contract of rational right: He must consider himself to be and behave as a representative of the subject of the contract, the universally united will of all'. To support this view, Kersting cites Kant's line of reasoning in *Theory and Practice* that the legislator 'must give his law as if it *could* have arisen from the united will of an entire people' (Kersting 1992, 355).

Reiss makes two interesting, related, observations about Kant's interest in sovereignty. He notes that the 'problem of sovereignty ... greatly occupied Kant; for he reverts to it again and again in his unpublished notes'. At the same time his consideration of sovereignty does register ambiguity and contradiction, and does indicate someone 'wrestling with a problem' that 'he had not solved entirely'. On the one hand Kant was clear that sovereignty 'originates with the people which ought to possess legislative power'. He also held that 'a monarch could possess it as a representative of the people in a derivative form'. But on the other hand Kant 'appears convinced that if the monarch is to exercise this power together with executive powers, his rule is despotic' (Reiss 1997a, 24–5).

However, having considered the key concepts for Kant's theory of sovereignty — right, international relations, publicity, law, and representation — the shape of Kant's conception of sovereignty, including its ambiguities, can be discerned. It is clear that the meaning of sovereignty for Kant resides in an abstract perspective, but it originates ultimately in the people who ought to possess (if only notionally and if only to grant to representatives) legislative power. In practice, and leaving open an interesting indeterminacy, sovereignty rests with whoever acts as the agent exercising the legislative power. In this way, a monarch could legitimately possess sovereignty as a representative of the people in a derivative form, so long as the monarch was not also the ruler, the executive. It is also the sovereign's moral duty to promulgate laws that are just and to introduce constitutional reforms so that a republican constitution is maintained. But this is a moral rather than a legal duty and citizens cannot resist or punish a sovereign who fails to follow up the duty. It is also an important feature of all the key concepts involved in Kant's theory of sovereignty with the exception of right, that Kant seeks to combine but more properly vacillates between positing the 'a priori necessity for an absolute sovereign agent that is beyond questioning' (Franceschet 2002, 46), and recognising a role for the agency of individuals, citizens, and an agent above sovereign states.

The key general features of sovereignty that are found in Kant are its moral character, the agency of the state as the locus of sovereignty, and the derivation of the external from the internal form. For Kant there is the potential to bring politics and international relations under the rule of morality and law. What this means depends in part, as we have seen, on the politics of interpretation of Kant's texts. This part of the chapter, in focusing on sovereignty, has given important weight to *The Metaphysics of Morals* and other texts, and not just to *Perpetual Peace*. Indeed, it needs to be remembered that Kant's commitment to the state as the locus of sovereignty takes place in the context provided by what Franceschet calls 'the sovereignty of the moral law' (Franceschet 2002, 10). Political action 'cannot have its own autonomous logic' as Machiavelli held, but 'must be subordinated to the requirements of morality' (Franceschet 2002, 12). The importance of the state is shown in the unconditional statement Kant makes in *Perpetual Peace* that 'states as such are not subject to a common external constraint' (Kant 1997, 103). The power to declare war and make peace is an urgent concern for Kant, as is the role of the sovereign in instituting political arrangements governed by right rather than by force, interest, expediency, or utilitarian motives. Franceschet underlines the importance of sovereignty — in the important sense of the moral and political agency of states — in Kant's thinking when he notes that 'sovereignty is the key mechanism of political reform' for Kant. It represents the means by which 'politics can be domesticated to approximate the formal principles of morality' (Franceschet 2002, 43). The derivation of external sovereignty from the internal form is the third key feature. For Franceschet it is precisely here that Kant's theory falters, on the grounds that the very need for 'international reform is a product of the problematic role that sovereignty plays within realising justice', for Kant (Franceschet 2002, 43). Thus, while sovereignty is 'a necessary cause of justice', it also presents Kant with 'a profound set of moral difficulties' and is a 'major cause of injustice' (Franceschet 2002, 43).

In assessing the strengths of Kant's system, it is clear that the strong moral framework that it sets out for political action can look attractive, and that its incrementalism — aiming towards peace and harmony in world politics in a gradualist manner — can look appealing. At least on Kersting's reading, Kant's deduction that politics takes places against the ideal of the 'rightful' state, is supplemented by a 'philosophy of compromise and reform' (Kersting 1992, 359). Kant's highlighting of the value of publicity and republicanism in politics can also be regarded as a strength. It opens up a space for politics as contestation and reasoned debate in a spirit of citizen participation, and reinforces Kant's fundamental belief that political issues should not be settled by force.

In addition, while many commentators regard Kant as setting up a gap between theory and practice that cannot be bridged in his system, Ellis makes a case for a distinction in Kant's work between provisional and conclusive right, as a means of overcoming contradictions in his work. Provisional right 'always leave[s] open the possibility of entering into a rightful condition' (Ellis 2005, 144). She highlights, for instance, Kant's view of property rights acquired before the civil condition has been established as requiring provisional respect, even though the ideal would call for the dissolution of all property rights at this point (Ellis 2005, 92). Ellis argues that the same logic applies for Kant at the international level, and that this 'provisional system includes the so-called right of nations ... the concept of sovereignty, which though it can be understood broadly as a people's right to determine the actions of their state independent of foreign interference, is perhaps best measured by and most widely understood to mean independence in the decision to go to war' (Ellis 2005, 93).

The major weakness of Kant's system is that it universalises from a culturally-specific set of preferences about reason, the individual, freedom and autonomy, and politics as a form of ethics, and does not recognise that there are substantial drawbacks in doing so. The history of Western colonialism and imperial power that developed on this basis, while not attributable to Kant (and indeed Kant censures European states for their treatment of other peoples (Wood 1999, xxix)), can be seen to have rendered many peoples in a condition of subjection. Kersting also picks up on another weakness when he makes the point that, while Kant's abstract and universalising political theory can be a force for self-empowerment, these qualities also indicate how it can discriminate against the needy. Kersting observes that Kant's concept of right concerns only 'the external sphere of the freedom of action', the internal sphere being that of morality. This means that only the 'effects of actions on the freedom of action of others are of interest to it'. Thus, inner 'intentions and convictions are excluded from the sphere of justice just like interests and needs'. It is only the 'formal compatibility of the external freedom of one person with that of others' that is important to Kant's notion of right. The consequence of Kant's reasoning is that 'no claims of right can arise from one's neediness. Right does not help powerless needs'. It follows that for Kant, 'a community of right is not a community of solidarity among the needy, but a community for self-protection among those who have the power to act' (Kersting 1992, 345). The sense of 'a community of solidarity' as a necessary dimension of politics, is alien to Kant's thinking.

Another weakness is that the highly abstract and formal injunctions of moral law, given the gulf between morality and the messy and contingent world of politics, cannot necessarily tell us very much about how to operate in political practice. Kant's theory cannot easily bridge the gap between those very general prescriptions and the political world of competing claims, entrenched inequalities and cultural differences, any more than can subsequent theories based on his approach, for instance by Habermas and Rawls. Relatedly, Kant is not necessarily convincing in his belief in the power of moral principle and precept by themselves to persuade people to subordinate other motives. Franceschet identifies how Kant's solution to Machiavelli's separation of politics and ethics, was to 'do much the same thing', to set out a 'depiction of subjectivity [that] separates (the pure, unconditioned realm of) morality and (the corrupted, conditioned realm of) politics' (Franceschet 2002, 10). Similarly, the progressive potential of Kant's theory is limited as well as enhanced by its debt to a strong philosophical framing. Kersting notes that 'the principle of right [can] make every politically inequitable distribution of freedom recognizable as not right'. However, if one seeks to discover from the principle of right itself 'how the domain of mutually compatible individual spheres of freedom is to be determined *a priori*, then Kant's principle is an unclear criterion' (Kersting 1992, 346).

As a conception of sovereignty the major and important strength of Kant's theory is that it pinpoints why the 'domestic analogy' cannot stand. Kant identifies sovereignty as the concept that prevents relations within a polity simply being mapped onto relations between states, and identifies international relations as a distinctive realm. Other strengths of Kant's

construction are that it focuses on the *Rechtstaat* and explicitly sees inter-
personal relations as mediated through impartial law. As Franceschet puts
it, Kant's theory of sovereignty is 'an attempt to reconcile politics with
what he views as the only plausibly solid ground of the modern subject: an
autonomous morality' (Franceschet 2002, 6). Also, on the reading of Kant
preferred here, it is a strength that it is by the terms of *sovereignty* that, for
Kant, on the one hand domestic interests are solidly prioritised over international ones, and on the other that relations between states should be
based on a commitment to peace and to a confederation of peaceful
republics.

The primary weakness is that, as Franceschet argues, Kant's conception
of sovereignty is strongly implicated in his 'quest to domesticate politics
through formal principles derived from morality' (Franceschet 2002, 7).
The scope of politics is heavily qualified, for Kant. Moreover, the absolute
separation Kant draws between knowledge from abstract and trans-historical principles of reason and knowledge from empirical inquiry, and
the priority of the first over the second, issues in a severely truncated
notion of popular sovereignty, an overly-trusting view of the value of law,
and no effective means of resistance to tyrannical government. Another
repercussion of this separation, this 'peculiarly Kantian alienation of politics and ethics' (Franceschet 2002, 10), is that it has given a licence to a subsequent mode of liberal theorising that concentrates on lofty prescriptions
which fail to engage sufficiently with power and with actual inequalities
in class, gender, ethnicity, and with indigenous populations, a point
recognised and analysed well by Tully (2002). While Reiss defends Kant's
view, holding that for Kant, '[p]ower cannot be ignored, but the real problem of politics is to ensure right, that is law and justice' (Reiss 1997a, 39),
the tradition that has developed from Kant has tended to focus on the latter and overlook the former. Franceschet goes so far as to argue that it is a
failing of Kant's theory of sovereignty that it is 'fundamentally dualistic
because of the bifurcated structure upon which justice depends'—caught
between 'a "dogmatic" and *a priori* formal justification' and attempts to
reform political practice (Franceschet 2002, 44).

A further weakness of Kant's conception of sovereignty is that, by
extrapolating from the domestic to the international sphere, Kant does not
adequately address the differences between the two spheres and politics
in them, and so licences a naïve and moralistic cosmopolitanism. The idea
of constructing a principled confederation of like-minded peaceful republics that acts as a moral rather than political force for peace, and does so
without coercion, is so unrealistic that it is problematic even as an aspiration. The superiority that such a confederation would obviously have in
economic and political, let alone military, resources (given the Western
character of Kant's thinking and location), together with the dominant

position in terms of international power politics that such a confederation would gain, militate against the operation of the purely moral purpose that is Kant's stated motive for such an alliance. Such a confederation would also automatically create an 'other' of states unwilling, for whatever reason, to join it. Kant's attempt to pacify the anarchy of the international realm by the imposition of moral principles is unsuccessful because it underrates the importance of political and power considerations.

HEGEL

Hegel was born in 1770 and died in 1831 of cholera. He grew up in the Duchy of Wurtemberg, one of the most constitutional of the German states, where his father was a civil servant. He took a great interest in politics, public administration, and political developments in the German states and elsewhere in Europe throughout his life, and was fascinated by the figure of Napoleon. In the late eighteenth century the extent of the fragmentation of the German states under the Holy Roman Empire meant that there were, as Plant notes, 'some 300 separate territories ... with badly defined boundaries and without clearly delineated areas of authority ... virtually sovereign states...each pursuing its own particular and isolated interests ... with no real political centre of gravity' (Plant 1973, 25). Napoleon made Hegel's home state of Wurtenberg into a kingdom in 1806 (Knox 1964, 246n). According to Pelczynski the turbulent series of events, portrayed by Hegel as 'tremendous political experiments' and 'colossal spectacles', of the French Revolution and its aftermath 'dominated Hegel's formative years'. In the *Phenomenology* Hegel criticised the French Revolution as an abstract and thus destructive force of freedom. Hegel witnessed 'the destruction of the *ancient regime*, the restoration and the second overthrow of the Bourbons; the foundation of the Republic and its degeneration into the Terror; the rise, apogee, and fall of Napoleon; the collapse and reconstruction of Prussia; the death of the Holy Roman Empire and the German Nation' (Pelczynski 1964, 9), and the Congress of Vienna.

Hegel's first published work (1798) was a commentary in a political booklet, remonstrating against the oligarchy of the Swiss canton of Berne for its treatment of the area of Vaud, and championing constitutional government. This was quickly followed by an examination of the inadequacy of the constitution of Wurtemberg and the urgent need for political reform, and a critique in the light of political reconstruction in western Europe of the constitution of the crumbling German Empire. Further examples of political writing included a long article in 1817 commenting on the turbulent proceedings of the Diet of Wurtemberg, and an essay in 1831 critical of the English Reform Bill.

In later years Hegel 'enjoyed the confidence' (Pelczynski 1964, 6) of one of the Prussian reforming ministers, but on the whole kept away from direct involvement in politics himself. Pelczynski describes the importance of German, French and British Enlightenment writings to Hegel, but also Hegel's debt to Ancient Greek and Roman authors. He notes that the 'concept of the state as an integral part of the ethical life of a people Hegel owes to the classical studies of his youth, as to some extent he does his belief in government by an intellectual elite or politics as education' (Pelczynski 1964, 8).

Whereas Kant turned to political matters only after explicating his philosophical system, Hegel exhibited a keen interest in politics and political and constitutional reform from early on. However, Hegel's *Philosophy of Right* of 1821, in which he outlines his theory of politics, follows in the tradition of Kant in examining politics through the lense of philosophical principle (although see Tunick (1992, 5–12) for the debate on the role of self-censureship in accounting for the differences between the *Philosophy of Right* and the lecture notes). His approach to politics takes as its starting-point that which is least concrete and most abstract. Hegel's political thought also owes much to Kant in working outward from what is significant about the individual person to what can be said about the possibility of an ethical politics. Both Kant and Hegel are systematic in the philosophical sense, in that there is a necessary line of logical development in the argument. Hegel is also indebted to Kant in seeing human freedom in moral terms as the exercise of the will in conformity with reason. There are also many differences between Kant's and Hegel's political theories, not the least of which are that Kant's abstraction is more abstract than Hegel's since the latter's contained a profound understanding of human reason as embedded in history and concrete social practices, and that Hegel's is a closely-argued theory in a single coherent text while Kant's is reconstructed from a set of different writings. Furthermore, while Hegel's thinking on politics follows in the Kantian tradition in being self-consciously regarded as part of a metaphysics of ethics, Hegel's political writings are shot through with that metaphysical edifice in a way that Kant's were not.

What is distinctive about Hegel's conception of sovereignty is the centrality of the state and the consistency between the role of the state in internal and external sovereignty, a consistency underpinned by a strong sense of groundedness in community. It is on this basis, moreover, that Hegel notably challenges liberal tenets, including the mechanism of the social contract, the natural rights tradition, and mechanistic relations between people. For Hegel individuals are not pre-formed but are in an important sense moulded by sovereignty. Also striking is Hegel's conception of sovereignty as uniquely expressing the 'whole' of the political community as an ethical substance, and his articulation of that abstract 'whole' in the concrete figure of the monarch.

The key concepts in Hegel's idea of sovereignty are the state, the constitution, the Crown, sovereignty at home, sovereignty in relation to foreign states, and war. The meaning of these concepts is framed by Hegel's specific understandings of the terms 'rational' and *Recht* (right or law). Pelczynski argues that Hegel's phrase, 'What is rational is actual and what is actual is rational', was intended to 'differentiate his political philosophy from the traditional *a priori* approach of his ... predecessors like ... Kant'. Rather than offering an ideal or utopia, Hegel sought to 'make men understand the ethical world to which they belonged' (Pelczynski 1964, 113). 'Actuality' referred to 'the whole complex of beliefs and ideals embodied in conventional religion and morality, social customs and institutions, as well as civil laws and political arrangements'. Reason for Hegel was 'concrete', and was distinguished from understanding — analytical reflection on general categories that was independent of empirical features. For example, for the understanding monarchy meant 'rule by one man', whereas 'the rational concept of "monarchy" means the form of government typical of early nineteenth-century Western Europe, ie constitutional monarchy with representative institutions, local autonomy, civil equality, etc' (Pelczynski 1964, 114). The convergence of the actual and the rational also means for Hegel that reason and sociality are inherently mediated. Truth is found in the whole and the meaning of the parts is enriched by their place in the whole. To align reason and sociality is the task of self-consciousness, and politics and the constitution are the practical expression of the mediation between them.

At the same time, however, the convergence of the rational and the actual did not lead Hegel into an unthinking conservatism, underwriting the status quo. Here the role of the philosopher is vital. As Pelczynski describes, for Hegel, if 'serfdom, slavery, and "the subjection of women", have been accepted in a society for centuries, the ordinary folk tend to see nothing wrong in them'. But they are not rational concepts, and the philosopher 'may more easily perceive that they are basically incompatible with the ideals of equality or freedom which the society professes and which pervade all the other aspects of ethical life'. Indeed, neither history nor utility are, for Hegel, strong grounds on which to justify old institutions (Pelczynski 1964, 115).

Hegel distinguishes between formal and material positive right or law (*Recht*). Knox notes that, for Hegel, *Recht* refers to 'not only civil law, but also morality, ethical life, and world history' (Knox 1967, vi). A law is positive in the formal sense by its authority within a particular legal system, but is positive in content, or materially, when it refers or applies to specific features of a particular country or through particular court judgments. The core of a positive system of law, as Pelczynski puts it, 'consists of rational, universally valid principles of justice', and it is the sign of a civilised country that law is codified with this rational character and is not simply customary or governed by the sentiment or interest of a ruling group. For Hegel it is crucial that law should be guided by clear and open principle rather than by vague, ambiguous, or implicit convention. A clearly-organised and well-formulated legal system that is transparent to the public is one of the greatest benefits a ruler can bestow, and reforming the positive law also has the advantage of resulting in greater fairness by disclosing 'outdated privileges, legal discriminations, and other irrationalities' (Pelczynski 1964, 116).

The *Philosophy of Right* is structured in three parts. The first part, entitled 'Abstract Right' concerns individuals as they interact with the outside world through the exercise of their will, freedom and right. The major ways in which this interaction takes place, according to Hegel, are through property, through contract, and through crime and punishment. The second part of the book introduces particularity and particular interests and explores the notion of morality in a social context. The third part, the real focus of the text, is entitled 'Ethical Life' and examines three ascending spheres of ethical life, in the family, in civil society and in the state, under the principle of universality. The character of civil society, an aspect of the distinctively modern state, allows individuals to pursue three aims with a degree of autonomy. As Pelczynski sums up, this realm 'secures its citizens an area of independent activity', and 'enables them to pursue subjective ends and seek happiness as they see it'. It also 'gives them the opportunity of the ethical, intellectual, and practical training which they need in order to be members of the state' (Pelczynski 1964, 120). Civil society contains three kinds of institution—courts of law, the police in the broad sense of all kinds of regulating authorities, and corporations (including municipal and religious bodies as well as trade and professional associations).

However, it is only in the highest of the three spheres of ethical life, the state, according to Hegel, that the individual can have not only the experience of natural relationships in the family, and can exercise self-interest in the competitive world of civil society, but can also identify with the common good of all citizens together. One of the meanings, for Hegel, of the state as the focus of ethical life lies in his metaphysical categories, aligning the expressiveness of political life with spirituality. As Houlgate observes, a rational state for Hegel is one that fosters the 'sense of freedom in its citizens and which so ensures that the rights which it enshrines in law are also laid claim to by the people themselves' (Houlgate 1991, 89). Another meaning rests in Hegel's search, as Dickey notes (1999 xiv), to delineate a form of state between 'machine states' of which Prussian absolutism was a contemporary example and the violent freedom expressed in the French Revolution. However the state had other meanings for Hegel too. For instance, patriotism is due towards the state, not on the basis of shared communal blood, history or glory, but on the pragmatic grounds that the state maintains the framework within which we can all pursue our own self-interest (Hegel 1967, 189). Likewise, Heiman points to one of the ways that Hegel cashes out his notion of the 'universality of the state'. He notes that this 'is attained by the individual not by virtue of his being a singular *per se*, but ... by this very individual's involvement in corporate and group affairs and thereby becoming legally and politically identifiable' (Heiman 1971, 129). This line of argument by Hegel cuts short an interpretation that seeks to see his state as monolithic. As Heiman registers, Hegel's 'state enters the field not as an absolute power but as the legal authority which maintains the orderly relationship between its constituent groups'. Such a state 'cannot act tyrannically against them, for its power depends upon the recognition by these diverse elements that their interests are protected by it' (Heiman 1971, 129).

Tunick remarks (1992, 94) that, in an earlier work Hegel defined the state as 'the society of people legally related in which each counts as a person; the immediate concern of the state is not to promote morality, religion or welfare, but to guarantee and actualize formal or abstract rights to person and property'. It was only in the *Philosophy of Right* that Hegel conceptualised the state as a normative 'ethical substance that is more than a mere collection of legally respected persons, and as the bearer of a right that is understood in a much broader sense than abstract Roman-law rights of personality', a 'whole'. Tunick also points to evidence that these two uses of the term 'state' reflected an ambiguity about the word in Hegel's day. The word 'state' was 'used often as a metaphor for a machine, or something external; but some used it as a moral concept of value' (Tunick 1992, 94). It is clear though, that in the *Philosophy of Right* Hegel is not jettisoning the first meaning for the second (although he would reject a mechanistic notion of the relations between people), for the sense of citizens as persons related juridically with each other, and of property as a concrete stake in the state expressed in representation as a legitimate 'interest', remain important to him.

Houlgate highlights another aspect of the meaning of the state for Hegel when he notes that a 'state, for Hegel, is a body of people held together by consciously willed general laws, rather than mere force or natural association'. He goes on that, in Hegel's view, states 'may be created by the forceful unification of people, but they must be sustained by some commonly acknowledged conscious purpose or identity if they are to count as true states' (Houlgate 1991, 31).

It is only in the state, the supreme public authority, says Hegel in the *Philosophy of Right*, that individuals can fully exercise and experience freedom and right and self-consciousness. The state is the highest ethical unity, grounded in the will of its members. Dickey refers to Schmitt's accurate grasp of what the ethical nature of the state meant for Hegel, namely that Hegel 'approaches the political sphere with the idea of promoting membership of a political association rather than with that of buttressing the sovereignty of the state'. Dickey notes that 'Carl Schmitt argues that, for Hegel, *Sittlichkeit* [ethical life] has less to do with abolishing individual morality for the sake of strengthening the sovereignty of the state than with creating within the political sphere an association in which citizens can think in common about the purpose and direction of public life' (Dickey 1999, xxxii). Moreover, while there is a strong parallel between the individual and the state, for Hegel, he is also keen to note the limits of that analogy. The 'welfare of the state has claims to recognition totally different from those of the welfare of the individual', he says. This is because, in contrast with the individual, the state 'has its determinate being, ie its right, directly embodied in something existent'. The being of the state is concrete where the being of the individual is abstract, with the consequence that the 'principle' of the state's 'conduct and behaviour' can only be this concrete content. The point of this distinction between individual and state, for Hegel, is that while the claim that politics should be subordinated to morality was at one time 'much canvassed', this concrete content of the state raises the status of politics as the appropriate form of activity in relation to states (Hegel 1967, 215).

It is in the third part of the *Philosophy of Right* that Hegel outlines his view of sovereignty, and he regards it as having two 'sides' (Hegel 1967, 180). He explicitly discusses the concept in two places. He considers the notion of 'sovereignty at home', or internal sovereignty in the section on 'The Crown'. The Crown is identified as one of the three aspects of the constitution, the other two being the executive and the legislative. And Hegel considers external sovereignty in a separate section entitled 'Sovereignty vis-a-vis foreign states'. We will look at the ideas he develops in these two places, but also at the complex relationship that Hegel envisaged as operating between these two 'sides' of sovereignty.

In terms of 'sovereignty at home', Hegel's line of argument begins with the view that a 'nation does not begin by being a state' (Hegel 1967, 218). For Hegel, '[s]o long as it lacks objective law and an explicitly established rational constitution, its autonomy is formal only and is not sovereignty' (Hegel 1967, 219). He goes on by way of illustration, that '[i]t would be contrary even to commonplace ideas to call patriarchal conditions a "constitution" or a people under patriarchal government a "state" or its independence "sovereignty"' (Hegel 1967, 219). For Hegel, a sense of membership of the state, along with representation, and the people's sense of fulfilling their obligations freely, are all part of what is meant by the public interest. Political rights are in this way different from rights accruing from belonging to the family and civil society, and make sense only in the context of the state.

According to Hegel's scheme, a key institution in government is the legislature. The upper chamber contains hereditary peers (and mediates in disputes between the lower chamber and the government) and the lower chamber contains representatives of the burgher class (and mediates between the nation and the government, expressing the views and grievances of the population and educating citizens in the law and government policy). For Hegel it is important and deliberate that the lower chamber expresses a political role in terms of representation rather than in terms of direct participation. The job of the lower chamber is facilitated by the public nature of its proceedings and by the operation of the press. Hegel was opposed to universal suffrage because of the arbitrariness and contingency in government that would result from democratic rule. In the *Philosophy of History*, in his theory of progress and historical change, Hegel rejected the historical models of democracy and republicanism for modern nineteenth-century nations, on the grounds that, as Pelczynski observes, 'modern nations are too large, heterogeneous, and individualistic to guarantee the sort of spontaneous self-identification of the citizen with the state which existed in ancient Greece and republican Rome' (Pelczynski 1964, 128-9).

Given Hegel's view that the state is the highest form of political society, the constitution plays a key role, for in the constitution the state can 'realise' (put into the real world) its rationality. For Hegel the term 'constitution' covers not just the legal framework for the political society as a whole (this supreme public authority of the state), but also the branches of executive government and the rational bureaucracy of the civil service, representative assembly and the Crown, the principle of positive law, transparent codification, and the progressive intent common to modern constitutionalism. All the features of a constitution should have rational form, embodying universal principles through, as Pelczynski puts it (1964, 118) the 'deeply rooted ideals, social conditions, and established institutions' of the country. It follows for Hegel that the Crown stands for the individual 'moment', the executive for particularity, and the legislative for universality, corresponding to the three sections of the third part of the *Philosophy of Right*. The best constitution is that headed by a constitutional monarch. As Hegel puts it, '[i]t is only as a person, the monarch, that the personality of the state is actual'. His reasoning is that '[p]ersonality expresses the concept as such; but the person enshrines the actuality of the concept, and only when the concept is determined as person is it the Idea or truth'. According to Hegel, the monarch, being a real person, exemplifies the sovereignty of the state much better than any 'artificial person' (such as Hobbes constructed in the figure of the Leviathan) could do, because an artificial person 'contains personality only abstractly, as one moment of itself' (Hegel 1967, 182). In Brod's words, for Hegel, '[s]overeignty requires that all the autonomous power centres of a society converge toward a single point of public authority' (Brod 1992, 151-2).

Monarchy represents for Hegel the best form of an effective common public authority. As he had argued in his early critique on the German Empire, in Pelczynski's words (1964, 16), 'true civil and political freedom lies in such organization and not in the independence of the "estates"', that is, in representative assemblies. According to Suter, for Hegel the sovereignty of the monarchy 'meant that a single monarch was legitimate only in so far as he respected the "public freedom" of which the nation was the real holder' (Suter 1971, 64). Indeed, Hegel argues that hereditary monarchy best expresses the role it plays as solid embodiment of the state, and also avoids the problem of conflicting factions around the throne at the death of a monarch. However, as Suter highlights, Hegel's advocacy of monarchy is not based on a nostalgia for the traditional rights and privileges of feudal monarchy, but in its appropriateness or 'fit'with the 'rationality of the constitution' (Suter 1971, 64).

The power of the crown contains three elements. The first is the universality of the constitution and the laws, and it is because of this that, for instance, only the monarch as sovereign has the right to grant pardons to criminals, so 'wiping out a crime by forgiving and forgetting it (Hegel 1967, 186). The second is the advisory capacity of council (this council and above it the monarch, form the apex of the levels of the civil service that constitute the executive branch), by which the universal is related to particular issues. The third element of the power of the crown is the decision-making function (as part of the legislative branch) in which the Crown is self-determining. Hegel puts great weight on the role of the Crown in promulgating law, arguing that 'by saying "I will" makes its decision and so inaugurates all activity and actuality' (Hegel 1967, 181), in contrast with the ancient world where law was seen as coming from a divine, extra-human source. It is this independence of the Crown from other powers of decision-making that is the distinctive principle of the power of the Crown, says Hegel.

The Crown is thus both chief executive, head of state in relation to the constitution and law-making (though in stable states this amounts only to rubber stamping the decisions of lower authorities), and in charge of foreign policy. Internal sovereignty is constituted by the first and second of these elements, that is in that the Crown is the touchstone for the universality of the constitution and legal structure, and is the living embodiment of the relation of the universal to specific issues through council. Hegel expresses an important element of his theory when he contends that 'sovereignty depends on the fact that the particular functions and powers of the state are not self-subsistent ... but have their roots ultimately in the unity of the state as their single self' (Hegel 1967, 179–80).

As well as conceiving of the Crown as the concrete incarnation of sovereignty, Hegel addresses the intangibility of sovereignty – that it is an idea rather than an existing thing – and accounts for it through an analogy between the state and an animal organism. In this sense sovereignty lies in the state rather than in any of its parts (Crown, estates, civil service). Sovereignty, says Hegel, 'is the same characteristic as that in accordance with which the so-called "parts" of an animal organism are not parts but members, moments in an organic whole' (Hegel 1967, 180). In the same way, the sovereignty of the state is the idea 'of all particular authorities within it' (Hegel 1967, 180). It represents and expresses legal, constitutional government. Sovereignty 'brings it about that each of these spheres [and functions of government] is not something independent, self-subsistent in its aims and modes of working, something immersed solely in itself, but that instead, even in these aims and modes of working, each is determined by and dependent on the aim of the whole (the aim which has been denominated in general terms by the rather vague expression "welfare of the state")' (Hegel 1967, 180). Moreover, Hegel has in mind a specific sense in which the parts relate to the whole. As Pelczynski explains, for Hegel, 'the only genuine unity is not an aggregate but a syllogism, ie a unity of differences, or of extremes united by the mediation of a middle term'. In Hegel's view (and underlining the significance of the mediating role performed by the lower chamber described above), a 'constitution becomes a rational unity ... only if the Crown on the one hand and its subjects on the other are united by the Estates Assembly as a mediating organ ... between the two' (Knox 1964, 249).

Hegel's conception of the intangibility of sovereignty as an idea, and as that which expressed the 'whole' of the state, does important work in his theory of politics, not least because, as Ilting notes, Hegel's theory deliberately lacks a social contract element found in other theories of the sovereignty of the modern state. Brod confirms this when he notes that for Hegel the 'state enters world history as one state among others' (Brod 1992, 156). Ilting describes how in other modern theories of the state, 'the doctrine of the social contract occurs at the point in the structure of the argument where it must be stated who has the right of the final decision and who is the source of all political and legal authority'. He observes that '[t]his doctrine Hegel explicitly rejected, and replaced it by the idea of a historically continuous political community which the individual finds already in existence'. Ilting also identifies that at the point where 'older theories proceeded from the state of nature to "civil society" (the state), Hegel inserted his doctrine of morality as a necessary condition of the state'. The significance of this (and attention to the structure of the text bears this out) is that Hegel defers his treatment of the idea of sovereignty until he discusses the different powers of the state, rather than considering it earlier in relation to his distinction between civil society and the state (Ilting 1971, 105). For Hegel, there is a moral rather than a contractual transition (whether historical or hypothetical) from civil society to the state. The moral rather than contractual basis of this transition in the argument is crucial to Hegel's conception of the state as an 'ethical substance'.

Hegel contrasts the modern state and the specific form of unity that is expressed in its internal sovereignty with societies in feudal times which, he argues, lacked the character associated with that form. He comes to the interesting conclusion that, under feudalism, external sovereignty was a feature of relations between political communities, but that 'at home however, not only was the monarch not sovereign at all, but the state itself was not sovereign either'. Hegel offers two arguments to substantiate his view. He contends that under feudalism 'the particular functions and powers of the state and civil society were arranged ... into independent Corporations and societies, so that the state as a whole was rather an aggregate than an organism'. Moreover, he holds that 'office was the private property of individuals', such that 'what they were to do in their public capacity was left to their own opinion and caprice' (Hegel 1967, 180).

Further explicating the meaning of sovereignty, Hegel rebuts the notion that '"sovereignty" is a synonym for "despotism"'. Despotism refers to a situation in which 'law has disappeared and where the particular will ... whether of a monarch or a mob ... counts as law or rather takes the place of law'. By contrast, Hegel holds, 'it is precisely in legal, constitutional government that sovereignty is to be found as the moment of ideality—the ideality of the particular spheres and functions'. In times of peace, according to Hegel, the parts work normally. But in both domestic and foreign crises, 'the organism of which these particular spheres are members fuses into the single concept of sovereignty' (Hegel 1967, 181), and sovereignty as an idea becomes 'actualised' in real work for the sovereign authority. At times of crisis, it is up to the sovereign to seek the state's salvation.

On the question of popular sovereignty, of whether there is a popular basis for sovereignty, Hegel gives four answers. His first answer is that, commonsensically, all sovereignty is popular because it is to the state that sovereignty belongs, and the state is made up of an identifiable group of people. 'Any people whatever', says Hegel, 'is self-subsistent *vis-à-vis* other peoples, and constitutes a state of its own'. For example, he says, the 'sovereignty of the people' exists in the British people, because they constitute a state of their own. But then the peoples of England, Scotland or Ireland 'are not sovereign peoples at all now that they have ceased to have rulers or supreme governments of their own' (Hegel 1967, 182). In his second answer Hegel maintains, however, that if the sovereignty of the people is meant in opposition to the sovereignty of the monarch, then it 'is one of the confused notions based on the wild idea of the "people"' (Hegel 1967, 182-3). Monarchy is critical to the formation of sovereignty, Hegel argues. 'Taken without its monarch and the articulation of the whole which is the indispensable and direct concomitant of monarchy, the people is a formless mass and no longer a state' (Hegel, 1967, 183). Later Hegel argues that while the will of the many 'tries to count' as the 'first thing in civil society', it is 'not the guiding principle of the family, still less of the state, and in short it stands opposed to the Idea of ethical life' (Hegel 1967, 186).

As a third answer, Hegel dismisses the notion of the 'sovereignty of the people' referring to a republican or democratic form of government. He argues that the benefits of democracy can be achieved in a constitutional monarchy without its drawbacks. It is here that Suter's comment is relevant, that for Hegel, to 'invest an undefined, amorphous mass with sovereignty is to surrender the state unconditionally to the discretion of private interests' (Suter 1971, 62). In the fourth answer Hegel contends that if the people are living 'instead as an inwardly developed, genuinely organic, totality, then sovereignty is there as the personality of the whole, and this personality is there, in the real existence adequate to its concept, as the person of the monarch' (Hegel 1967, 183). Hegel argues that self-consciousness, the sign of a mature state, must be experienced by actual people in order to be 'realised', in order to exist, and so the monarch as an actual person is best suited to express the sovereignty of the people. In this fourth answer, the concrete sovereignty of the monarch is fused with the intangibility of sovereignty expressed in the rational idea of the state. In sum, then, Hegel's first and fourth answers acknowledge indirect popular sovereignty, and his second and third answers reject direct popular sovereignty.

Looking more closely at Hegel's acceptance of the idea of indirect popular sovereignty, Brod makes the interesting point that links Hegel's understanding of popular sovereignty, public opinion, and the metaphysical dimension of Hegel's state. Brod's answer to the question of whether Hegel's citizens need to be Hegelian philosophers is that 'these principles are embodied in the institutions that constitute the Hegelian state', and that 'these institutions are structured with an eye toward the creation of a rational sphere of public opinion open to all'. For a 'key criterion of Hegel's evaluation of all Hegelian political institutions is their effect on the consciousness of those who participate in them' (Brod 1992, 136). In this way, indirect popular sovereignty operates in Hegel's system as a channel to nourish, define, and renew the rationality of the institutions of the Hegelian state and keep that state invigorated. Dickey also supports this view, observing that even in his earliest political works, 'Hegel proposes to revitalise public life in Wurttemberg in a relatively new and progressive way: by politicising citizens through "publicity"' (Dickey 1999, xi).

There is a lively debate among commentators on Hegel's conception of internal sovereignty that centres on the role Hegel assigns to the crown which is worth rehearsing here for the interpretative play it illustrates in Hegel's work. Pelczynski and Berki object to the role of the crown as an obstacle to the play of popular sovereignty. For Pelczynski (1971, 230) Hegel is guilty of rationalising existing practice as a philosophically timeless idea, while Berki agrees with Marx that monarchy and popular sovereignty are conflated by Hegel, and that there is a circularity in Hegel's mistrust of 'the people'. Ilting sees the crown as contingent in Hegel's system, whereas Smith argues that, in his own terms, Hegel's identification of the crown with internal sovereignty is reasonable.

Pelczynski challenges Hegel's notion of internal sovereignty, developing two objections to the role Hegel designed for the monarch. For Pelczynski, Hegel is led by an excessive fear of collective sovereignty to internal contradictions in his thinking. He takes issue with Hegel's view 'that the different organs of "the state as a political entity" must be seen as branches of a single public authority, and must be prevented by the constitution from becoming "self-subsistent", that is, functioning with excessive independence'. Internal sovereignty for Hegel is located in this 'unified character of the public authority'. Pelczynski argues that this logic should lead Hegel to think that 'the constitutional power of the monarch is limited by the equally legitimate powers of the other organs (the executive, the legislature, the electorate and the lower public authorities) which together with the crown form the "organism" or the constitution of the political and civil state'. Pelczynski contends that, according to Hegel's argument, the crown, notwithstanding its importance and power, 'as an institution is only one of the elements of the whole differentiated constitutional structure, which is logically prior and legally superior to him'. In sum, Pelczynski maintains that only the constitution as a whole, and not the crown, 'is able to "actualise" sovereignty in the Hegelian sense' (Pelczynski 1971, 230).

Pelczynski's second objection to the role of the monarch in Hegel's internal sovereignty, aims to demonstrate an internal incompatibility in Hegel's theory, rendering the monarch both absolutist and constitutional. Pelczynski argues that the role of the monarch in Hegel conception 'changes radically when Hegel begins discussing sovereignty in a conventional sense as the ultimate source of the validity of all legal acts and rules in a state, as the basis of a particular, positive legal system'. Here, says Pelczynski, in contrast with Hegel's misplaced attempt to identify the crown rather than the constitution as 'actualising' sovereignty, 'sovereignty seems to Hegel to be necessarily vested in one part of the constitutional system', namely the crown. In consequence, it would seem that all the other constitutional organs of the state 'are inferior to the crown, derive their power from it, and may be deprived of their power in certain circumstances'. Pelczynski reasons that 'Hegel thus seems to arrive at a doctrine of monarchical absolutism which is contrary to his belief that the rational form of the modern state is a constitutional monarchy'. Moreover, says Pelczynski, the problem is not solved by the reasonable self-limiting agency of the crown. Hegel's inconsistency here is 'modified only partially by Hegel's expectation that modern monarchs will in normal circumstances play a limited constitutional role and increasingly restrict their personal political influence' (Pelczynski 1971, 230–1).

Berki also raises objections to Hegel's theory of sovereignty when he argues that 'Hegel's argument is lumbered with metaphysical ballast and the two vital aspects of the question, that is, the necessity of structured unity in the state, and the individual monarch as the necessary expression of this unity, are conflated' (Berki 1971, 208). He quotes Marx's critique of Hegel's conception of internal sovereignty, 'here we are concerned with *two entirely opposed concepts of sovereignty*, of which one is such that it can come to existence only in a *monarch*, the other only in a *people*' (Berki 1971, 209, quoting Marx).

Berki also endorses Marx's further judgment that Hegel's argument that popular sovereignty is a 'wild' and 'confused' notion, is tautological. Hegel had argued that the 'people, taken without its monarch and without the structuring of the whole … is a formless mass, no longer a state'. But Marx points out the circularity involved in the line of reasoning that '[i]f the community is organised as a monarchy, which monarchical institutions, *then* to abstract these institutions from this community yields us indeed a people that is nothing but a formless mass' (Berki 1971, 209).

According to Ilting the role of the monarch is interchangeable, in Hegel's system, with an elected head of state, without loss of meaning. He maintains that whether the 'representative of the sovereignty of the state was a monarch who possessed the trust of the citizens, or an elected head of state, would have had no special importance in the framework of Hegel's political philosophy' (Ilting 1971, 106). Subsequently Ilting took the view that Hegel's continued commitment to the key role of the crown was a tactical and pragmatic ploy to assuage current dictatorial regimes (Ilting 1974).

Smith argues that some of the criticisms of the role Hegel specifies for monarchy are misplaced. He holds that the position of the monarch is reasonable, given Hegel's understanding of a 'rational constitution' and the way the organic analogy 'attempts to answer a real political problem, namely, how to guarantee the unity and integrity of the state' (Smith 1989, 154). The rationality of the constitution, for Hegel, is not a matter of deduction but, in Smith's words, 'depends on the historical development of a people's laws, moral sentiments, and manners. What is rational for some may not be rational for others' (Smith 1989, 152). What matters for Hegel is that 'a constitution is rational if it functions as an organic whole'. Smith makes the case that an 'organic whole' in the context of politics meant something quite specific and important for Hegel. This notion is far removed from the conservative notion of justifying 'social differentiation and hierarchy' but does draw on the sense of the need to adapt to the 'contingencies of experience'. For Hegel, says Smith, the rationality of the constitution 'is tied to his conception of the separation and division of powers', which has a specific meaning for Hegel in terms of his theory of inward differentiation. For Hegel the necessary division of powers guarantees public freedom, but he rejects the current notion of separation of powers on the grounds that it attributes a false 'absolute autonomy and independence to each of the powers' (Smith 1989, 153), and also leads to a 'general paralysis and the self-destruction of the state' (Smith 1989, 154).

For Hegel the organic whole of the rational constitution means that the powers are 'mutually supporting aspects of the same totality'. Smith quotes Hegel's explanation, that 'each of these powers is in itself the totality of the constitution, because each contains the other moments and has them effective in itself'. Smith argues that Hegel's notion of the organic amounts to an 'expressive totality', such that 'Hegel's point is not simply that every complex phenomenon consists of parts which get their meaning or function from their place within the whole'. Rather, Hegel's point is 'the stronger one that each part is somehow expressive of the nature of the entire organism' (Smith 1989, 153). Furthermore, the parts are 'internally related to one another in a way that makes the whole not a mere aggregation but a structured whole'. For Hegel, Smith argues, while the executive and legislative 'may have an important degree of de jure separation, the 'sovereignty of the state…is guaranteed by the interdependence of the three main branches of government'. At the same time the monarch is the 'rational apex' because it is the 'tangible expression of all the features of the constitution'. The popular will, for instance in an American-type president or elected head of state, would not fulfil the same role since the popular will, for Hegel, is 'only one part of the constitution' and the monarch 'must embody in his person the entire constitution, and not just a part' (Smith 1989, 154). As Brod makes clear, Hegel's conception of sovereignty 'required that political authority be self-grounded rather than being derived from the spheres of morality, religion, or any other source (Brod 1992, 173).

Smith gives credit to Hegel for attempting to solve the dilemma facing all theories of sovereignty, 'the very real juridical [problem] of finding a place where sovereignty resides'. Hegel rejects popular sovereignty on the grounds that 'the people' is only an abstraction. For Smith, Hegel's answer makes sense in the light of his understanding of the constitution as registering a community in a strong sense. The constitution for Hegel is 'more than a mere formal arrangement of offices', and more like 'the entire way of life of a people', the 'form or soul of a regime', a 'political culture'. It follows (and this addresses one of Marx's criticisms) that there 'is no people, but only peoples formed by the constitution of which they are a part' (Smith 1989, 155). Hegel does not subscribe to the liberal view of pre-political rational, free, autonomous and rights-bearing individuals. For Hegel, persons are crucially shaped by the societies and cultures they live in.

Smith also mounts a defence of another aspect of the role of the monarch for Hegel by stressing its symbolic function. He highlights that for Hegel, 'the sovereignty of the state is guaranteed, not by the person, but by the office of the monarch'. Hegel's monarch need not have determinate characteristics as in other systems, such as wisdom or virtue, but only needs to bring to the role 'a sense of the dignity of the office' and as Hegel puts it, 'to say "yes" and dot the "i"'. Smith maintains that more recent heads of state 'retain their sovereign majesty without the institution of monarchy' and so fulfil exactly this function, because 'any government requires some ceremonial power to confer dignity on it' (Smith 1989, 155).

Smith also answers the 'accusation that Hegel merely rationalises, and hence legitimises, certain contingent historical institutions, thus conferring a purportedly timeless validity on them', by coming back to what rationality means to Hegel. He points out that charges concerning the inadequate deduction of hereditary monarchy by Hegel are misconceived because they assume that Hegel used a deductive logic, strictly applying the categories of his dialectic method, in the *Philosophy of Right*. Smith argues convincingly that 'Hegel's method of analysis is not deductive'. Hegel's method is not to work from some 'ideal theory', but to 'bring out the rationality that is already there within existing institutions and forms of life, including the monarchy'. Rationality, for Hegel, 'is not something that we the philosophical onlookers are required to bring with us to the evaluation process, but is to varying degrees already realised within the world we inhabit' (Smith 1989, 156).

One of the valuable aspects of Smith's interpretation is that it brings together Hegel's own understanding of the metaphysical framework for understanding politics, with the more accessible pragmatic aspect of his work. This gives Smith's interpretation a richer feel and takes into account a wider range of Hegel's work, in contrast with the dismissal of Hegel's 'obscure metaphysical argument' by Pelczynski (1971 231) and 'metaphysical ballast' by Berki.

We come now to sovereignty vis-a-vis foreign states, the second of the two 'sides' of sovereignty that together explicitly form Hegel's conception of sovereignty. Hegel argues for the Crown as the embodiment of external sovereignty, and his reasoning is that because of the way mind and its ideas work, 'the state has individuality, and individuality is in essence an individual, and in the sovereign an actual, immediate individual' (Hegel 1967, 208). Sovereignty is necessarily mediated — by the crown — because the world and thought are mediated. Furthermore says Hegel, developing the analogy between a person and a state, '[i]ndividuality is awareness of one's existence as a unit in sharp distinction from others'. So states see themselves as autonomous from each other. He argues that '[t]his autonomy embodies mind's actual awareness of itself as a unit and hence it is the most fundamental freedom which a people possesses as well as its highest dignity' (Hegel 1967, 208). Avineri usefully points to the role of recognition in this individuality of states. He argues that, for Hegel, while 'sovereignty is absolute, a state's sovereignty needs recognition as such, just as a person's recognition as an individual and an independent being ultimately rests upon recognition by another'. Hence, he argues, 'even in war there are a number of norms which should be preserved, the foremost among them being that ultimately war is to be seen as something transient' (Avineri 1972, 204-5). However the limit of the analogy between the individual and state is reached when we realise that there is no corresponding groundedness in community and no sociality between states in the way there are between individuals, and so no potential for an ethical state writ large nor an elaborated system of law at the international level.

In consequence Hegel is dismissive of those who have cosmopolitan aims. Such people, he says, 'have very little knowledge of the nature of a collection or of the feeling of selfhood which a nation possesses in its independence' (Hegel 1967, 208). Thus while a state sees events that confirm its opposition to other states as contingent, as just happening by chance, that awareness of its opposition to other states is in fact characteristic of what it is to be a state, a moment when the state is most supremely its own, a moment when it expresses its Idea. It rises above its humdrum substance, above its finiteness and recognises itself as infinite. This is the absolute individuality of the state, rather than the contingent and unstable individuality that is perceived ordinarily (Hegel 1967, 209).

It follows for Hegel that citizens have a duty to promote this image of the state, even at the sacrifice of property and life. In this way the state is much more than 'a mere civil society and ... its final end ... only the security of individual life and property' (Hegel 1967, 209). Hegel, outlining one of his most controversial arguments, continues that war, therefore, as well as being an evil, an accident, requiring a substantive justification, a breakdown of international laws, and an activity whose scope should be limited (Hegel 1967, 215), is also an 'ethical moment' for the state. Looked at from the point of view of concrete existence, 'everything is mortal and transient' and the individual loss of property and life in war is a terrible accident. But from the point of view of the state as the 'ethical substance', the loss of property and life in war becomes recognised as a necessity, 'exalted to be the work of freedom, to be something ethical' (Hegel 1967, 209). Indeed Hegel argues that 'if the state as such, if its autonomy, is in jeopardy, all its citizens are in duty bound to answer the summons to its defence' (Hegel 1967, 210–11). The 'ethical moment in war' demonstrates that citizens value their state sufficiently to risk losing their property, lives and their settled and ordered way of life.

Commitment to war is also a way for citizens to reaffirm the internal domestic sovereignty of their state. Hegel draws a strong parallel here between internal sovereignty expressed in the sense of the state as whole greater than the sum of its parts, and external sovereignty expressed in the moment of war. He argues that the 'ideality which is in evidence in war, ie in an accidental relation of a state to a foreign state, is the same as the ideality in accordance with which the domestic powers of the state are organic moments in a whole'. An example of this direct parallel that Hegel provides is that 'successful wars have checked domestic unrest and consolidated the power of the state at home' (Hegel 1967, 210).

Smith makes a case that the idea of war offers Hegel's system a clear sense of 'what is, conceptually speaking, involved in statehood', as well as challenging the liberal tradition's elevation of the 'market model of politics' (Smith 1989, 160), in civil society, individualism, and the free play of self-interest. The proximity in Hegel's text of his condemnation of 'regarding the state as a mere civil society' with 'its final end as only the security of individual life and property' (a clear swipe at the liberal viewpoint) and his statement immediately afterwards that the 'ethical moment in war is implied in what has been said in this Paragraph' (Hegel 1967, 209) provides strong evidence for Smith's argument. Smith argues that, against the 'conceptual confusion between civil society and the state' of liberal theory (Smith 1989, 157), Hegel posed the state as an ethical community as a 'mode of relating which stresses shared values and common sacrifice at the expense of individual interests'. In liberal theory there is 'nothing specifically political' about our obligation to the state, for we only have privately incurred obligations, to property, family, and friends in civil society, and the state's role is simply to defend these things (Smith 1989, 157). Brod (1992 82) underlines the crucial difference for Hegel between civil society and the state, when he observes a parallel between Hegel's use of the two terms and Rousseau's distinction between government ('the collective will of the body politic considered as the compilation of all the individual wills of the society, as the will of all') and sovereignty ('this collective will considered as the truly universal general will').

The state in the liberal schema, as Smith notes, is only 'an instrument for the achievement of material satisfactions' (Smith 1989, 158). For Hegel, however, 'the individual is what he is only by virtue of his participation in some totality wider than himself', and one's obligation to the state derives from its being 'a community of persons united around some shared conception of the good life', around 'shared standards and principles', rather than because the state represents a superior force or the power to coerce (Smith 1989, 158). For Hegel, the weakness of the liberal theory of political obligation is that, if the state is an 'institution for the protection of private rights alone, then it is not clear why the citizen should ever obey the state's command to risk his life in time of war' (Smith 1989, 157).

As Smith clarifies, the ethical significance of war, for Hegel, then, is that it raises 'us above the level of mere civil association' and 'transcends attachment to things by uniting men for the purpose of a common ideal' (Smith 1989, 159), and so is an 'integral part of the life of the state' (Smith 1989, 163). Smith contends that Hegel articulated a notion of statehood between the 'market model of politics' and the idea of 'the state as controlling the monopoly of violence' expressed later by Weber. War 'becomes … a type of school for the civil education of the modern bourgeois', a 'means of promoting certain types of civic virtues for citizens who in normal times are used to consulting only their private interests' (Smith 1989, 160). War is 'the means whereby state sovereignty is expressed, as well as where the "ethical health" of a people, their sense of community and political solidarity, is put to the test'. But as well as these things, war for Hegel also has a 'philosophical function'. It 'prevents an excessive rootedness in an attachment to the more mundane interests of civil association', and it is the means whereby the 'state and the specifically political form of obligation can come to assert themselves over the cacophony of private rights engendered by civil society' (Smith 1989, 163). It follows for Hegel that the courage to go to war is not 'for the sake of personal honour' but 'in the service of something impersonal, the state' (Smith 1989, 161).

Smith also notes two other factors that should mediate our repugnance towards Hegel's sanctioning of war. Hegel predicted that the mechanisation of modern warfare would render it 'more humane and less barbaric', and he did not anticipate the 'slide into total war' of modern warfare (Smith 1989, 161). In addition, Hegel's philosophy of history envisaged an end of history whereby the 'growing rationalisation or Westernisation of humanity' would result in a 'mutual respect for persons' as well as 'the homogenisation' of humanity, leading to an 'increased agreement over all the fundamental aims of life'. The 'triumph of reason' would mean, according to Hegel, 'the elimination of the grounds of war and conflict, because there will be nothing left to fight about' (Smith 1989, 164). The effect of these two factors is to disclose the extent to which we tend to read back into Hegel our knowledge of wars since the mid-nineteenth century as well as different associations with and changed values towards war.

We can see that Hegel's view of sovereignty leads him to be very much opposed to the kind of cosmopolitanism that Kant sometimes advocates. Hegel refers explicitly to Kant's *Perpetual Peace*, and gives at least five reasons for rejecting its cosmopolitan argument, ranging from the pragmatic to the philosophical. Hegel says that 'the phrase "perpetual peace" ... must in the very nature of things be understood as carrying the proviso: until one party is attacked or treated like an enemy'. Hegel's line of argument is that '[n]o state can bind itself to let itself be attacked or treated as an enemy and yet not to arm itself but to keep the peace' (Hegel 1964, 208). Furthermore, Kant's proposal would 'always depend ultimately on a particular sovereign will and for that reason would remain infected with contingency' (Hegel 1967, 214). In addition Hegel argues that 'corruption in nations would be the product of prolonged, let alone "perpetual" peace' (Hegel 1967, 210).

Fourthly, a state must be allowed to defend its multiple interests and its welfare, since its 'infinity and honour' might be at stake (Hegel 1967, 214). Finally, as noted above in describing the meaning of the state for Hegel, there are strong limits on the analogy between the individual and the state, with the outcome that while morality is the relevant form of activity for analysing individuals, politics is the appropriate form for discussing states. Hegel's perspective is that state sovereignty is ultimate, and he is very clear that any higher commitment would infringe that sovereignty. While Kant stood by the sovereignty of the state in the face of the attractions of cosmopolitanism, Hegel's commitment to sovereignty is much more unequivocal, based as it is on a primary conviction that the state is the necessary focus of ethical life. The nation state, Hegel maintains, 'is therefore the absolute power on earth ... every state is sovereign and autonomous against its neighbours' (Hegel 1967, 212). In addition, while Hegel is positioned as a communitarian in contrast to Kant, it is clear that it is a potentially aggressive community that he promotes.

Smith notes that Hegel was 'especially critical of Kant' and that Hegel 'would have been critical of all Enlightenment liberals up to and including Woodrow Wilson, for believing that the reeducation of humanity through the spread of enlightenment or the rearrangement of political institutions will solve once and for all the problem of war' (Smith 1989, 162). For Hegel, it is precisely this kind of sacrifice by citizens that is 'the substantial tie between the state and all its members and so is a universal duty' (Hegel 1967, 210). Moreover, what effects this link is courage, a key part of the meaning of sovereignty. As Hegel puts it, '[t]he intrinsic worth of courage as a disposition of mind is to be found in the genuine, absolute, final end, the sovereignty of the state. The work of courage is to actualize this final end, and the means to this end is the sacrifice of personal actuality' (Hegel 1967, 211). In other words, giving your life for your state is the ultimate affirmation of its sovereignty. It follows for Hegel that because the monarch represents the sovereignty, the unity, the individuality of the state, the monarch must be the commander of the armed forces, and conduct foreign affairs through ambassadors, make war and peace and conclude treaties.

The central principle governing international law, for Hegel, is that it 'springs from the relations between autonomous states' (Hegel 1967, 212). Smith notes that Hegel's scepticism towards international law arose from his sense that 'the causes of war are sown deep in human nature' in a way that Enlightenment reason cannot alter (Smith 1989, 162). This scepticism adds to Hegel's argument that it is 'as particular entities that states enter into relations with one another', such that the differences in their histories and cultures are as important as what they have in common as states. Relations between states are thus characterised by 'external contingency' and 'inner particularity' (Hegel 1967, 215). These two aspects of the relationship between states limit the scope of international law, since such law depends upon the different wills of each sovereign state, and can not ever rule over a higher purpose. As Hegel puts it, 'what is absolute in it [international law] retains the form of an ought-to-be', since the nation state is 'the absolute power on earth'. However, Hegel adds, '[w]hether a state is in fact something absolute' hinges on two things — it 'depends on its content, ie on its constitution and general situation', and also upon recognition, which 'is conditional on the neighbouring state's judgment and will' (Hegel 1967, 212). The sovereign authority of each state 'receives its full and final legitimation through its recognition by other states' (Hegel 1967, 213). This recognition consists of reciprocal respect for the autonomy of other states. Nevertheless, says Hegel, the 'fundamental proposition of international law', in the sense of what is general, regardless of the content of specific treaties and contracts, 'is that treaties, as the ground of obligations between states, ought to be kept' (Hegel 1967, 213).

In addition to this rather weak qualification, the only other check that Hegel offers to the authority of states to make their own judgments is the perspective gained retrospectively in history. His argument that '[w]orld history is a court of judgment' (Hegel 1967, 216), is an important feature of his philosophy of history but does not carry much weight as an effective means to curb a ruler's or a state's unjust actions. In sum, then, Hegel's approach to international politics, working out the ramifications of the state-as-the-locus-of-ethical-life or 'ethical substance' in its relations with other states, is thus very different from Kant's more extensive mapping of the moral nature of the state onto the international realm which has been so influential in the contemporary debate.

While Hegel states clearly that his conception of sovereignty contains two 'sides', he does not address in any great detail the nature of the connections between them. But Brod raises an interesting point in this regard when he notes that, for Hegel, '[e]very state must speak with only one voice to other states, not primarily to avoid chaos in international affairs but to cement unity at home'. In other words, the role of the monarch, which Hegel discusses under the heading of 'sovereignty at home', has important repercussions for external sovereignty. As Brod observes, and thereby shows how the monarch straddles the two 'sides' of sovereignty for Hegel, the 'main reason the conduct of foreign affairs falls to the monarch is for internal rather than external considerations, because the complexity of international relations must not be allowed to shatter the internal unity of the state' (Brod 1992, 156). In this way we can see that, for Hegel, internal sovereignty looks outward as well as inward, and that the monarchy, as Brod puts it, is the key player in 'the transition from internal to external sovereignty' (Brod 1992, 157). Another connection that Hegel touches upon, and the example he gives is of feudal societies, is the possibility of a political society possessing external but not internal sovereignty. Hegel here lays open the idea that the two 'sides' of sovereignty are not always necessarily conjoint.

What Hegel does present clearly, in terms of the relation between internal and external sovereignty in his theory, is that external sovereignty is dependent on the internal 'side', for the justification of relations with other states lies in reaffirming the internal sovereignty of the state. As Brod notes, the 'logical priority of internal over external sovereignty is Hegel's most systematic way' of expressing his sense that 'a constitution cannot be imposed on a people externally but must grow out of the historical experiences of that people' (Brod 1992, 156). On the other hand, Hegel considers that war with another state is the highest way in which to realise the state and affirm its sovereignty. So whereas all the other theorists of sovereignty we have discussed so far regard external sovereignty as an extension of a predominant internal sovereignty, in a important sense for Hegel internal and external sovereignty are interdependent. Hegel's theory of the state accounts in large measure for this condition.

The key general features of sovereignty in Hegel's conception are a very strong identification of sovereignty with the state, and a further reduction of the role of popular sovereignty. For Hegel the sovereignty of the state means both the role of the monarch as the visible embodiment of sovereignty, and the introduction of the idea of sovereignty as expressing the organic 'whole' of the state that is greater than the collection of its members or the sum of its parts. The sovereignty of the state also imposes a clear limit on the possibility of international collaboration, and envisages international politics as necessarily a matter dominated by relations between states formally recognised as equals.

One of the strengths of Hegel's conception of sovereignty is his clear sense of the historical and cultural groundedness of particular states, and the value of this is reinforced by the absence of a social contract in Hegel's political thinking. In consequence Hegel is able to move away from the depoliticised individualism and supposedly 'neutral' state inaugurated by the liberal social contract tradition. The groundedness of states is also valuable because it means for him that differences between states are things to be respected, and such differences are not overridden by universal principles, duties or commitments. For Hegel, in contrast with Kant, the metaphysical framework around politics does not overshadow the need to acknowledge that particularity, context, and circumstance all play a vital role. Hegel's sense of the need for mutual respect between incommensurable cultures and societies is translated by him into his view of international politics.

The primary weakness of Hegel's conception of sovereignty for modern readers is the argument that leads to him identifying war as the ethical moment of the state. His conception of the state and of relations between states has enough other strong arguments supporting it and does not need to rest on this celebration of war. The same argument can be applied to Hegel's advocacy of monarchy and his antipathy to universal suffrage. Another weakness is Hegel's lack of attention to a seeming contradiction in his text, between his use of empirical arguments, for instance to reject popular sovereignty and to endorse the use of war by the state, and his conviction that empirical evidence has no place in philosophical reasoning. Berki defends the importance Hegel places on institutions to concretise political society, and criticises Marx's reluctance to specify such institutions in his discussion of democracy and, later, communism. Nevertheless, the contradiction in Hegel remains.

Finally, what kind of politics does this conception allow? In one sense Hegel provides a vigorous defence of politics, in that he is at pains to identify a field of politics, in the state, distinct from the field of the social and civil society (Hegel 1967, 198). Indeed, there is an important expressive dimension of politics, for Hegel, such that political activity is indicative and demonstrative of a particular kind of sociality. It is also clear that it was Hegel's self-conscious aim to carve out a sphere for politics in the context of the state form. Knox says that 'Hegel lived in a country where most citizens were simply "subjects", without participation in the work of government, and where, therefore, a political life and tradition, like the English, was almost wholly lacking'. Knox characterises the *Philosophy of Right* as 'an attempt to educate Germans beyond "civil" to "political" life' (Knox 1967, 376). Dickey makes a similar point, linking Hegel's aim to reinvigorate the idea of the political with the political context in which he was writing. Dickey claims that 'in Hegel's judgment, the boundaries of the political sphere were becoming so narrowly drawn in his own age that citizens were on the verge of becoming depoliticised'. In this 'context, he wished from the 1790s on to recall citizens to public life and civic engagement by identifying the political sphere' (Dickey 1999, ix). But in another sense Hegel severely restricts the scope of politics—through the very reduced role for popular sovereignty, through his strictures against democracy and a wide franchise, and because his notion of representation sharply limits the accountability of representatives to their constituents.

This chapter has sought to demonstrate once again a pair of thinkers whose conceptions of sovereignty are utterly distinctive. While sharing commonalities and self-consciously contributing to a tradition of thinking, each of the two theories is made up of a particular and tightly inter-related set of specific features. The two conceptions of sovereignty cannot be reduced without violent loss and misrepresentation to a single model of the concept. The following chapter outlines two further conceptions.

Chapter Five

SCHMITT AND FOUCAULT

SCHMITT

We turn now to two twentieth-century views of sovereignty, one which emphasises the deeply political, contestable nature of sovereignty, and the other which challenges the emphasis placed on its overtly political character and locates sovereignty in power relations in the social sphere. The first conception of sovereignty analysed in this chapter is by Carl Schmitt, who argues in his key work *Political Theology* that sovereignty is a profoundly political, not just a legal concept as the modern liberal tradition holds. Schmitt identifies sovereignty very firmly as state sovereignty. The second is by Michel Foucault, who argues that the modern Western intellectual tradition has highlighted the political and legal (or 'juridical') aspect of sovereignty and that this has disguised the more entrenched character of the disciplinary power that pervades our society.

The difference between Schmitt and Foucault can also be pinpointed around the concept of authority in relation to sovereignty. Schmitt argues for the primary importance of authority while Foucault insists on its utter irrelevance. Schmitt comes to the discussion of sovereignty as a public or constitutional lawyer keen to clarify the meanings of concepts in the light of new realities, while Foucault comes to sovereignty from the perspective of sociology, in that his focus of attention is the social realm. Schmitt envisages a realm for politics wrested away from the depoliticising legalisation and constitutionalisation of the public sphere, and recognises both the benefits and problems of a dynamic contestatory politics. Foucault subsumes the political under the social and only very late in his life did he acknowledge a slightly enlarged role for a form of politics. Neither writer has any faith in more mainstream notions of representative or participatory liberal democratic politics. Ideologically Schmitt was a conservative or even 'radical conservative' in Germany while Foucault was positioned on the radical left in France.

Schmitt and Foucault have a number of important things in common, though. Both writers indicate in important respects the limits of the concept of sovereignty. Both seek to unmask the pretensions of liberal ideology as understood in their different contexts, and to expose the power interests cloaked by liberal universalist claims. Schmitt questions the adequacy of the received notion of sovereignty to deal effectively with political crisis, while Foucault challenges the adequacy of sovereignty to account for political realities such as entrenched and naturalised inequalities. For both, the basic assumption of liberal theory and practice, the idea of reasonable agreement among free and equal persons, cannot be sustained. Moreover, neither rely on the linked ideas of a state of nature and social contract to underpin their theory. This is just one of the things that sets them apart from the collection of thinkers from Hobbes to Kant and from the liberal appropriation of those thinkers. Schmitt and Foucault also share a rejection of the kind of normative theorising undertaken by Kant and Hegel which sets out the ideal of the *Rechtstaat* and the rule of law as articulating a metaphysics of morals. For Schmitt such theorising left undefined who decided upon the exception, while Foucault regarded the normative edifice as a sham, used to cover up the real play of power relations of domination and subordination. Both address the problem left unacknowledged in the *Rechtstaat* tradition that, as Hoffman observes, this normative ideal 'rests not simply upon law but … upon a capacity to exercise superior physical force' (Hoffman 1996, 623).

Schmitt was born in 1888 in Germany into a devout Catholic background, and wrote his most important political works in the 1920s. He was very affected by the defeat of Germany in the First World War, and his reflections on politics were subsequently designed to sustain the Weimar Republic from threats to its existence from the far right (Nazi party) and the far left (Communist party). Indeed Kelly characterises the Weimar constitution as 'the premier catalytic moment for Schmitt's thought' (Kelly 2003, 11). Schmitt's concern with the fragility of the Weimar Republic was heightened by the sense of Germany's new and brittle constitutional arrangement, and the still recent unification of Germany. The German federal identity and its settlement of the relationship between the regional states and the federal state structure had occurred only in 1871.

Between 1930 and 1932 Schmitt played a key role as constitutional advisor in presenting the legal arguments to defend the republic and the constitution against the Nazi party, stressing the importance of the constitution's provision for the president to deploy exceptional measures. However, with the breakdown of the German state and Hitler's appointment as chancellor in 1933, Schmitt accommodated to the new regime. From 1933 until 1936 (when deprived by the Nazis of his government and party posts on the grounds of his opportunism, and because he had aligned himself with losing factions within the Nazi Party) he made serious concessions to the Nazi regime, and is notorious for having given legal support, after the event, to Hitler's accession to power. Strong notes that Schmitt 'remained a member of the [Nazi] Party as well as professor of law at the University of Berlin between 1933 and 1945' (Strong 2005, viii). It is important at this point in the chapter to come to a view about the relation between Schmitt's political theory and his practical political involvement, before going on to examine his theory of sovereignty.

Habermas suggests that Schmitt continued to harbour pro-Nazi sympathies, linking Schmitt's role as a lawyer at the post-war Nuremburg war crimes tribunal with Schmitt's argument against strong cosmopolitan law and international human rights. Habermas notes that Schmitt rejected the distinction between offensive and defensive wars on the grounds that 'only a morally neutral conception of war, which excludes the possibility of personal arrest of war criminals, is consistent with the sovereignty of the subjects of international law', namely states. According to this logic, 'the right to begin a war for any reason whatsoever, constitutes the sovereignty of states' (Habermas 1997, 141). Habermas details that Schmitt prepared a defence in 1945 for the Nuremburg defendant Friedrich Flick. In that brief Schmitt, says Habermas, 'rigorously distinguished between war crimes and "atrocities", stating that the latter transcend human understanding "as the characteristic expression of an inhuman mentality"'. Schmitt, says Habermas, 'could save the consistency of his purely juridical argument only by bracketing the mass crimes of the Nazi period as a sui generic category, in order to preserve at least the appearance of moral neutrality for war'. Habermas examines post-1951 writings for evidence of Schmitt's intention in making this line of argument and concludes that 'Schmitt not only wanted to see offensive wars decriminalised but also saw the absolute breakdown of civilisation in the extermination of the Jews on the same level' (Habermas 1997, 142).

Two important things emerge from this evidence, one about Habermas and one about Schmitt. It is clear from Habermas's argument that the force of his commitment to international law (a subject on which Schmitt also wrote, though taking a very different line) and a cosmopolitan public sphere comes in part from his revulsion against views such as the one he outlines about Schmitt, whereby a form of communitarianism and state sovereignty can be used to spuriously rebut charges of crimes against humanity. Habermas's attack on Schmitt helps to clarify and contextualise Habermas's own project. It also highlights the gap between the kind of theorising these two thinkers were engaged in and Habermas's desire to assimilate all theorising into his own kind. Habermas follows in the tradition of Kant and Hegel, of normative theorising establishing the conditions for working towards a moral ideal, reaffirming the centrality of law in a *Rechtstaat*. Schmitt, in contrast (and again there is a tradition of such theorising, another clear example of which might be Schumpeter), is concerned with identifying a reality and a crisis without making moral judgments about it and with providing a theoretical principle with concrete applicability.

More generally, Habermas implies a false dichotomy that needs to be resisted, in aligning cosmopolitan and state sovereignty positions with anti- and pro-Nazi sympathies. Habermas's commendation of 'the democratic transformation of morality into a positive system of law' (cited in Habermas 1997, 149) and Schmitt's plea for the depoliticisation of society and de-moralisation of politics do represent opposite poles, but they both have a valid meaning without being mapped onto the Nazi past.

What emerges about Schmitt from this evidence is that his defence of a Nuremburg trial defendant and his attempt to justify Germany's conduct under the Nazis do cast serious doubt on his political judgment, and do throw into question the wider value of his political thought. Further evidence for this view is provided by Müller's analysis of Schmitt's use of language in his political theory texts. Müller argues convincingly (1999 62) that Schmitt did not have a single 'doctrine' and was at times analytical 'neutral' jurist, authoritarian political theorist, irrational ideologue, political theologian, political actor, but that what did remain constant was Schmitt's sense of the 'primarily ideological nature of political battle' (Müller 1999, 63). At the same time it is clear that Schmitt lacked a sense of the difference between awareness of how politics is saturated with power interests and directly asserting one of those interests. Müller, like Habermas, sees Schmitt's right-wing Nazi allegiance as informing his political theory. Müller argues that Schmitt's sophisticated sense of the role played by language in politics was expressed in his 'desire to change a political situation by distilling it into a conceptual scheme', the clearest being his 'fashioning of a legal vocabulary centred on "concrete order thinking" … for the Nazis after 1933', using concepts with positive associations and distinguishing them from those with negative connotations. Müller contends that Schmitt's 'self-conscious construction of an ideological legitimation for the rulers was even more obvious in Schmitt's elaboration of the international law doctrine of "great spaces" … at the end of the 1930s, which was to underpin the Nazi conquest of Eastern Europe' (Müller 1999, 71).

Schmitt died in 1985. In recent years there has been a move to take seriously the significance of the terms of his political theory written in the 1920s, despite his later failures of political judgment. Schwab and others are keen to rehabilitate Schmitt's political theory and to discount his Nazi past. Evidence that, at the very least, Schmitt changed his political allegiance more than once, is used to downplay the Nazi episode. As well as the change noted above (from the 1920s and early thirties to the 1933-36 period) Schwab makes a case that Schmitt's 1938 work, *The Leviathan in the State Theory of Thomas Hobbes. Meaning and Failure of a Political Symbol*, contains a covert critique of the Nazi regime and 'insinuated the demise of the Third Reich' and signalled that 'he was reconnecting himself to the pre-1933 Schmitt' (Schwab 1996, x). In that work Schmitt reflects on the intellectual value of Hobbes's central thesis and argues for its ultimate lack of political impact, out of step with the English spirit and overtaken in continental Europe by the rise of 'indirect powers' such as modern political parties, trade unions, the church, and other interests. It is not clear that Schwab's optimism is warranted that the work demonstrates an unequivocal critique of the Nazi regime.

Huysmans makes a strong case for recognising Schmitt's Nazi past as necessarily a part of discussing his political theory, for 'introducing the spectre of Schmitt's political choice in any interpretation of theories which incorporate a Schmittean concept of the political' (Huysmans 1999, 328). He argues that if Schmitt's legacy is 'firmly placed in the social and political struggle of his time', then whether the origin of 'Schmitt's motivation for collaborating with the Nazis was conviction, opportunism or misjudged belief, is not of immediate concern'. Huysmans persuasively contends that the value of this sociological approach is that the 'relation between political positions and intellectual views emerges in an intersubjective understanding of social practices', rather than as simply a matter of an individual 'psychological or motivational question' (Huysmans 1999, 327). This approach is especially valuable in maintaining a political reading of Schmitt, and so finding a satisfactory alternative to those who 'decouple' Schmitt's Nazi past from the political theory and so silence discussion of the relation between them, while also providing an alternative to those who issue a blanket repudiation of the tainted political theory.

While agreeing with Huysmans's analysis, for the purposes of this chapter it is not the end of the story. We can also note here that Schmitt's changes of allegiance are explicable though not justified in terms of Hobbes's theory of the prudence of recognising as sovereign whomsoever captures and holds overwhelming power, a view which is echoed in Schmitt's own work. Indeed Schmitt explicitly applauds, and puts great emphasis upon in his own theory, the centrality that Hobbes places on the 'mutual relation between protection and obedience' (Hobbes, quoted by Schmitt 1976, 52). Strong's description of Schmitt's identification with a character in a Hermann Melville novel (Strong 2005, vii-x) also makes clear that Schmitt can be regarded as not simply a natural Nazi supporter, nor simply as an opportunist or as driven by ambition, but as someone who wrestled with the problem of 'how to do the right thing' in the shifting sands of a turbulent politics. Strong makes the further case that Schmitt was attracted to Hitler's actions when they demonstrated a clear capacity for decisionism and leadership (Strong 2005, xxxi).

Moreover we can see that Schmitt, like Hobbes, constructs a theory that is not simply politically loaded and which does more than simply respond to the political events of his day. It is in this theory that much of more general interest can be found apart from its local historical significance. Certainly in terms of Schmitt's conception of sovereignty there is a strong case for arguing that there is wider value in some of the principles and challenges he articulated, which are not invalidated by his, in some other areas, pro-Nazi stance. For instance, Koskenniemi takes the sound view that Schmitt's 'reprehensible association with the Nazis and his blatant antisemitism throw a well-founded shadow on his life as well as on some of his writings from that period'. But, Koskenniemi contends, 'they fail to undermine the force of many of his insights about law and the new political order'. He reasons that to 'deal with Schmitt is necessary', in order to 'understand the complex relationship between political utopias and struggles' (Koskenniemi 2001, 424).

In terms of his conception of sovereignty the shockingly radical novelty of Schmitt's theory was to question the *perpetual* character of sovereignty and to analyse the consequences of its impermanence and rupture in the absence of a given rule. He deals with the breakdown of sovereignty, and puts forward a perspective from outside the box. He turns the established view of sovereignty on its head — sovereignty lies in he who decides on the exception, rather than on he or they who decide on the rule. One of the most distinctive aspects of Schmitt's conception of sovereignty is that he thinks about sovereignty in the context of the inability of a self-proclaimedly neutral liberal tradition to provide a coherent account of the either politics or the state.

The key concepts informing Schmitt's idea of a sovereignty relevant to the modern state are pessimism, the contrast between 'politics-as-usual' and political conflict, the exception, the gap between the legal order and the state, the state, the theologisation of political conflict, decisionism, and dictatorship. In the course of examining these key concepts for sovereignty we also encounter other concepts important for his political theory more generally, such as the friend/enemy distinction and 'the political'.

Schmitt's theory of sovereignty occurs in the context of his disenchanted and pessimistic view of contemporary political life. The bourgeoisie had cultivated a romantic sensibility that aestheticised the meaning of events and normativism, as Koskenniemi puts it, 'sought to replace the State by its laws and to rid politics from the notion of sovereignty'. These two techniques for 'escaping politics' underpinned a broad trend toward depoliticisation in public and intellectual life, downplaying 'the conflictual character of the political realm' (Koskenniemi 2001, 427–8). To Schmitt, writing in the 1920s, liberal democracy was in crisis, and the question of political leadership in mass democracies was urgent and pressing. In Germany the Weimar constitution had been signed in 1919 but party politics was held in poor esteem. More than that, as Kelly puts it, '[b]orn of political defeat, the twin pole stars of Weimar's bloody birth were a fear for national unity and the spectre of Bolshevism' (Kelly 2003, 175). Kelly argues that Schmitt's dilemma was intensified by the tension he felt between his intellectual conviction that led him to remain an opponent of the new republic and his deeply-felt conviction (deriving from his Catholic upbringing) to accept the legality of and obey the newly constituted authority (Kelly 2003, 171).

What could the concept of sovereignty possibly have to offer in this situation? According to Schmitt, the nineteenth and twentieth centuries were witnessing the fragmentation of political authority, as the element of personal rule (in monarchy) receded under the impact of impersonal ideas. He had in mind impersonal principles such as democratic legitimacy, the separation of powers, the notion of checks on power as the central tenet of liberal constitutionalism, and the notion that the sovereignty of the law should supersede the sovereignty of the people. His works address different aspects of this theme. In *Political Theology* (published in 1922 and again in 1934 with a new forward), his key work for the theory of sovereignty, Schmitt's target is liberal constitutionalism and the liberal pre-eminence of the rule of law. In *The Concept of the Political* (published in 1927 and in elaborated form in 1932) his target is liberal pluralism (whereby the state is wrongly regarded as on a par with other forms of association within the state), the liberal bias 'directed against the intervention of the state', the liberal presupposition of the inherent goodness of man (Schmitt 1976, 60), and liberalism's 'negation of the political' in favour of a depoliticised individualism (Schmitt 1976, 70). He argues that 'liberalism's negation of state and the political, its neutralisations, depoliticalisations, and declarations of freedom' are not only mistaken, and dangerous, but also hypocritical. For they also have 'political meaning, and in a concrete situation these are polemically directed against a specific state and its political power' (Schmitt 1976, 61). The close connection between sovereignty and the political for Schmitt is demonstrated by his approval of the 1925 Weimar constitutional amendments that were made to strengthen the position of the President's emergency powers which, as Kelly notes, was 'precisely the arena Schmitt had immediately identified as central to the crucial issue of sovereignty, and hence the political, within the document' (Kelly 2003, 210).

Other works also relate to this theme. *Political Romanticism* (published in 1919 and 1925) argued that the liberal social order had been depoliticised by the 'European bourgeoisie as the class that had embraced romanticism' and 'its "poeticisation" of political conflicts' (Oakes 1986, xiii). In *Die Diktator* (published 1921) Schmitt made a case for the role of an authority to exercise emergency powers in times of extreme political crisis. *The Crisis of Parliamentary Democracy* (published 1923 and 1926) explores the tension between democratic and liberal principles. It identifies the President as upholding the democratic principle in the Weimar constitution and the only hope for overriding dangerous 'unconstitutional' parties. At the same time Schmitt criticises the 'endless conversation' of the liberal parliament because if it only represents particular interests it no longer operates effectively as a means of generating the public good, and so lacks legitimacy. In *Legalitat und Legitimitat* (published 1932), as Oakes puts it, 'Schmitt's target was a purely formal, value-neutral, and procedural jurisprudence that ignores the basic substantive values to which the Constitution is committed' (Oakes 1986, xiii).

According to Schmitt in *Political Theology*, action by the sovereign in the case of extreme emergency can only be successful if 'not subject to controls, if it is not hampered in some way by checks and balances, as is the case in a liberal constitution'. Only 'then it is clear who the sovereign is' (Schmitt 1985, 7). For Schmitt, 'the liberal constitutional state ... attempts to repress the question of sovereignty by a division and mutual control of competences' (Schmitt 1985, 11). In addition, Schmitt argues that '[t]oday nothing is more modern than the onslaught against the political'. Political problems are being reduced to economic or organisational-technical ones, whereas the 'core of the political idea', he maintains, is an 'exacting moral decision' (Schmitt 1985, 65).

But Schmitt's view was not only pessimistic. He regarded sovereignty positively as the key to resolving this situation in modern political life. To this end he sought to develop Hobbes's conception of sovereignty as a means of re-establishing in Weimar the legitimacy of the idea of personal intervention by the sovereign. Schmitt wanted to reinstate the notion of intervention by a president representing a personalised office-holder in political authority, who could protect the modern constitutional state.

The next of Schmitt's key concepts is 'politics-as-usual', and the contrast with political conflict. According to Schmitt, most political theorists were oriented only toward the conditions for 'politics-as-usual'. For Schmitt, faced with the turbulent constitutional politics of Germany in the 1920s and early 1930s, the kind of normal politics that most political theorists write for and aim at seemed unattainable. Political theorists generally seek to present their theories as a way of ensuring political security and stability, but Schmitt thought that in his own time this aspiration was hopeless. He was preoccupied instead with the idea of political conflict. Schmitt, in *Legalitat und Legitimitat* of 1932, considered that the meaning of 'political conflict' varied across different countries, and he compared Germany and England. The fragility of the political life of Weimar Germany, he maintained, was in marked contrast with what happened in England. According to Schmitt, Balfour had remarked of England that the 'whole political machinery presupposes a people so fundamentally at one that they can safely afford to bicker; and so sure of their own moderation that they are not dangerously disturbed by the never-ending din of political conflict' (Schmitt 1932, quoted by Schwab 1985, xxiii). In consequence of the more serious form of political conflict occurring in Germany, Schmitt argued, the kind of constitution advocated by the liberal legal tradition was insufficient to ensure its robustness in the face of bitter and divided political loyalties. As Schwab describes, Schmitt opposed the weak Weimar constitution that did not have adequate safeguards against its own overthrow. He 'challenged a basic liberal assumption ... that every political party, no matter how antirepublican, must be permitted freely to compete' for power, providing it proceed legally (Schwab 1976, 13).

Moreover, for Schmitt, the liberal tradition of legal theorists since Locke had defended the view of the principles of the constitution as scientific, unpolitical and 'rationalist' (Schmitt 1985, 13–14). But Schmitt argued that the acceptance of the legitimacy of the constitution depended upon its having an explicitly moral character. Under conditions currently obtaining in Germany, a legalistic interpretation of the constitution that attempted to be value-neutral simply served to facilitate its subversion. Only if the constitution embodied moral norms that are regarded as sacrosanct, would the constitution be strong enough to withstand political conflict in Germany (Schwab 1985, xxii). As Müller notes, for Schmitt 'even a decision on which concepts were political or not, was always already a political decision' (Müller 1999, 73).

The 'challenge of the exception', the next of Schmitt's key concepts in his theory of sovereignty to be analysed, was what political theory really had to deal with, Schmitt thought. But by 'exception' he did not mean anarchy and chaos. During an exception he says that 'the state remains, whereas law recedes', and 'order in the juristic sense still prevails even if it is not of the ordinary [routine] kind'. During an exception, order is provided by the temporary 'unlimited authority' of the sovereign, while the constitution is suspended (Schmitt 1985, 12). For Schmitt, addressing the exception was a way of confronting the fact that in 'political reality there is no irresistible highest or greatest power that operates according to the certainty of natural law' (Schmitt 1985, 17). As Kelly highlights, the '"exceptional situation" produces the "order" of the norm' for Schmitt, and the 'actual creation of political order is something that cannot be legislated for constitutionally'. Kelly notes that this insight, for Schmitt, stands in contrast to the constitutional tradition and of 'liberal constitutionalism in particular', which 'valorises the written document of the constitution' (Kelly 2003, 182).

Schmitt takes a very dim view of the history of the concept of sovereignty, arguing that the 'phases of its conceptual development are characterised by various political power struggles, not by a dialectical heightening inherent in the characteristics of the concept' (Schmitt 1985, 16–17). Again he argues against the politicised nature of sovereignty when he says that of 'all juristic concepts the concept of sovereignty is the one most governed by actual interests' (Schmitt 1985, 16).

However, while in general the tradition of thinking about sovereignty has overlooked the significance of this emergency state, Schmitt sees it as clearly present in Bodin. The way that 'this concept relates to the critical case, the exception, was long ago recognised by Jean Bodin', he says (Schmitt 1985, 8). Schmitt pays tribute to the way in which, for Bodin, 'commitments are binding because they rest on natural law; but in emergencies the tie to general natural principles ceases'. He contends that Bodin recognised that in crisis cases the relationship between the prince and the estates was reduced to 'a simple either/or' (Schmitt 1985, 8). Schmitt sees in Bodin a precursor of his own theory, arguing that 'the authority to suspend valid law ... is so much the actual mark of sovereignty, Bodin wanted to derive from this authority all other characteristics' (Schmitt 1985, 9). In addition, Schmitt argues, the definition of an occurrence as an exception and conversely of what constitutes public order and security, is relative and not absolute. As he says, public order and security 'manifest themselves very differently ... depending on whether a militaristic bureaucracy, a self-governing body controlled by the spirit of commercialism, or a radical party organisation decides when there is order and security and when it is threatened or disturbed' (Schmitt 1985, 9–10).

Schmitt argued, however — and making a general point about politics, the state, and sovereignty — that a crisis or exception is 'more interesting than the rule', and this is for two reasons. First a crisis confirms the rule, thereby reinvigorating the meaning of the rule of law. And second a crisis confirms the state's very existence. In day-to-day life we take the state for granted and are not aware of its moral meaning for us. As he puts it, in 'the exception the power of real life breaks through the crust of a mechanism that has become torpid by repetition'. Consequently, our self-consciousness of the importance of the state 'derives only from the exception' (Schmitt 1985, 15). An example of Schmitt's point here might be the nationalism and patriotism in Britain that was expressed during the Falklands War, which showed that a strong national feeling is often dormant: that just because it is not expressed in day-to-day life does not mean it is not there.

So the 'exception' is necessary in the sense that it plays an indispensable role, in reminding us of what coheres us as a nation, according to Schmitt. He explains what the concept of the exception means for him through a more general theory about the modern state resting on the secularisation of theological concepts. Schmitt argues that that derivation is not only historical, in terms of how (secular) political concepts 'were transferred from theology to the theory of the state', for instance in the way in which the transfer of 'the omnipotent God became the omnipotent lawgiver'. The derivation is also sociological, in the 'systematic structure' of the analogy between theological and juristic concepts. According to this logic, the 'exception in jurisprudence is analogous to the miracle in theology' (Schmitt 1985, 36).

For this reason, then, Schmitt opposed the aim of contemporaneous liberal legal constitutionalists like Hans Kelsen, who wanted to construct a watertight legal system that would eliminate the problem of the exception. He traces the liberal constitutionalist view back to Locke's claim that the 'law gives authority', and Locke's conscious choice of 'the word law antithetically to ... the personal command of the monarch'. But Schmitt identifies in this a failure by Locke to 'recognise that the law does not designate to whom it gives authority' (Schmitt 1985, 32). Schmitt ridicules Kelsen's attempt to erase or 'purge' politics of sovereignty, to provide 'in unadulterated purity a system of ascriptions to norms' and a 'uniform basic norm' in which 'all sociological elements have been left out' (Schmitt 1985, 18). He challenged Kelsen's reduction of the state to the legal order, arguing that on this basis 'Kelsen does not know what to do with the exception' (Schmitt 1985, 14). For Kelsen law is ultimately ungrounded since the 'state is thus neither the creator nor the source of the legal order'. Because Kelsen, seeking to elevate jurisprudence to a 'normative science' (Schmitt 1985, 20), subscribes to a 'dualism' between sociology and jurisprudence, he is led to the unsustainable position that the 'basis for the validity of a norm can only be a norm' (Schmitt 1985, 19). Kelsen can only, in the end, 'negate' or 'repress' the concept of sovereignty (Schmitt 1985, 21). Indeed, underlying the elevation of the rule of law by the liberal constitutionalists is their wholesale but mistaken rejection 'of the concept of sovereignty as a residue of the authoritarian state' (Schmitt 1985, 25).

Schmitt's work is committed to reinstating the central importance of the concept of sovereignty as a political concept. Politics, for Schmitt, and the organisation of politics, is not just about setting up a legal framework. Politics is an autonomous activity, and Schmitt feels the need to champion it very strongly in the face of threats it encounters. Liberal constitutionalists threaten to reduce politics to law, and there is the double menace that 'the political vanishes into the economic or technical-organisational' and that 'the political dissolves into the everlasting discussion' of liberal politicians

(Schmitt 1985, 65). As Schmitt importantly maintains, 'we know that any decision about whether something is *unpolitical* is always a *political* decision, irrespective of who decides and what reasons are advanced' (Schmitt 1985, 2, emphasis in original). The legal order is what is normally valid, but it cannot handle exceptional occurrences.

Coming to the next of Schmitt's key concepts, this argument prompted Schmitt to examine the gap between the legal order and the state that opens up because of the distinction between, as Kelly puts it, the 'substance and exercise of sovereignty'. For Schmitt, this distinction points out the false assumption that 'every juridical norm presupposes the homogeneity of the normal situation to give it meaning' (Kelly 2003, 178). The exception, Schmitt argued, is the occurrence that 'cannot be subsumed' under law (Schmitt 1985, 13). What is required in such a situation, according to Schmitt, is a 'command' rather than a norm (Schmitt 1985, 20). The exception is anomalous precisely because the law cannot anticipate it, and because its irregularity challenges the norms implicit in the law. The idea of civil disobedience is an example of such irregularity because it raises the question of how acts can be permitted that flagrantly go against the law and the legal system to which we are obliged.

Schwab summarises well (1985, xvii) the three questions that Schmitt poses in *Political Theology* to tease out the details of this cleft between the legal order and the state. The first concerns the identification of which authority in the state is competent to decide that an exception has taken place. The second asks which authority in the state is competent to determine the measures that should be undertaken to safeguard political unity, when an exception occurs. The third question was, which authority in the state is competent to conclude that order and stability have been restored? Schwab's elucidation aligns with Strong's explication of two constructive, non-accidental, ambiguities in the words 'decides' and 'exception' in the meaning of Schmitt's opening sentence in *Political Theology*, 'Sovereign is he who decides on the exception'. In the original German, the word 'decides' implies that sovereignty comprehends both deciding when an exceptional case has occurred, and deciding what to do about it (Strong 2005, xi–xii). The word 'exception' refers to a legal state of emergency but also more broadly to a political crisis or state of urgency (Strong 2005, xiii).

The answer to these three questions lies for Schmitt in the conception of sovereignty. For it is sovereignty, says Schmitt, that mediates between the legal order (which requires a 'normal situation' in order to operate and make sense) and political conflict. And whereas legal theorists conflate the legal and the political, Schmitt maintains that the definition of sovereignty is crucial in marking a clear separation between the legal and the political. For the essential definition of sovereignty is not in legal terms, as 'the highest, legally independent, underived power' (Schmitt 1985, 17), but in political terms as the authority to decide an exception. For Schmitt this definition takes account of the way that in 'political reality there is no irresistible highest or greatest power that operates according to the certainty of natural law' (Schmitt 1985, 17). The problem that legal theorists do not recognise, Schmitt argues, is that if you have a competent working legal order, then there is no need for sovereignty, but if that legal order is fundamentally challenged, it has no way of defending itself. Law is a blunt instrument for sovereignty. For if the authority of the law is effectively challenged, then its legitimacy is already compromised. A 'legal breach' (Schmitt 1985, 24), a breach of legal continuity, can only be overcome by a political decision.

In his search for a conception of sovereignty relevant to the modern state, Schmitt held that the problems of politics in the twentieth century could only be resolved through the key notion of sovereignty. But he argued that in order to be relevant to the modern world, the conception of sovereignty needed to be set free from the confusions and sterility of the liberal legal constitutionalist tradition epitomised by Kelsen. Liberal constitutionalism is self-defeating since, by saying that the 'state is confined exclusively to producing law', the liberal state ends up doing 'nothing but' assigning 'the legal value of [dominant] interests' (Schmitt 1985, 23). At the same time the liberal principle of pluralism serves to undermine the state as the sovereign body, since no association — not even the state — can be taken as primary (Schwab 1976, 12). The liberal tradition had attempted to construct a rational and scientific legal system which would insulate the state from the exception. But according to Schmitt, not only was that attempt futile, for 'the legal idea cannot translate itself independently'. Schmitt contends that a 'distinctive determination of which individual person or which concrete body can assume such an authority cannot be derived from the mere legal quality of the maxim' (Schmitt 1985, 31). The attempt was also damaging because exceptions have a positive role to play, in acting to remind people of their political identity — what the identity of their state is.

Schmitt argued that the relationship between politics and law is such that while in normal times sovereign authority is dormant and it is the normally valid legal order that governs, in times of exception the sovereign authority transcends that legal order. Sovereignty is tied to law, but in the final analysis is above the law. While the state (representing politics and sovereignty) and the constitution (representing law) are interdependent, the strategy of strengthening the constitution cannot, and should not, entirely dismiss the positive role played by the exception in political life. The core of the authority of the sovereign is his or her exclusive possession of the right of political decision-making, the right to decide 'what constitutes the public interest or interest of the state' (Schmitt 1985, 6). This is what Schmitt means when he defines the sovereign, in the very first line of *Political Theology*, as 'he who decides on the exception' (Schmitt 1985, 5), and sovereignty in turn as 'the highest power, not a derived power'. As he puts it, it is 'precisely the exception that makes relevant the subject of sovereignty' (Schmitt 1985, 6). The sovereign is the one who decides when an occurrence amounts to an exception, when political conflict mounts 'a danger to the existence of the state' (Schmitt 1985, 6). The sovereign has the authority to name a state of affairs as an exception, who decides that an issue is a 'borderline case and not ... routine' (Schmitt 1985, 5). And the sovereign is also the one who decides what to do about it, and decides when the exception has passed with stability restored and the rule of law again in place.

Kalyvas rejects the idea that for Schmitt 'the constitutive mark of sovereignty ... [is] the discretionary power of an unlimited supreme authority that is above and outside the restraints of the existing legal order'. Sovereignty for Schmitt is not simply 'the contingent, unpredictable subjective moment of the concrete manifestation of an undetermined will' (Kalyvas 2000, 345), Kalyvas articulates. He argues convincingly against the view that sovereignty for Schmitt amounts to a 'groundless, irrational will contained in an arbitrary personal decision of a plebiscitarian president' with absolute discretionary power (Kalyvas 2000, 346), and locates sovereignty for Schmitt instead in its 'norm-positing aspect', in 'its creative, instituting power to set new systems of fundamental laws, to instaurate new political and social orders' and especially in its 'power to create new constitutions' (Kalyvas 2000, 348).

We come now to the next of Schmitt's key concepts, the state. According to Schmitt the state is governed, not by Right and law, but by the ever-present possibility of conflict. Whereas in the German political tradition dominated by Hegel the state is seen as the realisation of the highest form of moral life, for Schmitt the role of the state is to provide the framework in which individual wills can operate. Schmitt argues strongly against the liberal constitutionalist idea of the 'sovereignty of law' (Schmitt 1985, 22) and in favour of the sovereignty of he who can command in the state of exception. This leads Kelly to argue that 'Schmitt's equation of the state and politics rested upon a quasi-existential, rather than a strictly legal basis' (Kelly 2003, 11). Schmitt agreed with Hobbes that the key political player is the one who holds authority and can command obedience, but he observed that it is not always the designated sovereign, the legally-constituted authority who possesses this power. Schmitt advocated a theory of sovereignty in which the sovereign represents the state, precisely because in a crisis 'the state remains, whereas law recedes' (Schmitt 1985, 12). The state has a monopoly on politics, according to Schmitt and so its representative, in the form of the sovereign, is the only one that can recognise and discriminate between friend and enemy (Schwab 1985, xxiv).

It follows from Schmitt's view of the state that, at the international level, 'international law, which governs relations between states, is law that does not distinguish between just and unjust, a nondiscriminating concept of war'. For Schmitt, '[w]ar between states derives its dignity and its honour and hence also its right from the fact that states wage wars only against states and that only states can face one another as enemies' (Schmitt 1996, 48). Schmitt develops this line of argument in his essays on *The Leviathan in the State Theory of Thomas Hobbes* of 1938, and he makes this point after outlining the consequences of Hobbes's theory of the state for the development of the overwhelming power of the 'consummate impartiality' (Schmitt 1996, 50) of the modern neutral state machine. The meaning of Schmitt's statement in relation to local events can be taken as providing a sham neutrality behind which the Nazis could perpetrate any kind of grossly immoral acts, wrongly taking moral judgments out of politics as Habermas suggests. It can also be taken as a critique of the hegemonic power of the Nazi state.

Kelly usefully explains Schmitt's position more fully when he links the fact that 'Kant's search for "perpetual peace" ... receives short shrift from Schmitt', with Schmitt's perception that 'the culmination of the 'search for neutrality (more bluntly peace) has been reached with modern liberalism and its "faith" in the neutrality of technicity and economic rationality', as well as its attempt to neuter the political sphere through its penetration of the state with multiple interest-groups (Kelly 2003, 196).

Added to all this was Schmitt's observation that, in politics, there is a widespread tendency to polarise political differences, and to view adversaries not just as opponents or competitors but to elevate them to the status of the forces of evil. This is also what he means when he says that there is a tendency to 'theologise' political conflict. This is the next key concept to be found in Schmitt's theory of sovereignty. Schwab's note, that in Schmitt's view, 'the church habitually meddled in affairs beyond its concern and that theology opened many avenues for politicising society' (Schwab 1985 xxiv), highlights the negative connotations of theology for Schmitt by the 1920s. Schmitt built upon the meaning of 'theologising' political conflict by developing the friend/enemy distinction in *The Concept of the Political*. The dominant realist strand of the Western tradition of international relations has regarded the friend/enemy distinction as characterising the international stage, but Schmitt contended that the same distinction applies also to domestic politics. He argued that '[t]o create tranquility, security, and order and thereby establish the normal situation is the prerequisite for legal norms to be valid'. However, for Schmitt, insofar as 'a state is a political entity, this requirement for internal peace compels it in critical situations to decide also upon the domestic enemy' (Schmitt 1976, 46).

The theologisation of political conflict also refers to Schmitt's 'secularisation thesis' in *Political Theology*, that 'all significant concepts of the modern theory of the state are secularised theological concepts', not only historically but also because of their 'systematic structure' (Schmitt 1985, 36). Müller skilfully analyses the way the relationship between legal and theological concepts remained profoundly ambiguous in Schmitt's work, asking whether the connection is a 'matter of analogy, of genealogy, of a secret, continuing dependence, or even a thinly veiled political demand to re-theologise politics'. Müller assesses that the relationship for Schmitt was 'more than a "research programme"' but 'less than the collapse of politics into theology', and ultimately 'amounted to a substantial demand to structure the political according to theological principles' (Müller 1999, 69).

For Schmitt, the enemy refers to a collective grouping (whether it be a political party, a church, or an economic interest group), and what is at stake here is a 'public enemy' and not just any competitor or a private adversary (Schmitt 1976, 28). Problems arise when internal antagonisms between, for instance political parties intensify to the extent that they take up the whole domain of politics (Schmitt 1976, 32). In his own situation in Germany, Schmitt contended, if the Weimar state was not prepared to identify as an enemy those forces on the left and right that threatened to subvert the state altogether, there was little hope for it. Schmitt stresses that, for him, the friend/enemy distinction is not a normative ideal but a description of how things stand in the real world (Schmitt 1976, 28). Thus sovereignty is the authority to decide on the exception, and the authority to designate the domestic enemy.

The importance of the friend/enemy distinction in Schmitt's work lies not only in the analytical capacity it gave for identifying the domestic enemy, but also and crucially in that it stands in place of a definition of politics. Kelly observes that, for Schmitt, 'the political is a supra-historical phenomenon, measuring the degree of intensity in the relationships between friends and (public) enemies' (Kelly 2003, 302). Schmitt significantly refused to provide a definition of politics, but argued that in the face of the overwhelming contingency, specificity and volatility of politics, the friend/enemy distinction serves as a constant, a 'criterion' of the political, which specifies 'the logic of the political' (Schmitt 1976, 79). Whether Schmitt envisaged the friend/enemy distinction along the lines of a temperature gauge measuring the degree at which a group was set on subverting the state rather than working within it, or in terms of a spectrum on which to plot political positions, or in some other way, is not clear.

Schmitt also maps the friend/enemy distinction appropriate to politics onto other intellectual fields. So, the distinction between good and evil is the key discriminator for Schmitt which governing morality, while the distinction between beautiful and ugly governs aesthetics, and that between profitable and unprofitable governs economics. The political is, like these other domains, an 'independent' and irreducible sphere of knowledge and action (Schmitt 1976, 26), and 'the autonomy of the political becomes evident by virtue of its being able to treat, distinguish, and comprehend the friend-enemy antithesis independently of other antitheses' (Schmitt 1976, 27). But, most importantly for Schmitt, the political is also different and in a sense superior to these other domains, because the 'political can derive its energy from the most varied human endeavours'. Crucially, the political domain 'does not describe its own substance, but only the intensity of an association or dissociation of human beings whose motive can be religious, national...economic, or of another kind' (Schmitt 1976, 38). It follows for Schmitt that a grouping like an extremist political party, oriented towards the 'most extreme possibility', is thereby 'the decisive entity' driving politics. It is 'sovereign in the sense that the decision about the critical situation, even if it is the exception, must always necessarily reside there' (Schmitt 1976, 38). In this way Schmitt's theory of sovereignty is predicated on a notion of the political as that which tests the limits of sovereign authority.

Müller adds an insight into the meaning of the political for Schmitt here. According to Müller, while Schmitt was highly aware of the politicisation of concepts, he 'did not say that every concept had to be political'. On the other hand Schmitt, on Müller's view, 'certainly did not want to restrict the political to one autonomous "sphere"'. For such a view, according to Schmitt's logic, 'would have left him within the modern liberal discourse of social differentiation' (Müller 1999, 74).

Underlying the friend/enemy distinction and the meaning of politics is Schmitt's view that 'all genuine theories [and this thereby disqualifies liberalism from the status of a 'genuine' political theory] presuppose man to be evil, i.e., by no means an unproblematic but a dangerous and dynamic being' (Schmitt 1976, 61). For 'the sphere of the political is ... determined by the real possibility of enmity' (Schmitt 1976, 64). According to Schwab, Schmitt felt he was witnessing a shift in Germany from 'politics' as a sphere of judgment over which the state necessarily held a monopoly (Schmitt 1976, 44), to 'the political' as an extended but fragmented and ill-defined area as 'new protagonists become the core of the entire complex of problems' (Schmitt, quoted by Schwab 1976, 12-13). If Schwab is correct, then the meaning of the friend/enemy criterion is also influenced by this shift. However, the evidence Schwab quotes for this view comes from Schmitt's 1972 Preface to Le categorie del 'politico', edited by Italian scholars late in Schmitt's career. Schmitt does not make this distinction in the 1927 text of *The Concept of the Political* or its 1932 elaborations, and it is not borne out by Schmitt's use of the terms there.

More plausibly, Schmitt's decision to call his book *The Concept of the Political* and not *The Concept of Politics* has to do with his enduring sense that the key question is 'what makes a situation political?' or 'what is "the political" situation', which brings us to identify friend and enemy groupings, rather than the question 'what is politics?' that only leads us down a definitional dead-end. Müller argues plausibly that 'the political' for Schmitt 'could be conceived of as a field of tensions between different authorities' (Müller 1999 65), so that political contest takes place between different concretely-represented or personified substantive ideas. For Schmitt, the question 'what makes a situation political?' is concrete and sharpens our antennae to look for areas of social conflict, whereas 'what is politics?' is only a dull, abstract academic question. This reading of politics is very important for understanding Schmitt's theory of sovereignty.

The next key concept of Schmitt's theory of sovereignty is 'decisionism'. This concept is crucial to Schmitt, given the unbridgeable gap he perceives between the normal rule of day-to-day life and the crisis situation, and the insurmountable problem of legal indeterminacy. Strong observes (Strong 2005, xv) that Schmitt is at pains to distinguish between decisionism in general (the view that any choice is better than none) and 'genuine decisionism' (which accurately differentiates politically between friend and enemy). Strong also highlights that for Schmitt the purpose of the decision is democratic legitimacy, not dictatorship (Strong 2005, xxv). Schmitt begins from the point that what 'matters for the reality of legal life is who decides', which is a question not just about the 'substantive correctness' of the decision but also about the crucial 'question of competence' (Schmitt 1985, 34). The matter of 'who decides?' — which becomes highly politicised in an emergency situation — is as much about the 'who' as the 'decides'. And it is a key element of Schmitt's theory that the 'who' must be a personal authority rather than a category like 'the people'. He argues when discussing Rousseau's theory that 'the necessity by which the people always will what is right is not identical with the rightness that emanated from the commands of the personal sovereign' (Schmitt 1985, 48). For the 'unity that a people represents does not possess this decisionist character' (Schmitt 1985, 49). It is this line of reasoning that leads Kelly to conclude that even where Schmitt discusses sovereignty 'in terms of the *pouvoir constituant* of the *Volk*, he actually develops further his assessment of the primary role of the *Reichsprasident* as the true representative of the political unity of the nation' (Kelly 2003, 209).

Decisionism relates directly to the notion of sovereignty because sovereignty is 'defined correctly, not as the monopoly to coerce or to rule, but as the monopoly to decide' (Schmitt 1985, 13). Schmitt places enormous weight here on the act of judgment made by the sovereign in deciding when an exception has occurred (and what to do about it, and when it has been resolved or overcome). Sovereignty for Schmitt thus has a performative quality, as it did in Rousseau. As Kelly observes, the sovereign 'not only resolves the exceptional situation, but also decides if the situation is indeed exceptional in the first place' (Kelly 2003, 185). The significance of that act for sovereignty lies in that 'no higher authority could review the decision' (Schmitt 1985, 56). Schmitt holds very strongly that the validity of settled legal prescriptions is entirely appropriate during times of normal politics, during politics-as-usual. As he says, every 'general norm demands a normal, everyday frame of life to which it can be factually applied and which is subjected to its regulations'. However, the problem is that there 'exists no norm that is applicable to chaos'. For 'a legal order to make sense, a normal situation must exist, and he is sovereign who definitely decides whether this normal situation actually exists'. It is in this sense, then, that '[a]ll law is "situational law"' (Schmitt 1985, 13).

While Schmitt argues that even during a crisis the sovereign acts through the law, and applies the law to an acknowledged political circumstance, he was aware that the latitude granted the sovereign to interpret politics and the law and to make a personal decision, was radical. He takes Hobbes as the 'classical representative' (Schmitt 1985, 33) of the personal and concrete conception of sovereignty associated with decisionism. Hobbes is an important theorist for Schmitt precisely because Hobbes refused to invert the value of sovereignty and law as the later liberal constitutional tradition did. Hobbes 'rejected all attempts to substitute an abstractly valid order for a concrete sovereignty of the state' (Schmitt 1985, 33). Schmitt quotes with approval more than once Hobbes's conclusion that authority, not truth, makes law (Schmitt 1985, 52). But the notion of 'decisionism' is also, in another sense, very abstract, and Schmitt recognised this as a problem. The decisionist, as Schmitt puts it, by 'focusing on the moment, always runs the risk of missing the stable content inherent in every great political movement' (Schmitt 1985, 3).

Between the 1922 and 1934 versions of *Political Discourse* Schmitt was influenced by the theory of Maurice Hauriou (Schmitt 1985, 3) that the state and its legitimacy can be strengthened through more concrete institutions, what he calls 'concrete orders'. This change softens considerably the radicalness of his vision. Schmitt is referring here to institutions in civil society, legally recognised institutions like occupational interest groups, the professional civil service, and religious associations (Schwab 1985, xxv). He envisaged such 'concrete orders' being represented in a parliament to which the sovereign authority—the popularly-elected president—also participated. Schmitt argues (1985, 2–3) that by 1934 he considered that as well as the impersonal rules advocated by the 'normativist' liberal legal tradition, and the 'decisionist' mode of relating law and politics which he had advanced, there was a third avenue, concerned with 'institutional guarantees'. For Schmitt, in this third mode, 'institutional legal thinking unfolds in institutions and organisations that transcend the personal sphere' (Schmitt 1985, 3). Whether he had in mind institutions in civil society set up by the Nazi regime would require further investigation, but the date of this change to his theory would be consistent with such a suggestion.

We come now to the last of Schmitt's key concepts, the notion of dictatorship. Given that the date of *Die Diktator* in 1921 coincided with his attempts to strengthen the Weimar constitution against extremist parties, this concept cannot be taken to refer to or endorse Hitler in any direct way. Schmitt meant something very specific by the term dictatorship. In using it he is taking issue with the liberal constitutionalist idea that in the modern state the sovereignty of legal norms 'replaces personal force', that we live under 'the rule of laws' rather than under 'the authority of persons, be they natural or artificial (legal) persons' (Schmitt 1985, 22). Schmitt set out an important and indeed crucial role for a personal sovereign, both in the sense of an authority capable of applying an abstract law to a 'concrete decision' in normal times (Schmitt 1985, 34), and in the sense of an authority above the law to intervene in political life in times of crisis. In doing so, Schmitt's theory of sovereignty follows closely those of Hobbes (for whom the personalised sovereign in this sense is permanently and necessarily above the law) and Rousseau (for whom the Lawgiver intervenes, only occasionally, to guide the sovereign body). Schmitt was aware that this role he laid down for the sovereign could lead to abuses of power, and indeed there is a tendency in his theory to seek to drain civil society of any negative political forces that could challenge the state's monopoly on politics.

With this problem of the potential abuse of presidential power in mind he considered the conditions and features of dictatorship. In *Die Diktatur* of the previous year Schmitt had distinguished between the more far-reaching 'sovereign dictatorship' (under which the president abrogates the constitution and a new one is introduced) and the less radical 'commissarial dictatorship' (under which the president can suspend the existing constitution and later restore it). This distinction hinges on Schmitt's crucial recognition of the difference between a particular legal order and the potential of a legal order as such, as well as on his sense that under both forms of dictatorship the president acts for legal reasons and not just on whim or personal interest. Schmitt's distinction contains a condemnation of liberal conceptions of dictatorship as being of the 'sovereign' type, putting its faith in the 'rational, technical nature of the constitution', and so 'always associated with the creation of a "new" order', and also of the 'unstable "combination" of commissarial and sovereign' types (Kelly 2003, 180, 179) in the Weimar constitution's description of the emergency powers at the President's disposal. In the case of an exception the 'two elements of the concept *legal order* are then dissolved' (Schmitt 1985, 12). Exceptions under a commissarial dictatorship could therefore be seen as critical interruptions to normal life, or more accurately as suspensions in order to 'succeed in reimposing the normal situation' with 'traditional, commissarial ways' (Kelly 2003, 178, 180), rather than as creating a complete break with the norm. But for Schmitt, since in both cases the very idea of a legal order persists, both sovereign and commissarial dictatorships 'remain within the framework of the juristic' (Schmitt 1985, 13). On the basis of the notion of commissarial dictatorship Schmitt argued that, in the Weimar republic, only those parties committed to the preservation of the existing constitutional order should be allowed to be active. Parties of the far right and far left that did not respect the constitution but were committed to its abolition, should be outlawed.

Kelly argues that in *Legalitat und Legitimitat* of 1932, Schmitt blurred the boundaries between the two forms of dictatorship, to the point where he had 'incorporated fully the idea of the *Reichsprasident* as both commissarial guardian of the constitution, and added to it the idea of the extraordinary legislator who may himself found a new constitution'. Kelly concludes that the 'merging of sovereignty and emergency powers was now complete', stemming for Schmitt from the necessity to respond to contemporary developments in modern politics (Kelly 2003, 244). Kalyvas puts forward an opposing interpretation, arguing that Schmitt's theory of sovereignty is based on a 'seminal notion of a popular sovereign will', enabling Schmitt to construct 'one of the most powerful and explicit theories of democractic legitimacy' (Kalyvas 2000, 350). However, Kalyvas's claim is made without acknowledging the very indirect nature of that popular sovereignty.

The logic of Schmitt's argument about commissarial dictatorship resembles the structure of Locke's two-fold notion of sovereignty. For Locke, sovereignty is held by the legislative power but is dependent on its conditional, fiduciary nature. If the trust is broken, it triggers a version of sovereignty to 'the people', in civil society. For Schmitt, in normal times sovereignty is exercised through government and the legal system, but in an emergency the president, on behalf of the people, takes over the sovereign role. In both Locke and Schmitt, real sovereign power is dormant unless triggered by an extreme situation. The nature of the extreme situation is very different in the two thinkers. But there are similarities too. In both writers the extreme situation can occur without it meaning a reversion to a state of nature. Both are performative notions — the act of resistance by the people in Locke and the actions of the president in Schmitt. Both are conservative in that neither theorist believes in a strong popular sovereignty. The irony of putting two such writers together, and the structural resemblance of the two arguments, would please neither of them.

In conclusion, Schmitt's central concern is to assert, as Kalyvas (2000, 345) puts it, 'the idea of the political as the original instituting moment', and that it is the state, the political entity of the state (represented in an emergency by the head of state), that is sovereign, not the law. As Kelly notes, for Schmitt 'sovereignty equates with "political" decision', which 'must rest on a transcendental source', given that Schmitt 'mistrusted the idea that the legal order rests on an abstract norm, as Kelsen had suggested' (Kelly 2003, 183). Schmitt was a strong critic of liberalism and liberal democracy and, if there is a viable distinction to be made between legal and political sovereignty, Schmitt comes down very strongly on the priority of political sovereignty. But along with this clear message, Schmitt's theory of sovereignty contains three interesting ambiguities. The first and the second involve a blurring of a particular case with a more general rule, while the third concerns positive and negative aspects of the same concept. First then, on the one hand Schmitt is arguing passionately about the fragile state of politics specifically found in Weimar Germany (and the consequent imperative to defuse political tensions in society), and contrasting that with the tradition of political stability found in England. But on the other hand he is saying that political conflict and the occurrence of the exception is a general feature of politics, and a 'general concept in the theory of the state'.

The second ambiguity concerns Schmitt's attitude to law. Sometimes he suggests that it is specifically the liberal conception of law, focussing upon checks and balances and constitutionalism, that is culpable in denying sovereignty its proper role. At other times, Schmitt argues that the problem lies in the tendency of jurists in general to reduce all politics to law, to see all political problems as legal problems, with legal solutions. Similarly, Schmitt is ambiguous about whether 'the political' sphere applies to the wider arena of political contestation that falls short of an emergency situation (an arena that is broader than the 'endless conversation' of discussion in a liberal parliament that Schmitt so despised), or whether it refers only to the crisis that threatens the state. Both the first and second ambiguity are to some extent about the conflicting claims to authority of tradition and reason. In terms of the authority of reason, Schmitt has his notion of commissarial dictatorship to fall back on. This provides some sense of the groundedness of politics in particular community, but only weakly and not in a strong Hegelian version whereby such groundedness provides stability, continuity and limits the impact of the extreme situation. But Schmitt also exhibits an element of blank slate rationalism in his sense of sweeping away and starting again, and this demonstrates the role of the authority of reason in his work.

Thirdly, Schmitt's attitude to the exception is ambivalent, double-edged. On the one hand the exception represents a breakdown of the political and legal order, and a failure of that order to prevent it occurring. And so what he wants is a strong state that will ensure peace, order and stability. But on the other hand, Schmitt sees the exception as playing a very positive role in political life, rejuvenating and rearticulating our political identity and bringing us together as one. In this respect, Schmitt diverges from Hobbes but is not so far from Hegel (in the revitalising effect of war) after all.

In terms of the contemporary relevance of Schmitt, some followers of Schmitt argue that in our contemporary world, the insecurities caused by supposed changes summed up in the term 'globalisation', make our political world a 'political world of exceptions' too. However, there is an important difference between the political and legal structure with which Schmitt was working and the globalisation hypothesis. Schmitt portrays a very strong image of the state, and holds that the head of state should have a monopoly over deciding the fate of the political, and internationally he was not a cosmopolitanist. It is an important aspect of the most familiar globalisation thesis, by contrast, that politics is fragmented in a globalised world, that governance is no longer captured by centralised states, and that the government functions of states have been eroded. Globalisation theorists tend not to advocate a dictator.

The general features of sovereignty that Schmitt sees as significant are ones whose traditional meaning he seeks to disrupt. He sees as problematic the relationship between sovereignty and the constitution, and takes issue with the equation of sovereignty with the establishment of the highest legal authority. One of the weaknesses in Schmitt's theory is that, while he can legitimately argue that the friend/enemy distinction is not a normative ideal but simply describes reality, he fails to acknowledge that the conceptualisation of that distinction as such is not empirical but normative. However, his view remains fresh because it has the effect of importing into the political theory debate a welcome politicisation of the legal constitutional point of view. The positive value of Schmitt's critique of sovereignty also lies in that it accents the political, contested character of sovereignty, and in that it shows as false the claim to sovereignty's perpetuity. Cristi comes to the same conclusion when he notes, 'sovereignty became visible only during exceptional circumstances, when a constitution was destroyed and another was born. In these circumstances, sovereignty showed up under the guise of constituent power' (Cristi, quoted in Kalyvas 2000, 351).

Schmitt's theory is also useful in the way it reinvests some of the key elements of Hobbes's theory with a sense of the political, an activity that Hobbes had sought to banish. Schmitt's insistence on the priority of the sovereign over the rule of law, his resoluteness to identify the internal or external enemy, and decisionism, all recall Hobbes's overwhelming fear of political breakdown and his drive to eliminate any kind of conflict (religious, political, or rhetorical) that threatened the settled order. Like Hobbes, Schmitt is aware that '[w]hat always matters is only the possibility of conflict' (Schmitt 1976, 39), by which he means extreme conflict that overthrows the state. But Schmitt adds to Hobbes's depoliticised realm the notion of politics as precisely describing the kind of conflict brought about by groupings dedicated to the 'most extreme possibility' and the kind of act of judgment that is necessary for the sovereign to make in this situation. Schmitt also argued, as Kelly observes, that 'the intimate connection between the political and the state had been perverted by a technical liberalism', and his solution was 'to call for a political process of depoliticisation, a "liberation" of the state for the sake of the state' (Kelly 2003, 300).

FOUCAULT

To great effect, Schmitt brought to political theory the perspective of constitutional law and its limitations while Foucault, highly influentially, brought to the question of sovereignty the viewpoint of sociology and a concern with the population considered as a regulated social realm. Both perspectives creatively disrupt and enlarge the settled discourse of political theory on sovereignty. But it is important to recognise from the outset the context in which Foucault is interested in sovereignty. Foucault's examination of sovereignty is part of his larger enterprise of demonstrating the myth of the sovereign subject and of delineating the operation of power — pre-eminently of disciplinary power over certain groups of the population and, later, of non-disciplinary biopower over the population as a whole. His challenge to the political theory discourse on sovereignty which valorises and fetishises the concept of authority while ignoring the effects of power is profound and well-placed, but at the same time his limited interest in sovereignty itself is problematic. The secondary significance of sovereignty for Foucault, in the light of this connection, will be examined later. Foucault was born in 1926 and died in 1984. His intellectual endeavour was shaped in part by living through the episodes of fascism and Stalinism, the 'two black heritages', and the threads he traced from them back to forms of power relation developed across liberal Western states (Fontana and Bertani 2003, 275–6).

Foucault's enormously radical step was to say that the effective location of power in the conditions of the modern contemporary world was no longer in the realm of formal politics, for instance in sovereignty, law and the constitution. Effective power was now to be found in the realm of micro-power and in the disciplinary practices (and later biopower) through which governmental techniques, ruling, and the relationship between ruled and rulers that establishes order, occurs. For Foucault (in the 1976 lectures where he discusses sovereignty at length) the *effective* location of political power is in the subject. That is, political power is now most accurately understood through the way power is inscribed into the body directly, and sovereignty in the old sense emerges as a supplementary effect from this process. The tradition of political theory was very vulnerable to this attack. The mainstream liberal tradition had not and still has not sufficiently recognised the import, for regulation and governing, of surveillance and punishment techniques and normalising sanctions. Nor has it fully accounted for the significance of mass industrial society described by Marx, Weber, Schumpeter and others, the knowledges of it based on behavioural norms developed for government use, and the consequent changes in the operation of power.

Foucault's formulations of these problems and his highlighting of the blindness to them of the mainstream liberal tradition, represents one of the most distinctive features of his theory of sovereignty. Another way of expressing this point begins by noting that especially Kant and Hegel both sought to conceptualise legitimate government on the basis of right rather than power. How can we respond to the serious Foucauldian three-pronged criticism of this position? First, since Kant and Hegel wrote, the reality of society and social power since the eighteenth century has been that the state and sovereign power are oppressive. Second, that the theories of Kant and Hegel themselves have contributed to the effect of producing masks for sovereign oppression by valorising the ideal of 'right'. And third, that such theorists were not sincere and their theories of sovereignty were shams for legitimising the power of an elite. After outlining the content of Foucault's theory of sovereignty we return to some of these questions.

The views of sovereignty developed by Schmitt and Foucault form an interesting contrast and the discussion of Foucault will operate through two comparisons with Schmitt. In the first comparison the two writers can be seen to represent the two directly-opposed positions of the twentieth-century ambivalence about sovereignty. On the one hand sovereignty has been regarded positively as a key element in the triumph of the form of political organisation of the nation-state (expressed for instance in the setting up of the United Nations), together with a sense of the superiority and success of liberal-democratic capitalism. On the other hand sovereignty has been regarded as the focus of a repressive politics. Schmitt, despite his pessimism, can be seen to represent at least the first half of the first view.

He identified sovereignty with state sovereignty, and sought to rejuvenate that identification in order to reclaim an autonomy for politics, in the sense of recognising a situation as political, as a bulwark in the face of threats from extreme political groupings. Schmitt sought to prevent politics being reduced to law, as he thought it had been in the liberal Western legal tradition. But for Foucault sovereignty is a charade and a smokescreen, used to deceive us into regarding repressive power as benign and as having a moral basis in consent and legitimacy.

Schmitt's view also acts as a critique of Foucault, from an unusual source, when Schmitt identifies one of the key concepts which Foucault was to take up, repression, with liberal political theory. Schmitt argues that the 'word repression is utilised in liberal theory as a reproach against state and politics' (Schmitt 1976, 73), and in this light Foucault is a libertarian liberal on the right of the political spectrum. Schmitt asserts the autonomy of politics from the field of his disciplinary background, namely law, while Foucault can be read as asserting the priority of his disciplinary background, sociology and the social realm, over politics. For Schmitt, sovereignty is the badge that proves that the state is a political entity while for Foucault sovereignty, the state and politics are all a sideshow to the real business of disciplinary power in social relations. The central text in which Foucault takes up the question of sovereignty is his 1976 lectures, and in particular Lecture Two, printed in the collection *Power/Knowledge* edited by Gordon (1980), and also as 'Disciplinary Power and Subjection' in Lukes (1986), and in Kelly (1994). The full lectures are found in *Society Must be Defended* (eds Bertani and Fontana 2003). This section of the chapter is also indebted to Tully's 1997 and 1999 explications of some of Foucault's vocabulary.

A key aspect of this first comparison is Foucault's two-pronged attack on sovereignty. His interest in sovereignty arises from his belief that the modern Western discourse of sovereignty has really done two things. It has anaesthetised the issue of political power. And it has concealed other relations of power that are going on in society. On the anaesthetising of political power, according to Foucault the discourse of sovereignty is properly defined as a discourse of power, centring on the concepts of 'right' and 'obedience'. 'The essential role of the theory of right, from medieval times onwards', Foucault argues, 'was to fix the legitimacy of power', in the form of sovereign power (Foucault 1980, 95). But more fundamentally 'right' and 'obedience' are defined in our intellectual tradition as defining the truth of political power. As he says, we 'are subjected to the production of truth through power and we cannot exercise power except through the production of truth'. As a result, says Foucault, through the notion of sovereignty, 'the essential function of the discourse and techniques of right has been to efface the domination intrinsic to power in order to present the latter at the level of appearance under two different aspects: on the one hand, as the legitimate rights of sovereignty, and on the other, as the legal obligation to obey' (Foucault 1980, 95). Foucault's aim, he says, is 'to give due weight ... to the fact of domination, to expose both its latent nature and its brutality'. He aims 'to show not only how right is ... the instrument of this domination ... but also to show [how] right ... transmits and puts in motion relations that are not relations of sovereignty, but of domination'. And when he uses the term 'right' Foucault means to refer 'not simply [to] the laws but the whole complex of apparatuses, institutions and regulations responsible for their application' (Foucault 1980, 95).

Consideration of the masking of other relations of power leads on to Foucault's real agenda here. For according to Foucault this discourse of sovereignty is, as Tully puts it, not really as 'central, constitutive, or 'sovereign' with respect to present politics' (Tully 1997, 4) as we think. Foucault is arguing that, in Tully's words, one will never find 'an alternative way of analysing politics and of thinking and acting politically', (Tully 1997, 11) while one is trapped in the discourse of sovereignty. That is, if one takes part in a 'debate in which you are either for or against sovereignty, one thus misrepresents and so misunderstands what is really going on in modern societies' (Tully 1997, 5). Tully holds plausibly that Foucault's 'demand to do away with political thought organised around the problem of sovereignty is part of his larger objection to any form of analysis organised around a sovereign subject' (Tully 1997, 6). Elsewhere Foucault develops the notion that there is 'no sovereign, founding subject ... on the contrary ... the subject is constituted through practices of subjection or ... practices of liberation' (quoted by Tully 1997, 7). It follow that, as Tully describes, 'all "actors" are constituted and self-constituting in relations of domination, power and confrontation' (Tully 1997, 26). It is the language of subjection and resistance, rather than of sovereign subject and right, that more accurately describes the operation of power in society, according to Foucault.

Thus the discourse of sovereignty and rights has disguised an underlying and much more insidious web of power relations. It is Foucault's claim that we have been more or less unaware of the operation of these more fundamental power relations. This is partly because the discourse of legitimate, state, power has deflected attention away from it, and partly because power operating at this level is not 'at the level of conscious intention or decision' (Foucault 1980, 97). It is Foucault's aim to disclose the operation of these underlying disciplinary practices, in 'local forms and institutions', where power 'becomes capillary' (Foucault 1980, 96). In contrast with the political theory tradition focusing on *sovereignty* in terms of power at the macro level, Foucault aims to reveal the operations of *power* where it can be observed—at the micro level (in institutions and social practices). Domination, he says, occurs not merely through 'the uniform edifice of sovereignty, but [in] the multiple forms of subjection that have a place and function within the social organism'. I want, he says, to 'substitute the problem of domination and subjugation for that of sovereignty and obedience' (Foucault 1980, 96). The question of sovereignty is for him a question of power.

Foucault's level of attention and methodology also raise a second form of comparison with Schmitt, through an interesting similarity here. Both writers want to bring into the light of intellectual analysis what has previously been excluded. In Schmitt's case it is the predicament of the 'exception' that has been denied and suppressed, by the liberal legal tradition. And in Foucault's case it is the full scope of the social relations of domination, the 'mechanisms of exclusion' as he calls them, which have been precluded from consideration. For both, sovereignty has operated to mark barriers of exclusion. For Schmitt it is axiomatic that 'every legal order is based on … the concept of the legal order' (Schmitt 1985, 10), while for Foucault the legal order is a mere smokescreen disguising the operation of power in the social realm.

Some of the key terms for Foucault in this second comparison can be represented through a set of contrasts—between the covert and overt operations of power, the ways in which subjects are constructed, sovereignty as descending compared with disciplinary power as ascending, and the operation of sovereignty through concrete acts contrasted with the operation of disciplinary power through surveillance, normalising sanctions and the panopticon. We will also examine the importance of Foucault's theory of the history of sovereignty.

The first contrast, then, concerns the covert and overt operations of power. Foucault argues that we need to examine how power operates to control, regulate and constrain the conduct and thinking of people, through the variety of material, concrete, disciplinary practices and institutions. Disciplinary power, as Tully notes, is 'organised around a statistical norm of individual and collective behaviour' (Tully1999, 127) and techniques that serve to bring behaviour in line with those norms and monitor the result. Such power operates in institutions both covertly and overtly. Included here is the implicit operation of power relations in the family, sexuality, schools and universities, bureaucracies, hospitals, factories, social work, and in the definitions of health, madness and delinquency. Explicitly, power operates in institutions such as prisons, armies, barracks, the police, and courts of law. Furthermore, Foucault holds that not only is power 'employed and exercised through a net-like organisation', but that we are all 'simultaneously undergoing and exercising this power' (Foucault 1980, 98). As he graphically puts it, 'we all have a fascism in our heads ... [and] we all have a power in our bodies', to be dominated and to subjugate others (Foucault 1980, 99). For instance in a school, as Tully conveys, 'although there is a relation of power between teacher and pupil, and the teacher is said to exercise ... authority over the student, the teacher him or herself is constituted in the school system' (Tully 1997, 13). It follows for Foucault that in contrast with the idea of the sovereign-subject relation, as Tully puts it, 'there is no sovereign subject transcendental to the field of events' (Tully 1997, 13). Furthermore, Tully elucidates, 'in this very general concept of power as a relationship of governance, by acting on the actions of others, it is not a necessary feature of power, for it to be legitimate, that it be exercised through the law or that it be based on consent' (Tully 1997, 14).

In addition, for Foucault, as Tully signals, 'power does not operate only through prohibitions. It is also productive. It aims to govern the conduct of others by inducing them to develop fairly regular habits of thought and behaviour through training' (Tully 1997, 15). Moreover, in his later work Foucault describes what freedom means in terms of 'governmentality', which is how he, in later works discusses disciplinary practice. Here, Tully sums up, 'freedom is not to be free of power, as in the sovereignty model, but rather is the condition of the putting-into-practice of a relationship of power in the sense of governance' (Tully 1997, 17). Thus Foucault has a more positive view of relations of power in his later work, from 1978 onwards, when he came to 'see that he could make sense of both power and resistance only if human subjects were active', as Tully puts it (Tully 1999, 132). In addition, Foucault criticises theorists like Habermas who seek to dissolve relations of power 'in the utopia of a perfectly transparent communication'. According to Foucault, 'relations of power are not bad in themselves', but should be exercised 'with a minimum of domination', (quoted in Tully 1999, 130-131) and a maximum of contestation and questioning.

Foucault argued in *Discipline and Punish* that 'although, in a formal way, the representative regime makes it possible, directly or indirectly ... for the will of all to form the fundamental authority of sovereignty, the disciplines provide, at the base, a guarantee of the submission of forces and bodies'. He makes the point that '[t]he "Enlightenment", which discovered the liberties, also invented the disciplines' (Foucault 1977, 222). Later on, Foucault theorised power in terms of biopower, 'a power over life that aims at the regulation of populations'. As Dean puts it, Foucault's 'genealogy of biopower suggests that law is transformed from a "juridical system" allied with the theory and practice of sovereignty to one that partakes of the regulatory functions of norms' (Dean 1999, 168).

This leads us to the next contrast, the way in which Foucault considers that subjects are constructed. Foucault contends that it is through these means, through the 'effects of power' that we become subjects and become conscious of ourselves as persons. 'We should try', he says, 'to grasp subjection in its material instance as a constitution of subjects'. He goes on to assess his project as 'the exact opposite of Hobbes' project in *Leviathan*', which in his view was concerned with 'the constitution of a unitary, singular body animated by the spirit of sovereignty — from the particular wills of a multiplicity of individuals' (Foucault 1980, 97). So rather than the top-down view taken by Hobbes, of subjects transferring their power to the sovereign, Foucault wants to establish the importance of a bottom-up view of subjects constituted by power in subjection. His project, as he spells out clearly in Lecture Three, is 'showing how actual relations of subjugation manufacture subjects' (Foucault 2003, 45).

Foucault is concerned to attack the view that he sees as having characterised the modern tradition of thinking about sovereignty which rests on the metaphor of sovereignty, whereby the individual subject is regarded as sovereign unto himself, with rights and effective autonomy, submitting to the dictates of the law only by consent, in relations untainted by power. For Foucault this is merely a 'juridical' model of the subject, which does not accord with and overlooks the reality of domination and subjection that characterise day-to-day life. Against this inflated juridical, sovereign subject, Foucault seeks to set out the reality of the subject who is constituted in social power relations. The discourse of sovereignty and the juridical subject does not help us, indeed hinders us, from recognising the operation of disciplinary power, for Foucault.

As Foucault holds in the Course Summary of the 1976 Lectures, 'to make a concrete analysis of power relations, we must abandon the juridical model of sovereignty', because it sets out an invalid conceptualisation of the subject. Foucault argues, '[t]hat model in effect presupposes that the individual is a subject with natural rights or primitive powers; it sets itself the talk of accounting for the ideal genesis of the State; and finally, it makes the law the basic manifestation of power'. Instead, '[w]e should be trying to study power not on the basis of the primitive terms of the relationship, but on the basis of the relationship itself, to the extent that it is the relationship itself that determines the elements on which it bears'. So, 'rather than asking ideal subjects what part of themselves or their powers they have surrendered in order to let themselves become subjects, we have to look at how relations of subjugation can manufacture subjects' (Foucault 2003, 265). Thus, the proper conceptualisation of the subject is crucial, for Foucault. It underpins our accurate understanding and identification of how power operates, and as a result it disbars sovereignty from serious consideration.

Coming to the last of these contrasts, Foucault distinguishes between sovereignty as descending and disciplinary power as ascending. He describes the bottom-up view of power as 'an ascending analysis of power'. It starts 'from its infinitesimal mechanisms, which each have their own history, their own trajectory, their own techniques and tactics'. The aim is to 'then see how these mechanisms of power have been — and continue to be — invested, colonised, utilised ... transformed, displaced, extended ... by ever more general mechanisms and by forms of global domination' (Foucault 1980, 99). The effect of these disciplinary powers is that 'more general powers and economic interests are able to engage with these technologies'. In this way Foucault asserts a clear link between the micro and macro levels of power. He sees the mechanisms of control in the family and in social relations as having a direct bearing on the exercise and distribution of economic and political power.

In sum then, through this set of contrasts Foucault maintains that we are able to focus, 'on the nature of power not towards the juridical edifice of sovereignty, the State apparatuses and the ideologies which accompany them', such as the ideology of education and the ideology of parliamentary democracy. In order to explain power and its operation we need rather to look 'towards domination and the material operators of power, towards forms of subjection'. In consequence, Foucault emphasises, we 'must eschew the model of Leviathan in the study of power. We must escape from the limited field of juridical sovereignty and State institutions, and instead base our analysis of power on the study of the techniques and tactics of domination' (Foucault 1980, 102).

We come now to Foucault's theory of the history of sovereignty, which seeks to provide a context for the contrast between sovereignty as descending and disciplinary power as ascending. The theory of history sets out to explain the manner in which the discourse of sovereignty masks the performance of disciplinary power through concrete acts like surveillance. In consequence, for Foucault, as Tully observes, the 'ability of the language and practice of sovereignty to appear more central and sovereign than it actually is can be explained historically' (Tully 1997, 5). Foucault outlines a history of sovereignty as having four stages. According to Foucault, in only the first stage is sovereign power an accurate description of the operation of power in society. As Tully sums up, sovereignty was used 'to refer to a mechanism of power that was effective under the feudal monarchy'. In the second stage sovereignty 'served as instrument and even as justification for the construction of the large-scale administrative monarchies'. Then in the sixteenth and seventeenth centuries, in the third stage, it was a weapon to limit or to reinforce royal power. Finally in the eighteenth century it was used to construct, 'in opposition to the administrative, authoritarian and absolutist monarchies, ... an alternative model, that of parliamentary democracy' (Foucault 1980, 103). Tully notes that for Foucault, sovereignty 'served ... as the great legitimation of the revolutions and constitution-building of the nineteenth and twentieth centuries' (Tully 1999, 125).

Schmidt and Wartenberg add the insight that in the lecture 'Qu'est-ce que la critique', Foucault argues that political discourse in the fifteenth and sixteenth centuries was concerned with the question 'how to govern?' The kind of resistance that emerged at that time was not in response to the general question 'how not to be governed?', but was a questioning of particular forms and applications of the sovereignty thesis, with respect to the spiritual authority of the church and the civil authorities' claim to sovereignty on the basis of natural law (Schmidt and Wartenberg 1994, 289). Moreover, according to Foucault's theory of history, in feudal societies sovereign power was meaningful in summing up the 'relationship of sovereignty' between the physical existence of sovereign and subject, encompassing 'the totality of the social body' (Foucault 198, 104). However, since the development of modern science, there has been a new mechanism of power, for instance through continuous surveillance and increasing regulation, rather than through concrete acts like levies and oaths of allegiance. Foucault holds that this 'new type of power ... can no longer be formulated in terms of sovereignty'. He argues that 'this disciplinary power ought by rights to have led to the disappearance of the grand juridical edifice created by' the theory of sovereignty. But, he says, 'in reality, the theory of sovereignty has continued not only to exist as an ideology of right, but also to provide the organising principle of the legal codes of Europe'. The theory of sovereignty has survived, he reasons, partly as an enduring criticism of monarchy, and partly it has 'allowed a system of right to be superimposed upon the mechanisms of discipline ... to conceal ... the element of domination' (Foucault 1980, 105).

The net result, says Foucault, is that the juridical systems 'have enabled sovereignty to be democratised through the constitution of a public right articulated upon collective sovereignty, while at the same time this democratisation of sovereignty was fundamentally determined by and grounded in mechanisms of disciplinary coercion' (Foucault 1980, 105). Modern society since the nineteenth century, says Foucault, 'has been characterised on the one hand, by a legislation, a discourse, an organisation based on public right, whose principle of articulation is the social body and the delegative status of each citizen; and, on the other hand, by a closely linked grid of disciplinary coercions whose purpose is in fact to assure the cohesion of this same social body' (Foucault 1980, 106). Furthermore, and in a crucial twist, the effects of disciplinary power cannot be overcome or limited by recourse to sovereignty (either in its popular, parliamentary or state forms), because the two mechanisms work together as power in our society (Foucault 1980, 108). As Smith elucidates, Foucault does not 'allow that sovereign power and law may be potentially liberating, because he casts them as closely implicated in the pre-modern form of government as a system of commands and prohibitions' and as 'subservient to disciplinary power' (Smith 2000, 301). Indeed, Foucault concludes Lecture Two by contending that both sovereignty and disciplinary power need to be resisted.

Having set out the features of Foucault's theory of sovereignty we can assess his challenge to mainstream liberal political theory. We can also address three questions that arise from ambiguities and problems in this conception, namely in the theory of history, the theory of power, and the conception of law. To begin with we can ask what work the historical stages that Foucault outlines are doing for him, and whether the series of stages is convincing. The history of sovereignty Foucault puts forward is problematic in that it does not pay sufficient attention to the complex continuities and similarities between the stages and variations within each stage, across time and place. For instance, Habermas justifiably takes issue with the way Foucault 'filters out the internal aspects of the development of law', and so 'the ungrounded impression arises that the bourgeois constitutional state is a dysfunctional relic from the period of absolutism' (Habermas 1994, 101). The 'critical history' of sovereignty that Foucault provides us with is a truncated model of four phases that is vulnerable to queries about how the criteria for the phases were constructed as well as about the narrowness of the understanding of sovereignty that the four phases exhibit. Moreover, by writing about sovereignty as only one of the 'genealogies of the juridical form of the subject', as Tully characterises his method (Tully 1999, 124), Foucault limits what he can say.

The way the genealogy of sovereignty is presented in the 1976 lectures also gives the impression that this model stands for the whole of what there is to be said about the theory of history of sovereignty. Indeed, it is problematic that Foucault is working with models rather than with historically accurate portrayals, and the credibility of the argument is subject to sound arguments which question the gap between a model and what it is meant to represent. Moreover, the use of the method of genealogy does not exhaust the realm of historical enquiry. History is in part contingent, it could have been different. For example there is the drama of the period through which Schmitt lived and wrote. Politics in Germany in the period 1930-32 could have been different, and Schmitt could have chosen in 1933 not to collaborate. The genealogical method does not adequately capture this feature of history.

On the question of the plausibility of the stages of the history of sovereignty, Foucault's characterisation of the feudal period can be questioned on the grounds that this period of history was not free of repressive social power relations and domination. Foucault uses a very narrow selection of historical evidence for his history. He maintains that the relationship between sovereign and subject does characterise 'the mode in which power was exercised' (Foucault 1986, 238) in the medieval period, but that thereafter power was exercised through disciplinary means though the language of sovereignty was retained. However, the church and feudal landlords exercised very powerful constraints on behaviours and thinking. Moreover, the extent of the divergence between Foucault and the mainstream political theory tradition in accounting for the beginnings of modern sovereignty is not addressed by Foucault. The mainstream canon sees Bodin and Hobbes as first conceptualising modern sovereignty, whereas Foucault's history starts three centuries or so before this. Moreover, Foucault can be seen as setting up a reverse of the Enlightenment story of progress from medieval to more enlightened times, a story which highlights the growth of scientific knowledge and emancipatory developments in the political realm. Foucault's story is one of progressive deterioration and intensification, but in portraying his story in this manner Foucault remains tied to that Enlightenment model. Furthermore, as Zizek points out, Foucault is unable to show how sovereignty emerges, and consequently 'the abyss that separates micro-procedures from the spectre of power remains unbridgeable' (Zizek 1999, 66).

The second issue at stake concerns power. We can understand Foucault's antipathy to sovereignty in the light of the enormous amount of work that the concept of power does in his theory. Foucault's belief that sovereignty masks the operation of, the more important, disciplinary social power relations, is true in its own terms because of how he defines power. In Lecture 1 his starting point is that 'the mechanism of power is repression' (Foucault 2003, 16) and he effectively conflates power and politics by identifying both with war, in his inversion of Clausewitz's proposition. Foucault maintains both that 'Power is war, the continuation of war by other means', and in the following sentence that 'politics is the continuation of war by other means' (Foucault 2003, 15). By erasing any meaning for politics other than that of the operation of repressive power, it is clear in Foucault's logic that sovereign power acts to suppress and cover up the wider disciplinary form of social power. There is no place in Foucault's system for sovereignty as a *political* concept as a result, both because the only meaningful political concept for him is repressive power, and because for him it is *social* power relations that have primary salience, not political ones. Focusing only on social power relations cancels the potential of the political sphere as one where inequalities can be voiced and contested. Foucault rightly highlights the role of disciplinary practices, but this does not annul or invalidate the possibility or need for politics. The juridical viewpoint and the disciplinary one, to use Foucault's vocabulary, do not take up the whole sphere of what we can say about politics and sovereignty. They do not represent the either/or that Foucault wants to make them. His two choices do not exhaust the field of politics.

The key liberal principles that accompany the sense of citizens related through law and sovereignty are the idea of the free, rational and autonomous individual as the basis for theorising, and a thin secular public realm. Foucault is right to highlight the social as a corrective to these two principles – that individuals exist and act within a network of social power relations, and that the 'thick' social world of values, power and inequalities deserves recognition in the public realm. But other theorists have taken this point further by making links between the social and politics, for instance showing how the social realm is important to politics in the form of the cultural communities (of class, religion, ethnicity etc) and civil associations that invest the notion of collective action with value.

Foucault is not fundamentally interested in the category of sovereignty but in the category of disciplinary power. His key concept is power, and sovereignty acts as a historical precursor to power, disciplinary power as well as now a mask to power, to give extra credence to the theory of power. Sovereignty is Foucault's 'other'. It is merely explicit but tamed and secondary power, in contrast with the much more damaging and insidious form of disciplinary power. As an 'other' sovereignty is certainly a very powerful metaphor in Foucault's line of argument. Sovereignty stands for the idea of being constituted, of subjectivisation itself. At the same time Foucault argues that sovereignty is really illusory, and that subjectivity is fragmented.

We can also ask whether Foucault is claiming too much, in attributing so much to the concept of sovereignty. Why fix on sovereignty? Foucault did not have to pick on sovereignty as his 'other' here. The choice of sovereignty seems in one light rather arbitrary. He could just have well, for instance, chosen 'obligation', 'legitimacy', or picked on the contractarian tradition through which the social contact is envisaged, in Kersting's words, as 'the place for a simultaneous socialization and establishment of domination' (Kersting 1992, 353), as well as its association with the institutionalisation of private property. As Kersting notes, [d]omination in the modern world is only to be justified through consensus and the freely willed self-obligation of the citizen'. This insight gains force when set against the background that '[m]odern contractualism is the expression of a revolution in the theory of legitimation, in which the traditional teleological and theological justifications in political philosophy has been deprived of power by the sovereign will of the individual' (Kersting 1992, 353).

Foucault could also have chosen the category of authority as his 'other', and this could have supported the logic of his argument more clearly since the nub of the idea of sovereignty that Foucault contests is the claim that sovereignty rests on an authority relationship. By conflating power and authority, and by talking about subjects' obedience rather than authority, Foucault misrepresents the sovereignty discourse in the political theory tradition. The problem with this conflation is that conceptualising power raises the question of resistance and agency, whereas the political theory tradition locates sovereignty in a cluster of concepts that are about the polity, rather than about denying agency to subjects. In this way Foucault's critique of sovereignty as anaesthetising and masking is to some extent misplaced. It may be that we have 'a fascism in our heads' but that is not all we have.

Another consequence of Foucault being actually much more interested in power, and specifically 'disciplinary' power, is that he only discusses sovereign power as a prelude, as a means of coming on to discuss power more fully. His priorities are clear when he says, at the end of Lecture Five, 'Once we begin to talk about power relations, we are not talking about right, and we are not talking about sovereignty; we are talking about domination' (Foucault 2003, 111). It is fair to ask, therefore, whether Foucault has a theory of *sovereignty* at all.

It is also the case that Foucault's focus on power rather than sovereignty leads him to effectively lump together all the canonical theories of sovereignty we have discussed, from Bodin to Hegel. The outcome of this homogenisation is that Foucault overlooks the diversity and distinctiveness of conceptions of sovereignty. For example he argues that freedom in the sovereignty model means to be free of power, in other words negative liberty. However, Rousseau's, Hegel's, and Spinoza's conceptions of sovereignty do not operate with that meaning of freedom, or not only it, and contain a much more complex view of freedom including positive freedom.

This book has sought to demonstrate that the meaning of sovereignty is not fixed and unified but malleable and diverse. Foucault accepts a very conventional definition of sovereignty, as state sovereignty, and as a 'uniform edifice' (Foucault 1986, 232). Foucault is attacking a very specific formulation of sovereignty, and one which is perhaps the easiest target. A strong reason for Foucault to introduce this meaning of sovereignty is because it enables him to construct a dichotomy between overtly repressive power and the covert but more treacherous social disciplinary practices. Foucault's aim can be read as engaging in a rhetorical strategy of setting up a dichotomy between two forms of power, rather than to examine sovereignty. Sovereignty plays the part of a prelude to Foucault's own discussion of what he sees as the much more important consideration of governmental power and it's unmasking. In 'Two Lectures', for instance, Foucault states explicitly that 'it is not through recourse to sovereignty against discipline that the effects of disciplinary power can be limited, because sovereignty and disciplinary mechanisms are two absolutely integral constituents of the general mechanism of power in our society' (1994, 45). Foucault is interested in sovereignty only because he is interested in power.

There is also the issue of the impact on his theory of sovereignty of the change in Foucault's work that takes place after these 1976 lectures, from seeing relations of power purely in terms of subjection, domination and subjugation, to seeing a possibility for freedom to be inserted into the discussion. In the later work freedom is being defined as operable within relations of power, making choices within relations of power, contesting power within relations of power. There is also a parallel change, from seeing sovereignty as the discourse of the state and official politics counterposed against a more comprehensive and insidious network of power, to seeing the state as itself more properly understood as a collection of 'multiple practical systems' (Tully 2002, 26). These changes make much more complex the clear distinction Foucault wanted to make between sovereign power and another type masked by it. The later formulation leaves significantly open and ambiguous the kinds of relation that obtain between sovereign and disciplinary (or governmental) powers.

The third question that arises from Foucault's depiction of sovereignty concerns law. Smith's analysis of evidence about the way law operates is interesting because it undermines Foucault's dichotomy between sovereign and disciplinary forms of power, and because it shows how sovereign power can be understood as still having an active role in conjunction with disciplinary power. Smith's critique of Foucault brings sovereignty back in, while recognising the force of his critique of disciplinary power. She notes that the distinction has become blurred between law as an autonomous, rational and neutral discourse and administrative forms of regulation informed by expert knowledges of medical, psychological and psychiatric sciences. But Smith argues that, contra Foucault, law (representing the sovereign state) has not 'ceded its power and authority to the disciplinary sciences and their expert practitioners'. Rather, the juridical field manipulates expert knowledge and 'itself operates a form of surveillance over the norm-governed exercise of expert knowledge' (Smith 2000, 283). Foucault's representation 'does not reflect our everyday experience of the means through which power and government are exercised'. It also 'necessarily leads him to neglect' that 'law may effectively re-define forms of disciplinary power in its own terms' and 'that law and legal rights may act to protect the subject from the coercive influence of such power' (Smith 2000, 291).

Another criticism of Foucault's position expressed by Smith argues that Foucault's highlighting of technologies of power has 'not effectively marginalised or superseded sovereign law as a primary site of power and as a potential source of protection against disciplinary forms of control' (Smith 2000, 303). Smith contends that 'in constructing government as significantly constituted through disciplinary power, Foucault is led to account for the persistent centrality of law and sovereignty by reference to their role in provide a legitimating "cover" for government by stealth' (Smith 2000, 302). A 'society where compliance is ensured by largely dispersed and invisible forms of discipline has, at the same time', and here Smith quotes Foucault (*Power/Knowledge* (1980), 105) 'allowed a system of right to be superimposed upon the mechanisms of discipline in such a way as to conceal its actual procedures, the element of domination inherent in its techniques, and to guarantee to everyone, by virtue of the sovereignty of the State, the exercise of his proper sovereign rights'. Foucault goes on to say 'once it became necessary for disciplinary constraints to be exercised through mechanisms of domination and yet at the same time for their effective exercise of power to be disguised, a theory of sovereignty was required to make an appearance at the level of the legal apparatus' (Foucault 1980, 106). Smith observes from these quotations that for Foucault, while 'law remains impotent as a source of power', it 'is necessary to cast a legitimating gloss on those "real" technologies of power which are essentially invisible, norm governed and discretionary'. Smith has shown in her analysis of specific forms of case law that 'far from performing only an ideological function, law as part of the liberal sovereign state continues to constitute a pre-eminent site of power'. This criticism is part of a wider criticism of Foucault, 'that the sociological passion for privileging methodological attention to "writing" and "power" over "action" and "structure" simply obscures important areas of proper sociological concern' (Smith 2000, 303).

In conclusion, the general features of sovereignty that Foucault focuses upon—in order to contest—are sovereignty as a form of power, and the claim to the monopoly of violence. He regards as a sham the idea of sovereignty as setting up the authority and rule of law. He is also keen to critique the notion of sovereignty as a one-to-one authority relationship between ruler and subject, and to criticise the validity of a distinction between absolute and popular sovereignty. Like libertarian liberals, Foucault poses as the central question the negative effects of state sovereignty on the goal of freedom.

The great strength of Foucault's account of sovereignty is that it highlights the importance of power in social relations, and its relevance to political discussion. His critique of the depoliticised political theory discourse on sovereignty which highlights autonomy and independence but ignores its effects in terms of domination and repression is well targeted. One of the weaknesses of Foucault's account is that it sees resistance to social power as the only possible form of politics, thereby failing to recognise and so nullifying politics as a separate sphere of action and level of attention from the social. Relatedly, if the distinction between legal and political sovereignty is a meaningful one beyond liberal thought, Foucault not only castigates legal sovereignty as a sham, but leaves no room at all for political sovereignty. The other important problem with Foucault's conception is that it isn't a theory of sovereignty at all, but part of a theory of power. Tully is right that Foucault's method is designed to 'enable us to think and act differently by means of critical histories that exhibit the singularity, contingency and arbitrary constraints of our forms of subjectivity' (Tully 1999, 107). But while Tully argues convincingly for the soundness of Foucault's method, in the case of sovereignty, Foucault's argument is, ultimately, unsatisfactory.

Chapter Six

CONCLUSION

This book has examined a range of conceptions of sovereignty. It has sought to highlight the diversity of ideas about sovereignty found in this set of thinkers, and to demonstrate how history and theory are integrated in the examination of these thinkers' conceptions of sovereignty. In a sense a substantive conclusion to this endeavour is not possible. The aim was to open up the interpretive field of conceptions of sovereignty, and so there can be no resolution of the differences that are exhibited. The focus of this short concluding chapter is instead to turn now to analyse what this set of examples tells us about the scope and meaning of politics. What space for politics is there to be gleaned from these conceptions of sovereignty?

There are several reasons for focusing on this question. In the Introduction we touched upon some of the ways in which this project was political, both in terms of constructing and reconstructing meanings and interpretations in the history of political thought, and in terms of the volatile and dynamic nature of political concepts themselves. Thus, on the one hand, we noted Ball's perceptions into how histories of political concepts are 'histories of political arguments, and of the conceptual contests and disputes on which they turned and to which they gave rise' (Ball 1997, 42), so that histories of *political* concepts cannot be discussed 'apart from the political conflicts in which they figure'. We also referred to Skinner's insight that 'our social practices help to bestow meaning on our social vocabulary' while at the same time 'our social vocabulary helps to constitute the character of those practices' (Skinner 1989, 22). On the other hand we saw how political concepts are 'weapons of war, tools of persuasion and legitimation, badges of identity and solidarity' (Ball 1997, 41), and observed with Ball, Farr and Hanson the importance of recognising the mutability of political meanings. These insights demonstrate not only that doing history is political, but also that because of the political nature of political concepts, sovereignty can be seen as political, and so as not unpolitical after all.

Secondly, studying conceptions of sovereignty is an opportunity to explore the consequences of how politics is described and analysed in the different theories. Sovereignty performs a very political function in establishing the source of political power. Where the locus of rule-making power resides in a given political community, irrespective of how that power is derived (force, authority, bottom up consent) is only one part of the meaning of sovereignty. There is also a very close conceptual connection between sovereignty and politics. Sovereignty shapes the way politics is envisaged and conducted in specific ways in a particular community. The chapters in this book have sought among other things to identify the space for politics in Bodin, Hobbes, Spinoza, Locke, Rousseau, Kant, Hegel, Schmitt, and Foucault. This involved identifying in each case the different specific locations for sovereignty, the cluster of conceptual relations and the different features of political life central to the meaning of sovereignty in the different theories. It also involved clarifying the characterisation of the realm for politics in each case and so asking what kind of politics each conception allows for, and whether this includes room for the play of contestation to take place.

The history of political thought up to the present crucially consists of debates about the meaning of politics and the expansion of that meaning. We can take politics to refer not just to government policy-making and legislation, the narrow lines of party competition to capture that government access to 'ruler sovereignty', and a field of tensions between different authorities in institutional structures. In its broader designation, politics can refer to the scope of 'debate and action in concert' in relation to a number of things. What is to be done when different ideas about an aspect of living in a political community clash and conflict? Practices and ideas can be contestable and unstable and in need of negotiation or renegotiation —sometimes because of the distribution of scarce resources, and sometimes through an engagement with structural inequalities and structural exclusionary mechanisms, on egalitarian and emancipatory grounds. Political conflict is also due to the always-unfinished play of different interests and competing centres of power and influence, and to deep-seated intractable and incommensurable differences in values and beliefs. Politics also deals with mutability, contingency and change in the social and political world. Politics takes account of decisions which are arbitrary in the sense of being indeterminate in the wider scheme of things and so subject to determination according to specific values and norms. Politics is also expressed in what gets on the political agenda and what doesn't. Politics signifies the need for public scrutiny and for public accountability and justification. Politics so defined is a much broader category than that of democracy, meaning the settled democratic procedures of competiton for the stable and ordered organisation of political life and for mediating conflict through representatives elected to parliament. The claims of democratic politics, for instance, are made precisely because they are claims and not given by nature, reality, power, or a foundational rational logic. It is not simply 'natural' that, as democratic politics holds, the content of politics should focus on redistribution and equality, that its procedures should be open to all and participatory, that its limits should be the limits of perceived publicly-relevant equality, and that the boundary between political and unpolitical should be capable of being renegotiated by the people. All these categories are contestable and interactive, and shaped by specific cultural, political and historical traditions and dispositions of power, and so arranged differently in different polities.

Part of what is meant by the broader category of politics here also refers to strands of Honig's (1993) ideas about the dangers of a politics of justification (justifying inequalities), the importance of a fidelity to agonism, and of attention to the remainders of politics — both in terms of people who do not fit the requirements of the order they live in, and people who are ill-fitted to dominant norms, for instance of gender or sexuality. Honig's ideas about the remainders of politics also recall Rancière's discussion (1999) of those who do not 'count' because not accorded full rationality and speech and so are not counted or visible in political debate.

I am reluctant to invoke the politics/the political distinction to formalise this understanding of politics at this point, agreeing with Schmitt, who refused to give a definition of politics. For Schmitt, as we saw, 'the sphere of the political is ... determined by the real possibility of enmity' (Schmitt 1976, 64). While we can take issue with Schmitt and argue that it is only in cases of crisis that politics becomes characterised in terms of the polarisation of friend and enemy, and argue that equally important is everyday politics which exhibits a more pluralistic, interactive and complex field of play, we can still agree with him that politics is a sphere of judgment over which the state does not necessarily hold a monopoly. As noted in Chapter 5, Schmitt has an enduring sense that the key question is 'what makes a situation political?' or 'what is "the political" situation', which brings us to identify friend and enemy (or multiple interest and value) groupings, rather than the question 'what is politics?' that only leads us down a definitional dead-end. Schmitt articulated an important insight into politics when he identified that the question, 'what makes a situation political?', is concrete and sharpens our antennae to look for areas of social conflict, whereas 'what is politics?' is only a dull, abstract academic question.

In the third place, *Sovereignties: Contemporary Theory and Practice* (Prokhovnik 2007) developed the analysis of a property of sovereignty which highlights the political dimensions of the concept. In conditionally stabilising the identity of the political community and specifying the boundary between the political and the unpolitical within it, theories of sovereignty have direct and crucial implications for the scope of politics, whether or not they give specific attention to this matter. At the same time the complex work that we want the concept of sovereignty to do for us tends to keep implicit the political quality of the concept. We ask sovereignty to capture for us our sense of the wholeness of our political community and political identity, and so be neutral and above the fray of politics. We also ask sovereignty to perform the role for us of specifying the boundary between what is political and contestable (within the scope of lawful dissent and legitimate re-examination) and what must be unpolitical and given. And yet we overlook that this very setting of the boundary, and the conditional settlement of the conditions of and limitations on politics, is also political. In this respect, sovereignty is political in a sense which is not directly related to governance. For instance, in terms of the European Union a substantial group of British and other citizens regard the invitation to share and jointly exercise sovereignty as necessarily having the outcome of depleting and endangering national sovereignty. In the light of the argument developed in that book, it is useful to look back here at some of the conceptions in the modern mainstream canon and elicit the role for politics in relation to sovereignty allowed or imagined by those thinkers.

If we can take politics reasonably unproblematically to be among other things the search for social cooperation, the articulation and negotiation of contestation and difference, and the designation of political identity, then sovereignty is a condition of and for politics, in two ways. We use sovereignty to specify the boundaries of politics, for instance in the end or limits to politics in Schmitt, the condition of politics in Spinoza and Rousseau, the elimination of politics in Hobbes. In addition sovereignty helps to define (the nature of) politics and political practice in any particular society, through its links with a constitution, the kind of law established and the importance given to it, the dominant political mentality and how it relates to minority ethnic and cultural groups, where the boundary between participation and dissent is set, customary ways of doing politics, and the sense of political identity. It also regulates norms, in social values, rules regarded as obligatory and habitually practiced, routines of conduct, moral beliefs, and in standards that constitute the identities of actors, as well as in patterns of behaviour that arise from fear of sanctions.

Condren (1994b, 1997, 2000) rightly warns against an anachronistic use of the term 'politics', elucidating how, before the modern period, questions of what we call politics were dealt with, within the discourse of their times, under the rubric of legal thinking and civil philosophy. The activity of politics as we understand it (as well as sovereignty and all other political concepts) is the product of our modern Western intellectual and political inheritance. We need to remember that ideas of large-scale representative politics, let alone modern ideas about democracy in its representative, deliberative and agonistic meanings, would have been quite foreign to most of the thinkers studied in this book. Arguments such as that by Kant for publicity and public debate can be seen in hindsight as ideas which have been taken as moves towards our contemporary meanings of politics and democracy.

We turn now to rehearse the scope for and meanings of politics in the theories of sovereignty of the different thinkers we have examined.

We noted in Chapter 1 that Bodin's focus of attention was in theorising sovereignty and not just dealing with the practical question of marks of sovereignty etc. Indeed, the value of Bodin's conception of sovereignty lies in its articulation of the asymmetrical character of absolute sovereignty for him, and straight away this severely limits the scope for politics in Bodin's theory. For Bodin, the sovereign commands but cannot be commanded. The analytical approach Bodin takes to sovereignty, its legislative form, and the pinpointing of sovereignty as perpetual power all militate against a strong sense of politics. However, Bodin's insistence that, at the same time, sovereignty is not unlimited and the way in which Bodin combines absolute, perpetual and limited dimensions of sovereignty, opens up the conceptualisation of sovereignty to politics and weakens its supposed link with early-modern absolute monarchy.

At the level of procedure and use, Bodin does not seek with his theory of absolute sovereignty to eliminate or foreclose political debate, and in this sense his theory is more open than Hobbes's to a space for politics. The *Parlement*, the Estates, and magistrates may all engage in real debate. However, their role in political life is circumscribed by only being able to advise and counsel the sovereign, and by holding only delegated authority. For Bodin, so long as the line of authority and its one-way, non-reciprocal nature is fully comprehended, then on the one hand political life as understood in the sixteenth century can flourish, while on the other hand the sovereign can exercise power, most importantly to legislate, in an effective fashion. Sovereignty, properly understood and adhered to, allows some room for politics to occur.

Bodin's place in the canon as the primary author of the early-modern theory of sovereignty rests upon his conception of absolute sovereignty (or sometimes a misrepresentation of it) and upon his theorising of sovereignty in the context of an impersonal state, whereby the distinction between the person holding the office and the office itself is a crucial element of the theory. But more importantly, and underpinning these aspects of Bodin's work is his formidable legalism, and it is interesting that this does not disqualify a role for politics for him. We saw that his legalism covers the importance he accords to law within a political community; his understanding of sovereignty as primarily a legal concept; the way his thinking is rooted in a jurisprudence discourse; the pre-eminence he gives to legislating as the key function of the sovereign and in the definition of sovereignty; in his preoccupation with legal distinctions; the political significance he invests in legal technicalities; and the centrality of the legal relationship between subject and sovereign.

As we noted, Bodin's legalism is of course closely linked to the absolute sovereignty and state sovereignty for which he is famous. It is precisely as a consequence of the legal character of sovereignty for Bodin that there exists that asymmetrical relationship whereby the sovereign prince alone can make law for his subjects, and the way that he is not answerable to the people for any infringements that his positive law might have against natural and divine law. This absolutism then denies the possibility of a right of resistance. Likewise it is as a direct implication of the status of the sovereign prince as lawmaker within the political community rather than as personal ruler that the necessary framework in which the sovereign operates is a modern state as we understand it. The other interesting dimension of Bodin's conception that Chapter 1 noted is that sovereignty, according to Bodin, and notwithstanding his (even if mistaken) emphasis on its indivisibility and his own preference for monarchy, can perfectly legitimately be expressed in democratic and aristocratic as well as monarchical forms of commonwealth.

Hobbes's and Spinoza's theories of sovereignty result in very different conceptions of politics and political activity. The legitimacy of collective action, of the expression of competing interests, and of the openness of political outcomes, are not in dispute for Spinoza, while for Hobbes these things are abhorrent and prohibited. Spinoza has a positive view of political practice in the context of the polycentric structure of power vested in the provinces and their towns, and as a matter of dynamically negotiating disputes and differences toward consensual outcomes within the framework of the constitutional tradition embodying customary practice and conventional usage. It is the sovereignty settlement which provides the framework in which politics can be allowed to take place. For Hobbes, however, as Kraynak aptly notes, the 'power that sets the limits must itself be the supreme power and hence must be sovereign' (Kraynak 1990, 167). Politics is abolished by Hobbes because in his eyes any play of difference and debate represents a potential threat to the authority of the sovereign and could result in putting in jeopardy the stability and unity of the commonwealth. Politics, for Hobbes, is reduced to and breeds irresolvable conflictual positions, and in an important sense sovereignty disbars politics, according to Hobbes.

We saw in Chapter 2 that for Hobbes sovereignty is absolute in several senses, the most important of which in the comparison with Spinoza, is that Hobbes regarded sovereignty as analytically absolute. Furthermore, Hobbes saw himself as disclosing the inherently universal and transcendental character of sovereignty. In addition, for Hobbes sovereignty is associated with centralised political control and power, a natural territorial boundary, and is unchallengeable by supremacy claims by rival powers. For Hobbes, these qualities of the theory have the effect of marginalising a role for politics much more than they do for Bodin. For Spinoza however, it is perfectly possible for sovereignty to be mediated through other institutions and loyalties. This reflects the persistence of the medieval mentality of the United Provinces, which persevered in the seventeenth century and beyond despite the United Provinces being highly aware of the development of modern states in England and France. Furthermore, in a radical difference with Hobbes's analytical absolutism, Spinoza stipulates in his second political treatise that no-one can be considered as holding a position above the law in any of the three forms of dominion. The king in a monarchy, and patricians, syndics and senators in aristocracies, are all bound by the law (TP 364). Spinoza is also explicit about the accountability of judges and senators (TP 360, 366). For Hobbes, in comparison, it is a defining attribute of sovereignty that a sovereign is not only the maker of positive law but is also above that law.

Chapter 3 concluded that like Hobbes, Locke is not keen to allow for a political realm of debate about the conditions or moral standing of public policy. Hobbes regarded politics as too unruly and disruptive an activity to be tolerated, and all that is left for him is the public law-making of the sovereign and court politics around the sovereign. For Locke, an active political realm could conflict with and jeopardise the primacy of individuals pursuing their business and other interests in the 'private' realm, and a restricted politics of problem-solving is left to the political elite to manage. The strength of Locke's theory of sovereignty is that it explicitly articulates a robust notion of individual rights. The weaknesses are that it dismisses any positive sense that sovereignty can play in expressing a shared political world, and that its individualism conceals, even for his day, a strongly elitist political commitment.

We saw that Locke's attitude toward politics is underpinned by the clever piece of logic he employs in relation to sovereignty. Ultimately sovereignty for Locke rests with the pre-political natural rights from which derive the residual powers held by the people in perpetuity, but they hold this power individually, unless it is triggered by a resistance to government and a dissolution of government. In this way Locke's sovereignty is 'popular' only in a formal and foreshortened sense. Locke has a profound distaste for individuals taking on a collective, group persona as a strong part of their identity, and so only legitimises the utilisation of this perpetual residual power as an extreme measure. Sovereignty, for Locke, certainly does not function as a collective political identity nor licence collective action. For the most part Locke's persons in civil society operate as individuals in the 'private' sphere. Because of his individualist stance, Locke is reluctant to discuss either obligation or sovereignty, because he does not want to emphasise duties but rights, and because sovereignty implies a unified group identity in which individuals are interdependent in the group. However, he does consider that one's legitimate obedience is owed to the legislative so long as that branch of government operates within the trust, and he does have a strong though reluctant sense of popular sovereignty in the notion of the right of resistance specifying a rigorous limit on the scope and actions of government.

The residual power of the people (understood as a collection of individuals) to abolish the government is what Locke's conception of popular sovereignty ultimately amounts to. This minimalist and weak conception stands alongside Locke's fierce and positive championing of pre-political individual rights. Furthermore, while Hobbes's conception of sovereignty results in individuals being radically equal as 'subjects', in Locke's conception individuals in a sense become citizens (or at least some of them — propertied males — do), but more meaningfully they remain individuals. In sum then, we noted that while Locke does have a conception of sovereignty as a unity, a whole, he denies a notion of sovereignty as a collectivity. For Locke we are individuals first and foremost, and sovereignty exists only in order to further the rights of individuals. Locke's championing of individualism is necessarily a stronger element in his political theory than the notion of sovereignty. Indeed, Locke's individualism sits uneasily with his majoritarianism and with the principle of a right of resistance as a group, and his inclinations are not towards democracy. The upshot of Locke's theory is that the collectivist resonances of the conception of popular sovereignty are the cost he is prepared to bear in order to be able to reinforce the rights of the individual with a right of resistance.

Chapter 3 argued that Locke utilises two general features of sovereignty in his conception. In order to confirm the ultimate 'supremacy of the people' over government, Locke reluctantly takes on the idea of a weak popular sovereignty designating the unity of the political community. As Laslett circumspectly observes, 'this residual power must be called Locke's idea of what we now think of as popular sovereignty' (Laslett 1965, 134). The 'supreme power' of the people is exercised, under strict limits and on a conditional basis, by the legislative branch of government. Sovereignty also serves to seal the relationship between rulers and ruled, but only on the proviso that the relationship is established through the trust extended in a one-way direction from latter to the former. It is a conception of sovereignty that is wholly negative, in that its only purpose is to confirm the pre-eminence in political society of something else, namely pre-political individual rights. Indeed, Locke turns the concept of sovereignty on its head, by positing the sovereignty of (necessarily disaggregated) individual natural rights and so rejecting the idea of sovereignty as a *political* concept. Locke's grudging acceptance of the role played by sovereignty in his theory is consistent with his approach to all such political concepts and derives from the suspicion he has for any positive outline of the terms of government and political society.

In Chapter 3 we also noted that, of all the conceptions of sovereignty in the mainstream political theory tradition, Rousseau's is one of the ones that has the strongest sense of politics as a positive and active realm of deliberation and contestation between equal citizens in pursuit of the common good. There is a self-consciously intimate connection between sovereignty and politics for Rousseau since sovereignty is transformative in creating active citizens. We saw that Rousseau argues that 'the essence of the political body lies in the union of freedom and obedience so that the words *subject* and *sovereign* are identical correlatives, the meaning of which is brought together in the single word *citizen*' (Rousseau 1968, 138). Politics here is understood as the appropriate realm for the exercise of the general will and not of particular wills. Thus, in answer to Strong's question, 'what claim [does] the common ... have on me'? (Strong 1994, 78), Rousseau would reply 'a great deal' while Locke would respond, 'a minimal amount'.

We saw that the key general features of sovereignty that preoccupy Rousseau are the relationship between rulers and ruled, sovereignty as self-government within a moral framework, and sovereignty specifying the highest legal authority. The meaning of all these features for Rousseau leads to a robust sphere of politics for Rousseau. Wokler points to one of the strengths of his theory when he notes that, '[p]rior to the meaning he ascribes to it in the *Social Contract*, the concept of sovereignty had been connected by its interpreters to the idea of force, power, or empire'. Wokler also accents the novelty of Rousseau's theory of sovereignty and politics, and how this way of envisaging the political realm follows as a consequence from sovereignty, when he notes that, 'it had generally pertained to the dominion of kings over their subjects, however that had been acquired, rather than to citizens' freedom'. Wokler argues that for 'both Bodin and Hobbes in particular—the best-known advocates of absolute sovereignty before him ... [sovereignty meant the] unequalled power of the ruler'. In contrast, for Rousseau 'the idea of sovereignty is essentially a principle of equality, identified with the ruled element, or the subjects themselves, as the supreme authority, and it is connected with the concepts of will or right, as he defines them, rather than force or power' (Wokler 1995, 64).

We observed that Gourevitch teases out another aspect of the importance of politics for Rousseau. He notes that there are 'three basic principles of his politics, that man is by nature good, that political society corrupts him, and that everything is radically dependent on politics'. In Gourevitch's insightful reading, 'Rousseau categorically denies that any political solution can transform "men as they are" into "men as they ought to be"'. Rousseau 'holds out no prospect whatsoever of an end to politics, be it by men's rationally choosing what is in their enlightened self-interest, or by their becoming "moralised", or by the "withering away of the state"'. In Rousseau's nuanced understanding of politics there is both 'no alternative to politics' and no political solution which can be definitive (Gourevitch 1997, xxxi). The tensions are at best held in place by the workings of politics.

Despite its evident strengths, the major weakness of Rousseau's conception remains the threat of degeneration into tyranny, notwithstanding the nobility of his ideal and the safeguards he puts in place. The energetic vigilance of the sovereign body, the set of dualistic prescriptions in which the theory is couched, the generality of the law enacted by the sovereign body, the limits placed on the institutions of lawgiver and dictator, the mechanism by which citizens recover their natural freedom if the social pact is broken through the degeneration or corruption of the state, are yet insufficient to overcome that threat. The problems of preventing the merger of political and public interest (in the form of government despotism), or the fusion of political and private interest (and the dominance of certain particular interests), or of majoritarian tyranny, persists.

Chapter 4 found that Kant allows a broad scope for politics — understood now in terms of rational political reform — at both domestic and international levels, within the terms of his key general features of sovereignty, namely its moral character, the agency of the state as the locus of sovereignty, and the derivation of the external from the internal form. For Kant there is the potential to bring politics and international relations under the rule of morality and law, though what this means depends in part on the politics of interpretation of Kant's texts. Kant's commitment to the state as the locus of sovereignty takes place in the context provided by what Franceschet calls 'the sovereignty of the moral law' (Franceschet 2002, 10). For Kant, political action 'cannot have its own autonomous logic' as Machiavelli held, but 'must be subordinated to the requirements of morality' (Franceschet 2002, 12). The importance of the state is shown in the unconditional statement Kant makes in *Perpetual Peace* that 'states as such are not subject to a common external constraint' (Kant 1997, 103). The power to declare war and make peace is an urgent concern for Kant, as is the role of the sovereign in instituting political arrangements governed by right rather than by force, interest, expediency, or utilitarian motives.

Franceschet underlines the prominence of sovereignty — in the important sense of the moral and political agency of states — in Kant's thinking when he notes that 'sovereignty is the key mechanism of political reform' for Kant. It represents the means by which 'politics can be domesticated to approximate the formal principles of morality' (Franceschet 2002, 43). But, the argument found Franceschet's line of thinking convincing that it is precisely in the derivation of external sovereignty from the internal form that Kant's theory falters, on the grounds that the very need for 'international reform is a product of the problematic role that sovereignty plays within realising justice', for Kant (Franceschet 2002, 43). Thus, while sovereignty is 'a necessary cause of justice', it also presents Kant with 'a profound set of moral difficulties' and is a 'major cause of injustice' (Franceschet 2002, 43).

It is clear that the strong moral framework that it sets out for political action is one of the strengths of Kant's system, and its incrementalism — aiming towards peace and harmony in world politics in a gradualist manner — can look attractive. At least on Kersting's reading, Kant's deduction that politics takes places against the ideal of the 'rightful' state, is supplemented by a 'philosophy of compromise and reform' (Kersting 1992, 359). Kant's highlighting of the value of publicity and republicanism in politics can also be regarded as a strength. It opens up a space for politics as contestation and reasoned debate in a spirit of citizen participation, and reinforces Kant's fundamental belief that political issues should not be settled by force. Another positive aspect of Kant's construction is that the conception of sovereignty focuses on the *Rechtstaat* and explicitly sees interpersonal relations as mediated through fair and impartial law. As Franceschet puts it, in Kant's terms sovereignty is 'an attempt to reconcile politics with what he views as the only plausibly solid ground of the modern subject: an autonomous morality' (Franceschet 2002, 6).

We also noted that another important strength of Kant's theory is that the conception of sovereignty pinpoints why the 'domestic analogy' cannot stand. Kant identifies sovereignty as the concept that prevents relations within a polity simply being mapped onto relations between states, and identifies international relations as a distinctive realm. Also, on the reading of Kant developed in this book, it is a strength that it is by the terms of *sovereignty* that, for Kant, on the one hand domestic interests are solidly prioritised over international ones, and on the other that relations between states should be based on a commitment to peace and to a confederation of peaceful republics.

However, Chapter 4 also argued that it is a major weakness of Kant's approach to politics that, notwithstanding Ellis's interpretation, the highly abstract and formal injunctions of moral law cannot necessarily tell us very much about how to operate in political practice, given the gulf between morality and the messy and contingent world of politics. Neither Kant nor Ellis resolve the meta issue of how the two can be effectively related. Kant's theory cannot easily bridge the gap between those very general prescriptions and the political world of competing claims, entrenched inequalities and cultural differences, any more than can subsequent theories based on his approach, for instance by Habermas and

Rawls. Politics as the application of moral principles to guide social life towards 'justice' leads also to a truncated and heavily qualified form of political life. As Franceschet argues, Kant's conception of sovereignty is strongly implicated in his 'quest to domesticate politics through formal principles derived from morality' (Franceschet 2002, 7). Moreover, the absolute separation Kant draws between knowledge from abstract and trans-historical principles of reason and knowledge from empirical inquiry, and the priority of the first over the second, issues in a severely limited notion of popular sovereignty, an overly-trusting view of the value of law, and no effective means of resistance to tyrannical government. Another weakness of Kant's system is that it universalises from a culturally-specific set of preferences about reason, the individual, freedom and autonomy, and politics as a form of ethics, and does not recognise that there are substantial drawbacks in doing so. Kersting also makes a point that, while Kant's abstract and universalising political theory can be a force for self-empowerment, these qualities also indicate how it can discriminate against the needy.

A further weakness of Kant's conception of sovereignty is that, by extrapolating from the domestic to the international sphere, Kant does not adequately address the differences between the two spheres and politics in them, and so licences a naïve and moralistic cosmopolitanism. Chapter 4 argued that the idea of constructing a principled confederation of like-minded peaceful republics that acts as a moral rather than political force for peace, and does so without coercion, is so unrealistic that it is problematic even as an aspiration. The superiority that such a confederation would obviously have in economic and political, let alone military, resources (given the Western character of Kant's thinking and location), together with the dominant position in terms of international power politics that such a confederation would gain, militate against the operation of the purely moral purpose that is Kant's stated motive for such an alliance. Such a confederation would also automatically create an 'other' of states unwilling, for whatever reason, to join it. Kant's attempt to pacify the anarchy of the international realm by the imposition of moral principles is unsuccessful because it underrates the importance of political and power considerations.

Coming on now to Hegel, in one sense Hegel provides a vigorous defence of politics, in that he is at pains to identify a field of politics, in the state, distinct from the field of the social and civil society (Hegel 1967, 198). Indeed, there is an important expressive dimension of politics, for Hegel, such that political activity is indicative and demonstrative of a particular kind of sociality. It is also clear that it was Hegel's self-conscious aim to carve out a sphere for politics in the context of the state form. Knox underlines that 'Hegel lived in a country where most citizens were simply "subjects", without participation in the work of government, and where, therefore, a political life and tradition, like the English, was almost wholly lacking'. Knox characterises the *Philosophy of Right* as 'an attempt to educate Germans beyond "civil" to "political" life' (Knox 1967, 376). Dickey makes a similar point, linking Hegel's aim to reinvigorate the idea of the political with the political context in which he was writing. Dickey claims that 'in Hegel's judgment, the boundaries of the political sphere were becoming so narrowly drawn in his own age that citizens were on the verge of becoming depoliticised'. In this 'context, he wished from the 1790s on to recall citizens to public life and civic engagement by identifying the political sphere' (Dickey 1999, ix). But in another sense Hegel severely restricts the scope of politics — through the very reduced role he envisages for popular sovereignty, through his strictures against democracy and a wide franchise, and because his notion of representation sharply limits the accountability of representatives to their constituents.

We saw in Chapter 4 that the key general features of sovereignty in Hegel's conception are a very strong identification of sovereignty with the state, and a further reduction of the role of popular sovereignty. For Hegel the sovereignty of the state means both the role of the monarch as the visible embodiment of sovereignty, and the introduction of the idea of sovereignty as expressing the organic 'whole' of the state that is greater than the collection of its members or the sum of its parts. The sovereignty of the state also imposes a clear limit on the possibility of international collaboration, and envisages international politics as necessarily a matter dominated by relations between states formally recognised as equals.

One of the strengths of Hegel's conception of sovereignty is his clear sense of the historical and cultural groundedness of particular states, and the value of this is reinforced by the absence of a social contract in Hegel's political thinking. In consequence Hegel is able to move away from the depoliticised individualism and supposedly 'neutral' state inaugurated by the liberal social contract tradition. The groundedness of states is also valuable because it means for him that differences between states are things to be respected, and such differences are not overridden by universal principles, duties or commitments. For Hegel, in contrast with Kant, the metaphysical framework around politics does not overshadow the need to acknowledge that particularity, context, and circumstance all play a vital role. Hegel's sense of the need for mutual respect between incommensurable cultures and societies is translated by him into his view of international politics.

The primary weakness identified in Chapter 4 in relation to politics of Hegel's conception of sovereignty in modern eyes is the argument that leads to him assimilating war to the ethical moment of the state. His conception of the state and of relations between states has enough other strong arguments supporting it and does not need to rest on this celebration of war. The same argument can be applied to Hegel's advocacy of monarchy and his antipathy to universal suffrage. Another weakness we registered is Hegel's lack of attention to a seeming contradiction in his text, between his use of empirical arguments, for instance to reject popular sovereignty and to endorse the use of war by the state, and his conviction that empirical evidence has no place in philosophical reasoning. Berki defends the importance Hegel places on institutions to concretise political society but nevertheless, the contradiction in Hegel remains.

The upshot of the discussion of Schmitt in Chapter 5 is that the positive value of Schmitt's critique of sovereignty lies in that it accents the political, contested character of sovereignty, and in that it shows as false the claim to sovereignty's perpetuity. Cristi highlights the same point when he notes, 'sovereignty became visible only during exceptional circumstances, when a constitution was destroyed and another was born. In these circumstances, sovereignty showed up under the guise of constituent power' (Cristi, quoted in Kalyvas 2000, 351). Schmitt's view remains fresh because it has the effect of importing into the political theory debate a welcome rectification of the de-politicisation of the legal constitutional point of view.

The general features of sovereignty that Schmitt sees as significant are both closely related to the operation of politics, and are ones whose traditional meaning he seeks to disrupt. He sees as problematic the relationship between sovereignty and the constitution, and takes issue with the equation of sovereignty with the establishment of the highest legal authority. The reliance on law, in Schmitt's perspective, undervalues the sphere and scope of politics to resolve political problems, both under normal conditions and in times of crisis.

Schmitt's theory is also useful in the way it reinvests some of the key elements of Hobbes's theory with a sense of the political, an activity that Hobbes had sought to banish. Schmitt's insistence on the priority of the sovereign over the rule of law, his resoluteness to identify the internal or external enemy, and decisionism, all recall Hobbes's overwhelming fear of political breakdown and his drive to eliminate any kind of conflict (religious, political, or rhetorical) that threatened the settled order. Like Hobbes, Schmitt is aware that '[w]hat always matters is only the possibility of conflict' (Schmitt 1976, 39), by which he means extreme conflict that overthrows the state. But Schmitt adds to Hobbes's depoliticised realm the notion of politics as precisely describing the kind of conflict brought about by groupings dedicated to the 'most extreme possibility' and the kind of act of judgment that is necessary for the sovereign to make in this situation. Schmitt also argued, as Kelly observes, that 'the intimate connection between the political and the state had been perverted by a technical liberalism', and his solution was 'to call for a political process of depoliticisation, a "liberation" of the state for the sake of the state' (Kelly 2003, 300).

Chapter 5 also argued that one of the weaknesses in Schmitt's theory is that, while he can legitimately argue that the friend/enemy distinction is not a normative ideal but simply describes reality, he fails to acknowledge that the conceptualisation of that distinction as such is not empirical but normative.

The great strength of Foucault's account of sovereignty for politics is that it highlights the importance of power in social relations, and its relevance to political discussion. His critique of the depoliticised political theory discourse on sovereignty which highlights autonomy and independence but ignores its effects in terms of domination and repression is well targeted. The primary value to politics of Foucault's theory, then, is his critique of the notion of sovereignty as a one-to-one benign authority relationship between ruler and subject. This idea is central to the liberal tradition of political theory and Foucault rightly points out that this attention to exalted ideal principles has the outcome of overlooking or ignoring the regulative effects of social power relations of domination in the governmentalising techniques applied to the people as a whole.

At the same time it is one of cardinal weaknesses of Foucault's account that it downplays the role of politics, and it does so in several ways. Chapter 5 noted that Foucault's theory identifies resistance to social power as the only fully specified and worked out form of politics. It thereby fails to recognise sufficiently the character of the political sphere, and so consequently nullifies politics as a separate sphere of action and level of attention from the social. Relatedly, if the distinction between legal and political sovereignty is a meaningful one beyond liberal thought, Foucault not only castigates legal sovereignty as a sham, but leaves no room at all for political sovereignty. Thirdly, because Foucault's conception is not a theory of sovereignty at all, but part of a theory of (social) power, the scope of politics is again delimited. Tully is right that Foucault's method is designed to 'enable us to think and act differently by means of critical histories that exhibit the singularity, contingency and arbitrary constraints of our forms of subjectivity' (Tully 1999, 107). But Chapter 5 argued that, while Tully argues convincingly for the soundness of Foucault's method, in the case of sovereignty and its implications for politics, Foucault's argument is, ultimately, unsatisfactory.

Another problem with Foucault's account concerns the general features of sovereignty that Foucault focuses upon—in order to contest—namely sovereignty as a form of power, and the claim to the monopoly of violence. He regards as a sham the idea of sovereignty as setting up the authority and rule of law. This draws Foucault into an unlikely and unholy alliance with libertarian liberals. Like them, Foucault poses as the central question the negative effects of state sovereignty on the goal of freedom.

We can see in sum that the character of each theory of sovereignty has far-reaching consequences for the way politics can be conducted and the kinds of political claims that can and cannot be made. Politics and sovereignty are crucially interconnected ideas. At the same time, the way the scope for politics, the content of politics, and the parameters of politics are envisaged are not simply given by the concept of sovereignty but vary widely in the different conceptions we have studied.

BIBLIOGRAPHY

Henry Allison (1987) *Benedict de Spinoza: An Introduction*, New Haven, Yale University Press.

Karl Ameriks (1992) 'The Critique of Metaphysics: Kant and Traditional Ontology', in Paul Guyer ed. *The Cambridge Companion to Kant*, Cambridge, Cambridge University Press.

Hannah Arendt (1977) *Between Past and Future: Eight Exercises in Political Thought*, London, Penguin.

David Armitage (1998) in 'Literature and Empire', in Nicholas Canny ed. *The Origins of Empire. Volume 1 British Overseas Enterprise to the Close of the Seventeenth Century*, Oxford, Oxford University Press.

Richard Ashcraft (1994) 'Locke's Political Philosophy' in Vere Chappell ed. *The Cambridge Companion to Locke*, Cambridge, Cambridge University Press.

Shlomo Avineri (1972) *Hegel's Theory of the Modern State*, Cambridge, Cambridge University Press.

Terence Ball (1988) *Transforming Political Discourse*, Oxford, Blackwell.

Terence Ball (1995) *Reappraising Political Theory. Revisionist Studies in the History of Political Thought*, Oxford, Clarendon Press.

Terence Ball (1997) 'Political Theory and Conceptual Change' in Andrew Vincent ed. *Political Theory. Tradition and Diversity*, Cambridge, Cambridge University Press.

Terence Ball, James Farr and Russell Hanson (1989) 'Preface' in T Ball, J Farr and R Hanson eds *Political Innovation and Conceptual Change*, Cambridge, Cambridge University Press.

Ernest Barker (1971) 'Introduction' to *Social Contract. Essays by Locke, Hume, Rousseau*, Oxford, Oxford University Press.

Jens Bartelson (1995) *The Genealogy of Sovereignty*, Cambridge, Cambridge University Press.

Deborah Baumgold (1988) *Hobbes's Political Theory*, Cambridge, Cambridge University Press.

Richard Bellamy and Dario Castiglione (1997) 'Review Article: Constitutionalism and Democracy – Political Theory and the American Constitution', *British Journal of Political Science*, Vol. 27.

R N Berki (1971) 'Perspectives in the Marxian Critique of Hegel's Political Philosophy', in Z A Pelczynski ed. *Hegel's Political Philosophy. Problems and Perspectives*, Cambridge, Cambridge University Press.

Isaiah Berlin (1991) 'Two Concepts of Liberty', in D Miller (ed.), *Liberty*, Oxford, Oxford University Press.

Christopher Bertram (2004) *Rousseau and 'The Social Contract'*, London, Routledge.

Jean Bodin (1992) *On Sovereignty. Four Chapters from 'The Six Books of the Commonwealth'*, ed. Julian Franklin, Cambridge, Cambridge University Press.

James Bohman and Matthias Lutz-Bachmann (1997) 'Introduction', in J Bohman and M Lutz-Bachmann eds. *Perpetual Peace. Essays on Kant's Cosmopolitan Ideal*, Cambridge Mass., MIT Press.

Chiara Bottici (2003) 'The Domestic Analogy and the Kantian Project of *Perpetual Peace*', *Journal of Political Philosophy*, Vol. 11.

Harry Brod (1992) *Hegel's Philosophy of Politics. Idealism, Identity, and Modernity*, Boulder, Colorado, Westview Press.

Chris Brown, Terry Nardin and Nicholas Rengger (2002) 'Introduction', in C Brown, T Nardin and N Rengger (eds) *International Relations in Political Thought. Texts from the Ancient Greeks to the First World War*, Cambridge, Cambridge University Press.

Govert Buijs (2003) '"*Que les Latins appellant* maiestatem": An Exploration into the Theological Background of the Concept of Sovereignty', in Neil Walker ed. *Sovereignty in Transition*, Oxford, Hart.

Glen Burgess (1991) 'Revisionism, Politics and Political Ideas in Early Stuart England', *The Historical Journal*, Vol. 34.

Glen Burgess (1992) *The Politics of the Ancient Constitution: An Introduction to English Political Thought 1603-1642*, Basingstoke, Palgrave Macmillan.

Alfred Cobban (1964) *Rousseau and the Modern State*, London, Allen & Unwin.

G D H Cole (1973) 'Introduction' to *Jean-Jacques Rousseau. The Social Contract and Discourses*, ed. G D H Cole, New York, Everyman.

Janet Coleman (2005) 'Pre-Modern Property and Self-Ownership Before and After Locke', *European Journal of Political Theory*, Vol.4.

Conal Condren (1994a) 'The Paradoxes of Recontextualization in Early Modern Intellectual History', *The Historical Journal*, Vol. 37.

Conal Condren (1994b) *The Language of Politics in Seventeenth-Century England*, London, Macmillan.

Conal Condren (1997) 'Political Theory and the Problem of Anachronism' in Andrew Vincent ed. *Political Theory. Tradition and Diversity*, Cambridge, Cambridge University Press.

Conal Condren (2000) *Thomas Hobbes*, New York, Twayne Publishers.

William Connolly (1993) *The Terms of Political Discourse*, 2nd ed., Oxford, Blackwell.

William Connolly (2004) 'The Complexity of Sovereignty', in J Edkins, V Pin-Fat and M Shapiro (eds) *Sovereign Lives. Power in Global Politics*, New York, Routledge.

David Cooper (1971) 'Hegel's Theory of Punishment', in Z A Pelczynski ed. *Hegel's Political Philosophy. Problems and Perspectives*, Cambridge, Cambridge University Press.

Charles Covell (2004) *Hobbes, Realism and the Tradition of International Law*, Basingstoke, Palgrave Macmillan.

Maurice Cranston (1968) 'Introduction' to Rousseau, Jean-Jacques *The Social Contract*, trans. Maurice Cranston, London, Penguin.

E Curley (1988) *Behind the Geometrical Method*, Princeton, Princeton University Press.

Mitchell Dean (1999) 'Normalising Democracy: Foucault and Habermas on Democracy, Liberalism and Law', in Samantha Ashenden and David Owen eds. *Foucault contra Habermas. Recasting the Dialogue between Genealogy and Critical Theory*, London, Sage.

R J Delahunty (1985), *Spinoza*, London, Routledge.

N J H Dent (1988) *Rousseau. An Introduction to his Psychological, Social and Political Theory*, Oxford, Blackwell.

Nicholas Dent (2005) *Rousseau*, London, Routledge.

O L Dick (1946) *Aubrey's Brief Lives*, Harmondsworth, Penguin.

Laurence Dickey (1999) 'General Introduction', *G W F Hegel, Political Writings*, Laurence Dickey and H B Nisbet eds., trans. H B Nisbet, Cambridge, Cambridge University Press.

Robert A Duff (1903), *Spinoza's Political and Ethical Philosophy*, Glasgow, James Maclehose & Sons.

Alfred Dufour (1991) 'Pufendorf', in *Cambridge History of Political Thought, 1450-1700*, J H Burns (ed.), Cambridge, Cambridge University Press.

Siegfried Van Duffel (2004) 'Natural Rights and Individual Sovereignty', *Journal of Political Philosophy*, Vol. 12.

C N Dugan and Tracy Strong (2001) 'Music, Politics, Theater, and Representation', in Patrick Riley ed. *Cambridge Companion to Rousseau*, Cambridge, Cambridge University Press.

John Dunn (1984) *Locke*, Oxford, Oxford University Press.

John Dunn (1994) 'Introduction', *Political Studies Special Issue*, 'Contemporary Crisis of the Nation State?', Vol. 42.

Elisabeth Ellis (2005) *Kant's Politics. Provisional Theory for an Uncertain World*, New Haven, Yale University Press.

Jean Elshtain (1987) *Women and War*, New York, Basic Books.

Markus Fischer (1992) 'Feudal Europe, 800-1300: Communal Discourse and Conflictual Practices', *International Organisation*, Vol.46.

Alessandro Fontana and Mauro Bertani (2003) 'Situating the Lectures', in Michel Foucault *'Society Must Be Defended' Lectures at the College de France, 1975-76*, eds. Mauro Bertani and Alessandro Fontana, London, Allen Lane.

Murray Forsyth (1981) 'Thomas Hobbes and the Constituent Power of the People', *Political Studies*, Vol. XXIX.

Michel Foucault (1977) *Discipline and Punish: The Birth of the Prison*, London, Allen Lane.

Michel Foucault (1980) *Power/Knowledge: Selected Interviews and Other Writings 1972-77*, ed. Colin Gordon, Harlow, Essex, Pearson Educational.

Michel Foucault (1986) 'Disciplinary Power and Subjection', in Steven Lukes ed. *Power*, Oxford, Oxford University Press.

Michel Foucault (1994) 'Two Lectures', in Michael Kelly (ed.) *Critique and Power. Recasting the Foucault/Habermas Debate*, Cambridge MA, MIT Press.

Michel Foucault (2003) *'Society Must Be Defended' Lectures at the College de France, 1975-76*, eds. Mauro Bertani and Alessandro Fontana, London, Allen Lane.

Antonio Franceschet (2002) *Kant and Liberal Internationalism. Sovereignty, Justice, and Global Reform*, Basingstoke, Palgrave Macmillan.

Julian Franklin (1981) *John Locke and the Theory of Sovereignty*, Cambridge, Cambridge University Press.

Julian Franklin (1992) 'Introduction', in Jean Bodin, *On Sovereignty. Four Chapters from 'The Six Books of the Commonwealth'*, ed. Julian Franklin, Cambridge, Cambridge University Press.

Elizabeth Frazer (1997) 'Method Matters: Feminism, Interpretation and Politics' in Andrew Vincent ed. *Political Theory. Tradition and Diversity*, Cambridge, Cambridge University Press.

Hans-Georg Gadamer (1975) *Truth and Method*, London, Sheed and Ward.

Hans-Georg Gadamer (1987) 'The Problem of Historical Consciousness', in Paul Rabinow and William Sullivan eds *Interpretive Social Science. A Second Look*, Berkeley, University of California Press.

Moira Gatens (1996) *Imaginary Bodies. Ethics, Power and Corporeality*, London, Routledge.

Clifford Geertz (1973a) 'Thick Description: Toward an Interpretive Theory of Culture', in Clifford Geertz *The Interpretation of Cultures*, New York, Basic Books.

Clifford Geertz (1973b) 'The Impact of the Concept of Culture on the Concept of Man', in Clifford Geertz *The Interpretation of Cultures*, New York, Basic Books.

Clifford Geertz (1973c) 'The Politics of Meaning', in Clifford Geertz *The Interpretation of Cultures*, New York, Basic Books.

H Gildin (1973) 'Spinoza and the Political Problem', in Marjorie Grene, ed. *Spinoza. A Collection of Critical Essays*, New York, Doubleday.

M M Goldsmith (1980) 'Hobbes's "Mortall God": Is There a Fallacy in Hobbes's Theory of Sovereignty?', *History of Political Thought*, Vol. 1.

M M Goldsmith (1993) 'Hobbes's "Mortall God': Is There a Fallacy in Hobbes's Theory of Sovereignty?', in P King ed. *Thomas Hobbes. Critical Assessments*, Volume 3 Politics and Law, London, Routledge.

J W Gough (1973) *John Locke's Political Philosophy*, Oxford, Clarendon Press.

Victor Gourevitch (1997) 'Introduction', in *Rousseau. 'The Social Contract' and Other Later Political Writings*, ed. and trans. Victor Gourevitch, Cambridge, Cambridge University Press.

Jürgen Habermas (1991) *Moral Consciousness and Communicative Action*, Cambridge Mass., MIT University Press.

Jürgen Habermas (1994) 'Some Questions Concerning the Theory of Power: Foucault Again', in Michael Kelly (ed.) *Critique and Power. Recasting the Foucault/Habermas Debate*, Cambridge MA, MIT Press.

Jürgen Habermas (1995) 'Citizenship and National Identity: Some Reflections on the Future of Europe', in Ronald Beiner (ed.), *Theorising Citizenship*, New York, State University of New York Press.

Jürgen Habermas (1997) 'Kant's Idea of Perpetual Peace, with the Benefit of Two Hundred Years' Hindsight', in James Bohman and Matthias Lutz-Bachmann eds. *Perpetual Peace. Essays on Kant's Cosmopolitan Ideal*, Cambridge Mass., MIT Press.

Iain Hampsher-Monk (1992) *A History of Modern Political Thought*, Oxford, Blackwell.

Stuart Hampshire (1951) *Spinoza*, Harmondsworth, Penguin.

Errol E Harris (1992) *Spinoza's Philosophy: An Outline*, New Jersey, Humanities Press.

Errol E Harris (1995) *The Substance of Spinoza*, New Jersey, Humanities Press.

Ian Harris (1998) *The Mind of John Locke. A Study of Political Theory in its Intellectual Setting*, 2nd edition, Cambridge, Cambridge University Press.

Ross Harrison (2003) *Hobbes, Locke, and Confusion's Masterpiece. An Examination of Seventeenth-Century Political Philosophy*, Cambridge, Cambridge University Press.

G W F Hegel (1964) *Hegel's Political Writings*, ed. Z A Pelczynski, trans. T M Knox, Oxford, Clarendon Press.

G W F Hegel (1967) *Philosophy of Right*, trans. T M Knox, Oxford, Oxford University Press.

G Heiman (1971) 'The Sources and Significance of Hegel's Corporate Doctrine', in Z A Pelczynski ed. *Hegel's Political Philosophy. Problems and Perspectives*, Cambridge, Cambridge University Press.

F H Hinsley (1969) 'The concept of Sovereignty and the Relations Between States', in W J Stankiewicz ed. *In Defense of Sovereignty*, Oxford, Oxford University Press.

F H Hinsley (1986) *Sovereignty*, Cambridge, Cambridge University Press.

Thomas Hobbes (1946) *Leviathan*, ed. M Oakeshott, Oxford, Blackwell.

Thomas Hobbes (1984) 'Considerations Upon the Reputation, Loyalty, Manners and Religion of Thomas Hobbes of Malmesbury, Written by Himself, By Way of Latter to a Learned Person (John Wallis, D. D.)', in W. Molesworth ed., *The English Works of Thomas Hobbes*, Vol.IV, London, John Bohn.

Thomas Hobbes (1991), *Hobbes. 'Leviathan'*, ed. R Tuck, Cambridge, Cambridge University Press.

John Hoffman (1996) 'What on Earth have Sovereignty and the State to do with the Question of Gender?', in I Hampsher-Monk and J Stanyer (eds) *Contemporary Political Studies 1996*, Belfast, Political Studies Association.

Sarah Williams Holtman (2002) 'Revolution, Contradiction, and Kantian Citizenship', in Mark Timmons ed. *Kant's 'Metaphysics of Morals'. Interpretative Essays*, Oxford, Oxford University Press.

Bonnie Honig (1993) *Political Theory and the Displacement of Politics*, New York, Cornell University Press.

Stephen Houlgate (1991) *Freedom, Truth and History. An Introduction to Hegel's Philosophy*, London, Routledge.

Kimberly Hutchings (1996) *Kant, Critique and Politics*, London, Routledge.

Jef Huysmans (1999) 'Know Your Schmitt: A Godfather of Truth and the Spectre of Nazism', *Review of International Studies*, Vol. 25.

K-H Ilting (1971) 'The Structure of Hegel's *Philosophy of Right*', in Z A Pelczynski ed. *Hegel's Political Philosophy. Problems and Perspectives*, Cambridge, Cambridge University Press.

K H Ilting (1974) 'Introduction' to Vol.4 of K H Ilting ed. *Vorlesungen uber Rechtsphilosophie*, Stuttgart, Fromman Verlag.

Duncan Ivison (2003) 'Locke, Liberalism and Empire' in Peter Anstey *The Philosophy of John Locke. New Perspectives*, London, Routledge.

Robert Jackson (1999) 'Introduction: Sovereignty at the Millennium', *Political Studies*, Vol. 47.

Alan James (1986) *Sovereign Statehood*, London, Allen and Unwin.

Bertrand De Jouvenel (1957) *Sovereignty. An Inquiry into the Political Good*, Cambridge, Cambridge University Press.

Andreas Kalyvas (2000) 'Hegemonic Sovereignty: Carl Schmitt, Antonion Gramsci and the Constituent Prince', *Journal of Political Ideologies*, Vol. 5.

Immanuel Kant (1952) *The Critique of Judgement*, trans. J C Meredith, Oxford, Clarendon Press.

Immanuel Kant (1997) *Political Writings*, ed. H. S. Reiss, trans. H. B. Nisbet Cambridge, Cambridge University Press.

Immanuel Kant (1999) 'Appendix' to the *Metaphysics of Morals*, in Mary Gregor ed. and trans. *Immanuel Kant. Practical Philosophy*, Cambridge, Cambridge University Press.

M A Kaplan (1993) 'How Sovereign is Hobbes's Sovereign?', in Preston King ed. *Thomas Hobbes. Critical Assessments*, Vol.3, London, Routledge.

Paul Keal (2003) *European Conquest and the Rights of Indigenous Peoples. The Moral Backwardness of International Society*, Cambridge, Cambridge University Press.

Duncan Kelly (2003) *The State of the Political. Conceptions of Politics and the State in the Thought of Max Weber, Carl Schmitt and Franz Neumann*, Oxford, Oxford University Press.

Michael Kelly (1994) ed. *Critique and Power. Recasting the Foucault/Habermas Debate*, Cambridge MA, MIT Press.

Wolfgang Kersting (1992) 'Politics, Freedom, and Order: Kant's Political Philosophy', in Paul Guyer ed. *The Cambridge Companion to Kant*, Cambridge, Cambridge University Press.

Preston King (1974) *The Ideology of Order: A Comparative Analysis of Jean Bodin and Thomas Hobbes*, New York, Barnes & Noble.

Preston King ed. (1993) *Thomas Hobbes. Critical Assessments*, Vol.3, London, Routledge.

M Knox (1967) 'Translator's Foreward' and translator's notes, in G W F Hegel *Philosophy of Right*, trans. T M Knox, Oxford, Oxford University Press.

Martti Koskenniemi (2001) *The Gentle Civilizer of Nations: The Rise and Fall of International Law 1870-1960*, Cambridge, Cambridge University Press.

Stephen Krasner (2001) 'Problematic Sovereignty', in S Krasner (ed.) *Problematic Sovereignty. Contested Rules and Political Possibilities*, New York, Columbia University Press.

Robert Kraynak (1990) *History and Modernity in the Thought of Thomas Hobbes*, Ithaca, NY, Cornell University Press.

Robert Kraynak (1993) 'Hobbes's *Behemoth* and the Argument for Absolutism', in Preston King ed. *Thomas Hobbes. Critical Assessments*, Vol.3, London, Routledge.

Peter Laslett (1965) 'Introduction' to *John Locke. Two Treatises of Government*, New York, Mentor.

Hans Lindahl (2003) 'Sovereignty and Representation in the European Union', in Neil Walker (ed.) *Sovereignty in Transition*, Oxford, Hart.

Genevieve Lloyd (1994) *Part of Nature. Self-Knowledge in Spinoza's Ethics'*, Ithaca, NY, Cornell University Press.

Genevieve Lloyd (1996) *Spinoza and the 'Ethics'*, London, Routledge.

Genevieve Lloyd and Moira Gatens (1999) *Collective Imaginings: Spinoza, Past and Present*, London, Routledge.

S A Lloyd (1992) *Ideals as Interests in Hobbes's 'Leviathan'*, Cambridge, Cambridge University Press.

John Locke (1965) *Two Treatises of Government*, ed. Peter Laslett, New York, Mentor

John Locke (1988) *Two Treatises of Government*, Cambridge, Cambridge University Press.

Martin Loughlin (2003) 'Ten Tenets about Sovereignty', in Neil Walker (ed.) *Sovereignty in Transition*, Oxford, Hart.

E J Lowe (2005) *Locke*, London, Routledge.

A MacIntyre (1981) *After Virtue*, London, Duckworth.

Iain MacKenzie (2005a) 'General Introduction, in Iain MacKenzie ed. *Political Concepts. A Reader and Guide*, Edinburgh, Edinburgh University Press.

Iain MacKenzie ed. (2005b) *Political Concepts. A Reader and Guide*, Edinburgh, Edinburgh University Press.

Noel Malcolm (1991a) *Sense on Sovereignty*, London, Centre for Policy Studies.

Noel Malcolm (1991b) 'Hobbes and Spinoza', in J. H. Burns ed., *Cambridge History of Political Thought 1450-1700*, Cambridge, Cambridge University Press.

Noel Malcolm (2002) *Aspects of Hobbes*, Oxford, Clarendon Press.

James Martineau (1882) *A Study of Spinoza*, London, Macmillan.

A P Martinich (1992) *The Two Gods of Leviathan: Thomas Hobbes on Religion and Politics*, Cambridge, Cambridge University Press.

Karl Marx (1975) 'Economic and Philosophical Manuscripts', in L Colletti ed., *Karl Marx Early Writings*, Harmondsworth, Penguin.

John Stuart Mill (1974) *On Liberty*, Harmondsworth, Penguin.

Chantal Mouffe (1992) 'Preface: Democratic Politics Today', in C Mouffe ed., *Dimensions of Radical Democracy*, London, Verso.

Jan Müller (1999) 'Carl Schmitt's Method: Between Ideology, Demonology and Myth', *Journal of Political Ideologies*, Vol. 4.

Martha Nussbaum (1997) 'Kant and Cosmopolitanism', in J Bohman and M Lutz-Bachmann eds. *Perpetual Peace. Essays on Kant's Cosmopolitan Ideal*, Cambridge Mass., MIT Press.

Guy Oakes (1986) 'Translator's Introduction' in Carl Schmitt *Political Romanticism*, Cambridge Mass, MIT Press.

Timothy O'Hagan (1999) *Rousseau*, London, Routledge.

Onora O'Neill (1992) 'Vindicating Reason', in Paul Guyer ed. *The Cambridge Companion to Kant*, Cambridge, Cambridge University Press.

Susan Moller Okin (1993) '"The Soveraign and His Counsellours": Hobbes's Reevaluation of Parliament', in Preston King ed. *Thomas Hobbes. Critical Assessments*, Vol.3, London, Routledge.

Anthony Pagden (1998) 'The Struggle for Legitimacy and the Image of Empire in the Atlantic to c.1700', in Nicholas Canny ed. *The Origins of Empire. Volume 1 British Overseas Enterprise to the Close of the Seventeenth Century*, Oxford, Oxford University Press.

Anthony Pagden (2002) 'Introduction', in Anthony Pagden ed. *The Idea of Europe. From Antiquity to the European Union*, Cambridge, Cambridge University Press.

Geraint Parry (1978) *John Locke*, London, George Allen & Unwin.

Z A Pelczynski (1964) 'Introduction', Z A Pelczynski ed. *Hegel's Political Writings*, trans. T M Knox, Oxford, Clarendon Press.

Z A Pelczynski (1971) 'Hegel's Political Philosophy: Some Thoughts on its Contemporary Relevance', in Z A Pelczynski ed. *Hegel's Political Philosophy. Problems and Perspectives*, Cambridge, Cambridge University Press.

Daniel Philpott (1999) 'Westphalia, Authority, and International Society', *Political Studies*, Vol. 47.

Raymond Plant (1973) *Hegel*, London, George Allen & Unwin.

Thomas Pogge (1994) 'Cosmopolitanism and Sovereignty', in Chris Brown ed. *Political Restructuring in Europe. Ethical Perspectives*, London, Routledge.

Ulrich Preuss, Michelle Everson, Mathias Koenig-Archibugi and Edwige Lefebvre (2003) 'Traditions of Citizenship in the European Union', *Citizenship Studies*, Vol. 7.

Raia Prokhovnik (1991) *Rhetoric and Philosophy in Hobbes's 'Leviathan'*, New York, Garland Press.

Raia Prokhovnik (2004) *Spinoza and Republicanism*, London, Palgrave Macmillan.

Raia Prokhovnik (2005) 'Hobbes's Artifice as Social Construction', *Hobbes Studies*, Vol.18.

Raia Prokhovnik (2007) *Sovereignties: Contemporary Theory and Practice*, London, Palgrave Macmillan.

Paul Rabinow and William Sullivan eds (1987) *Interpretive Social Science. A Second Look*, Berkeley, University of California Press.

Jacques Rancière (1999) *Disagreement: Politics and Philosophy*, Minneapolis, University of Minnesota Press.

D D Raphael (1990) *Problems of Political Philosophy*, London, Palgrave.

H S Reiss (1997a) 'Introduction', in *Kant. Political Writings*, ed. H. S. Reiss, Cambridge, Cambridge University Press.

H S Reiss (1997b) 'Postscript', in *Kant. Political Writings*, ed. H. S. Reiss, Cambridge, Cambridge University Press.

Christian Reus-Smit (2001) 'Human Rights and the Social Construction of Sovereignty', *Review of International Studies*, Vol. 27.

Melvin Richter (2005) 'A Family of Political Concepts. Tyranny, Despotism, Bonapartism, Caesarism, Dictatorship, 1750-1917', *European Journal of Political Theory*, Vol.4.

Paul Ricoeur (1973) 'The Model of the Text: Meaningful Action Considered as a Text', *New Literary History*, Vol.5.

Jean-Jacques Rousseau (1968) *The Social Contract*, trans. Maurice Cranston, London, Penguin.

Jean-Jacques Rousseau (1993) *The Social Contract and Discourses*, trans. and Introduction by G D H Cole, revised and augmented by J H Brumfitt and John Hall, updated by P D Jimack, London, Everyman.

David Runciman (2003) 'The Concept of the State: the Sovereignty of a Fiction', in Q Skinner and B Strath eds. *States and Citizens*, Cambridge, Cambridge University Press.

Michael Sandel (1982) *Liberalism and the Limits and Justice*, Cambridge, Cambridge University Press.

J Scanlan and O Kent (1988) 'The Force of Moral Arguments for a Just Immigration Policy in a Hobbesian Universe. The Contemporary American Example', in M Gibney ed. *Open Borders? Closed Societies?*, New York, Greenwood Press.

James Schmidt and Thomas Wartenberg (1994) 'Foucault's Enlightenment: Critique, Revolution, and the Fashioning of the Self', in Michael Kelly (ed.) *Critique and Power. Recasting the Foucault/Habermas Debate*, Cambridge MA, MIT Press.

Carl Schmitt (1976) *The Concept of the Political*, New Jersey, Rutgers University Press.

Carl Schmitt (1985) *Political Theology. Four Chapters on the Concept of Sovereignty*, Cambridge Mass., MIT Press.

Carl Schmitt (1986) *Political Romanticism*, Cambridge Mass, MIT Press.

Carl Schmitt (1988) *The Crisis of Parliamentary Democracy*, Cambridge Mass., MIT Press.

Carl Schmitt (1996) *The Leviathan in the State Theory of Thomas Hobbes. Meaning and Failure of a Political Symbol*, trans. George Schwab and Erna Hilfstein, Westport, Conn., Greenwood Press.

George Schwab (1976) 'Introduction', in Carl Schmitt *The Concept of the Political*, New Jersey, Rutgers University Press.

George Schwab (1985) 'Introduction', in Carl Schmitt *Political Theology. Four Chapters on the Concept of Sovereignty*, Cambridge Mass., MIT Press.

George Schwab (1996) 'Introduction', in Carl Schmitt *The Leviathan in the State Theory of Thomas Hobbes. Meaning and Failure of a Political Symbol*, trans. George Schwab and Erna Hilfstein, Westport, Conn., Greenwood Press.

Melissa Schwartzberg (2003) 'Rousseau on Fundamental Law', *Political Studies*, Vol.51.

Roger Scruton (1986) *Spinoza*, Oxford, Oxford University Press.

Robert Simon (2002) 'Introduction: Social and Political Philosophy – Sorting Out the Issues', in Robert Simon ed. *The Blackwell Guide to Social and Political Philosophy*, Oxford, Blackwell.

Gerry Simpson (2004) *Great Powers and Outlaw States. Unequal Sovereign in the International Legal Order*, Cambridge, Cambridge University Press.

Quentin Skinner (1975) 'Hermeneutics and the Role of History', *New Literary History*, Vol.7.

Quentin Skinner (1978) *The Foundations of Modern Political Thought. Volume Two: The Age of Reformation*, Cambridge, Cambridge University Press.

Quentin Skinner (1988) 'A Reply to My Critics', in James Tully ed. *Meaning and Context: Quentin Skinner and His Critics*, Cambridge, Polity.

Quentin Skinner (1989) 'Language and Political Change', in T Ball, J Farr and R Hanson eds *Political Innovation and Conceptual Change*, Cambridge, Cambridge University Press.

Quentin Skinner (1992) 'On Justice, the Common Good and the Priority of Liberty', in C Mouffe ed. *Dimensions of Radical Democracy*, London, Verso.

Quentin Skinner (1993) 'Hobbes on Sovereignty: An Unknown Discussion', in P King ed. *Thomas Hobbes. Critical Assessments*, Vol.3, London, Routledge.

Quentin Skinner (1994) 'History and Ideology in the English Revolution', 'Thomas Hobbes and his Disciples in France and England', 'Thomas Hobbes and the Nature of the Early Royal Society', all reprinted in Preston King ed., *Thomas Hobbes. Critical Assessments*, London, Routledge.

Quentin Skinner (1996) *Reason and Rhetoric*, Cambridge, Cambridge University Press.

Quentin Skinner (2002) *Visions of Politics. Volume 1: Regarding Method*, Cambridge, Cambridge University Press.

Carole Smith (2000) 'The Sovereign State v Foucault: Law and Disciplinary Power', *Sociological Review* Vol. 48 (2).

Steven B Smith (1989) *Hegel's Critique of Liberalism. Rights in Context*, Chicago, Chicago University Press.

Johann Sommerville (1991) 'Absolutism and Royalism', in J H Burns ed., *Cambridge History of Political Thought 1450-1700*, Cambridge, Cambridge University Press.

Johann Sommerville (1992) *Thomas Hobbes: Political Ideas in Historical Context*, London, Macmillan.

B Spinoza (1951) *B. de Spinoza. A Theologico-Political Treatise. A Political Treatise*, ed. R H M Elwes, New York, Dover.

B Spinoza (1955) *Benedict de Spinoza. On the Improvement of the Understanding, The Ethics, Correspondence*, ed. R H M Elwes, New York, Dover.

Baruch Spinoza: Theological-Political Treatise (1998) trans. S Shirley, Indianapolis, Hackett Publishing Company.

Hendrik Spruyt (1994) *The Sovereign State and Its Competitors. An Analysis of Systems Change*, Princeton, Princeton University Press.

Leo Strauss (1952) *Persecution and the Art of Writing*, Chicago, University of Chicago Press.

Tracy Strong (1994) *Jean-Jacques Rousseau. The Politics of the Ordinary*, London, Sage.

Tracy Strong (2005) 'Forward', *Carl Schmitt 'Political Theology'*, trans. G Schwab, Chicago, University of Chicago Press.

J-F Suter (1971) 'Burke, Hegel, and the French Revolution', in Z A Pelczynski ed. *Hegel's Political Philosophy. Problems and Perspectives*, Cambridge, Cambridge University Press.

Adam Swift (2001) *Political Philosophy*, Cambridge, Polity.

Charles Taylor (1987) 'Interpretation and the Sciences of Man', in Paul Rabinow and William Sullivan eds *Interpretive Social Science. A Second Look*, Berkeley, University of California Press.

Charles Taylor (1990) *Sources of the Self*, Cambridge, Cambridge University Press.

Charles Taylor (1992) *Multiculturalism and 'The Politics of Recognition'*, Princeton, Princeton University Press.

Benno Teschke (2003) *The Myth of 1648. Class, Geopolitics, and the Making of Modern International Relations*, London, Verso.

V T Thayer (1993) 'A Comparison of the Ethical Philosophies of Spinoza and Hobbes', reprinted in King ed., *Thomas Hobbes. Critical Assessments*, Vol.2, London, Routledge.

Richard Tuck (1989) *Hobbes*, Oxford, Oxford University Press.

Richard Tuck (1991) Introduction and A Note on the Text, in T Hobbes, *Hobbes. 'Leviathan'*, ed. R Tuck, Cambridge, Cambridge University Press.

Richard Tuck (1999) *The Rights of War and Peace. Political Thought and the International Order from Grotius to Kant*, Oxford, Oxford University Press.

James Tully (1997) 'One Way of Thinking Differently About Sovereignty. An Interpretation of Foucault on Sovereignty', paper presented to the 'Sovereignty and Identity' Seminar, University of Victoria, Canada, 13 March 1997.

James Tully (1999) 'To Think and Act Differently: Foucault's Four Reciprocal Objections to Habermas' Theory', in Samantha Ashenden and David Owen eds. *Foucault contra Habermas. Recasting the Dialogue between Genealogy and Critical Theory*, London, Sage.

James Tully (2002) 'The Kantian Idea of Europe: Critical and Cosmopolitan Perspectives', in Anthony Pagden ed. *The Idea of Europe. From Antiquity to the European Union*, Cambridge, Cambridge University Press.

Mark Tunick (1992) *Hegel's Political Philosophy. Interpreting the Practice of Legal Punishment*, Princeton NJ, Princeton University Press.

Martin Van Gelderen (1993) ed., *The Dutch Revolt*, Cambridge, Cambridge University Press.

Jeremy Waldron (2002) *God, Locke, and Equality. Christian Foundations in Locke's Political Thought*, Cambridge, Cambridge University Press.

Michael Walzer (1967) 'On the Role of Symbolism in Political Thought', *Political Science Quarterly*, Vol. 82.

Robert Wokler (1995) *Rousseau*, Oxford, Oxford University Press.

Jonathan Wolff (1996) *An Introduction to Political Philosophy*, Oxford, Oxford University Press.

H A Wolfson (1934) *The Philosophy of Spinoza. Unfolding the Latent Processes of His Reasoning*, Cambridge MA, Harvard University Press.

Sheldon Wolin (1960) *Politics and Vision: Continuity and Innovation in Western Political Thought*, Toronto, Little, Brown & Co.

Allen Wood (1999) 'General Introduction', in Mary Gregor ed. and trans. *Immanuel Kant. Practical Philosophy*, Cambridge, Cambridge University Press.

David Wootton ed. and into. (1993) *John Locke. Political Writings*, Indianapolis, Hackett.

Yirmiyahu Yovel (1989) *Spinoza and Other Heretics. Vol.1 The Marrano of Reason*, Princeton, Princeton University Press.

Jacques Ziller (2003) 'Sovereignty in France: Getting Rid of the Mal de Bodin' in Neil Walker ed. *Sovereignty in Transition*, Oxford, Hart.

Slavoj Zizek (1999) *The Zizek Reader* (eds) Elizabeth Wright and Edmond Wright, Oxford, Blackwell.

INDEX